Schema Therapy – A Phase-Oriented Approach

Targeting Tasks and Techniques in Individual and Group Schema Therapy

Rosi Reubsaet

Schema Therapy – A Phase-Oriented Approach: Targeting Tasks and Techniques in Individual and Group Schema Therapy

English translation of *Schematherapie: werken met fases in de klinische praktijk*

Published by:
Pavilion Publishing and Media Ltd
Blue Sky Offices, 25 Cecil Pashley Way
Shoreham by Sea, West Sussex
BN43 5FF

Tel: 01273 434 943
Email: info@pavpub.com
Web: www.pavpub.com

Published 2021

A catalogue record for this book is available from the British Library.

ISBN: 978-1-914010-56-9

Pavilion Publishing and Media is a leading publisher of books, training materials and digital content in mental health, social care and allied fields. Pavilion and its imprints offer must-have knowledge and innovative learning solutions underpinned by sound research and professional values.

This is a translation of Reubsaet, R.J. (2018) Schematherapie: werken met fases in de klinische praktijk. Houten: Bohn Stafleu van Loghum. ISBN 9789036821148.

Author: Rosi Reubsaet
Translation: Mirjam van Bommel
Cover design: Anthony Pitt, Pavilion Publishing and Media Ltd
Page layout and typesetting: Anthony Pitt, Pavilion Publishing and Media Ltd
Printing: CMP Digital Print Solutions

Contents

Acknowledgements

I have found great satisfaction in writing this book, and I am grateful to everyone who has contributed to it in one way or another. I would like to explicitly mention some of them.

First, my colleagues at the Academy for Schema Therapy: Judith Hollands (dramatherapist), Judith Vanhommerig (psychodramatherapist), Wiesette Krol (clinical psychologist) and Guido Sijbers (clinical psychologist). I've learned so much from our collaboration and I'm happy that we can continue working together. I feel very proud to have been able to write this book on behalf of the Academy.

Second, the many clients with whom I have been involved over the years. Their courage and perseverance motivated me to keep looking for openings.

Further, I am indebted to my mentors in schema therapy: Arnoud Arntz, Hannie van Genderen and Remco van de Wijngaart in the Netherlands, and Joan Farrell and Ida Shaw in the United States. I consider myself privileged to have been able to learn 'the trade' from them.

Then I would like to thank some of the people who have been involved in this book. Firstly, Mirjam van Bommel who translated the book for me – an adventure for both of us. Then Marleen Rijkeboer, who wrote the Foreword and provided feedback on the text, and Eveline Timmermans-Lenders and Saskia de Koning who also offered comments. My Dutch publisher Yulma Perk and my English publisher Darren Reed supported me throughout the process. Also thanks to Susan Simpson, who introduced me to Darren, and Eva Fassbinder for supporting our phase-based work in Germany.

Last but not least thank you, the reader, for taking the time to study this book. I hope that it provides enjoyment, gives confidence and stimulates creativity.

Rosi Reubsaet
May 2021

About the author

Rosi Reubsaet is a clinical psychologist, schema therapy supervisor and behavioural and cognitive therapy supervisor who has specialized for seventeen years in working with people who suffer from severe personality disorders. She is the co-founder and general director of the House for Schema Therapy, a mental health care facility in the Netherlands where, together with colleagues, she treats people with personality disorders with schema therapy. With the same colleagues she also runs the Academy for Schema Therapy, an institution for delivering training and supervision in schema therapy. Rosi gives workshops and training courses around the world, and she is a board member of the personality disorders division of the Dutch Association for Behavioral and Cognitive therapy.

Foreword

Schema therapy has boomed over the past decade. The underlying concepts have been explored in numerous studies. Questionnaires for schemas, coping styles and modes have been tested for their psychometric qualities. Schema and mode models for the different personality disorders have been developed and validated. And the effect of schema therapy has been researched worldwide in extensive clinical trials taking place over many years. Most of these trials concern individual schema therapy for borderline personality disorder, but other personality disorders have also been investigated. The results are remarkably robust: there is relatively low dropout and a strong decrease in personality pathology. In recent years, the effect of schema therapy as a group treatment has also been investigated. Various trials are ongoing, with the first results appearing favourable; more certainly will only come over time. Schema therapy is offered in more and more mental healthcare institutions around the world, and the number of therapists officially certified by the International Society of Schema Therapy (ISST) is increasing exponentially.

Schema therapy is an effective therapy, then, but not exactly an easy one. While the concepts are generally easily recognizable to both clients and therapists and the treatment appeals to many, the implementation is often complicated. How do you logically build up this therapy, which sometimes takes two or three years? Which pitfalls do you encounter, how do you recognize them and what do you do with them? These are some examples of questions that are frequently asked in daily practice. Rosi Reubsaet, a well-known and experienced supervisor, trainer and practitioner in schema therapy, offers an answer to these and many other questions in this practical book. Taking readers by the hand in a pleasant way, she offers a step-by-step guide to the entire schema therapy process. This process is divided into phases, analogous to the journey from childhood to adulthood. Each phase is accompanied by clear explanations, attention is also paid to areas such as goals, therapeutic attitudes and pitfalls, and the text is richly interspersed with beautiful and insightful examples from practice. Readers are also provided with numerous inventively conceived experiential exercises that can be applied in both individual and group schema therapy.

In short, this is a well-structured and easy to read practice book, which absolutely invites and inspires us to actively work with clients and literally get out of the chair to bring about a lived change.

Prof. Dr. Marleen Rijkeboer
Extraordinary Professor of Personality Disorders, Maastricht University
Chairman of the Dutch Association for Behavioral and Cognitive Therapy (VGCT)

Preface

>> **Therapist:** "Schema therapy really appeals to me. I can easily explain to clients what the therapy is all about and I love the fact that there's a range of working methods to choose from. At the same time, I find it difficult to structure the complex therapy process. I also feel slightly unsure about some of the exercises. Therefore, I think my sessions sometimes lack depth. I'd like some more guidance with regard to supporting clients to keep developing themselves."

Schema therapy is a popular and successful form of psychotherapy designed primarily for people with personality disorders. A wide range of techniques, drawn from a variety of existing therapies, are available to enable the schema therapist to intervene at cognitive, experiential and behavioural levels. But how can these techniques be integrated in a positive and useful way? How can you focus on experiential work without forgetting the other components? When is such a long and intense form of therapy finished? And how, when working with clients with complex problems, can you be sure to take good care of yourself? These are questions that cause problems not only for the newly qualified, but also for many experienced schema therapists.

First-hand experience of the pitfalls and difficulties involved in day-to-day work with clients with borderline personality disorder has produced strategies for gaining more control over the process and, at the same time, increasing the emotional depth. Distinguishing between four different phases of therapy, each with a fixed duration and a specific therapy climate, has proved to be a very helpful approach. The phases relate to the different basic needs which form the foundation of schema therapy, and they are inspired by the typical stages of normal child development. Each includes goals for development for the client, areas of focus for the therapist, guidelines for therapeutic attitudes and interventions, integrative exercises, and tips for collaborative clinical practice.

This practical book is intended to pass on the working method outlined above in order to inform and hopefully inspire other therapists. The gradual development of an intense therapy for people with serious difficulties is described in a lively manner. Readers are given practical guidance with regard to keeping the complex therapeutic process transparent, while simultaneously achieving more depth and accessing more emotions. The importance of creativity, enthusiasm and self-confidence to successful outcomes is also discussed.

Background

The phase-oriented method can be applied when working with clients with one or more personality disorders, in individual schema therapy (ST) and group schema therapy (GST).

The classification of four phases and the examples in this book have arisen from individual and group work with clients who have a borderline personality disorder. However, the principles, approach and exercises of the phase-oriented method can also be applied in other settings and with other target groups. For example, there have been experiments with a phase-oriented group schema therapy for clients with a cluster C personality disorder; see Chapter 6 for an illustration.

It is possible to combine individual and group schema therapy. Under these circumstances, a phase-oriented approach means that the individual and group therapists must agree on the therapy phase, so that they can aim for the same development goals and adopt the same therapeutical attitude.

Working with phases can take different forms within group schema therapy. Firstly, there is regular group schema therapy where clients join a group according to a semi-open or open format and take part in it for a certain amount of time (for example, two years). A phase-oriented working method within a group like this means that the therapists and clients will take into account which phase each participant is working at. The therapists adjust their interventions and attitudes to the individual. For example, with a chair technique in the group, the therapists will ask a client who has only just started therapy and is therefore in phase 1 very different questions to those they ask a client who has been with the group for eighteen months and is therefore close to finishing phase 3.

Secondly, there is a closed group approach in which all the clients are in the same therapeutic phase at all times. This enables the therapists to narrow down their interventions to a specific focus, because all clients have the same development goals and need the same approach and attitudes.

Finally, it is possible to create phase-oriented groups. This means there are different groups running simultaneously. Clients who are at the same level with regard to their development form a group together, so each phase has its own group. In this set-up there is an optimal flow of clients and the therapists can target their interventions and attitudes with the aim of stimulating the clients' development in the best possible way. This is comparable to a primary school class being divided into sub-groups within which all the children have the same approximate level of reading skills.

Example of phase-oriented group schema therapy

The personality disorders team has chosen a phase-oriented approach with a homogenous, semi-open group for clients with a borderline personality disorder. The team believes that there are advantages to a more homogeneous group with regard to the clients' disorders, anxiety tolerance and levels of development. The therapy has been separated into four different phases and each has its own development goals. Each phase applies to a specific group, so four phases result in four separate groups and therefore quite a few of the therapists in the team have a role to play.

Before starting the therapy, the clients have two individual introductory interviews in which they receive information about schema therapy and an initial set-up of the mode model is created. Thereafter, each phase of the therapy lasts for six months, which means the therapy finishes after two years. In phases 1 and 2 there are weekly group schema therapy sessions combined with an individual meeting once a fortnight. In phase 3 the weekly group sessions continue; however, the individual meetings take place only once a month. In phase 4 the group sessions are held every other week and the individual meetings only happen upon request. Clients always join an existing group in a pair, to ensure that each new person has a 'buddy'.

Today, Amber and Nico are starting therapy. They will join six other clients in the phase 1 group: Anna, Marc, Clara, Kim, Esther and Susan. Susan and Marc have been in therapy for five months. They have been in the group the longest and it's their task to make Amber and Nico feel welcome. In four weeks' time Susan and Marc will leave the phase 1 group and join the phase 2 group which also consists of six other clients. If the process runs smoothly for Amber and Nico, they themselves will join the phase 2 group in six months' time. There they will meet Susan and Marc again who, four weeks later, will depart for the phase 3 group. So clients know that that they will re-encounter their fellow group members in subsequent phases. This allows them to experience that a connection isn't 'all or nothing' and it can continue to exist. They also get to know each other very well during the process and, through the re-encounters, they can observe each other's progress.

Finally, in all three versions of phase-oriented group schema therapy it's possible to choose between a homogeneous and a heterogeneous group in terms of disorder. A homogeneous group means that participation is only open to clients with a specific disorder, such as a borderline personality disorder. A heterogeneous group means that clients with various personality disorders take part in the same group at the same time. Both models can be set up according to the phase-oriented method. The advantage of a homogeneous group is that the clients have identical basic needs, which the therapists can target with more specific interventions.

Reading guide

In the interest of simplicity and readability, the male pronoun ('he', 'his') is used throughout this book when referring to both the client and the therapist. The many quotations and case studies, which are derived from real life examples and described in anonymised form, showcase the practical approach. While the examples are portrayed in a positive light for educational purposes, in reality procedures are seldom this smooth and straightforward. Schema therapy for clients with a personality disorder is a complex process, in which every therapist will encounter obstacles. Therefore, the ideas and exercises presented in this book have been developed through trial and error in working through many rigid barriers, tough processes and difficult sessions. Hopefully, the book will instil the guidelines and confidence to overcome these challenges rather than avoid them.

Layout

This book consists of six chapters. The first offers a brief outline of the theoretical frameworks of individual and group schema therapy and explores reasons why things can go awry in real-life situations. Depth and transparency for both therapist and client are then created by separating the treatment into four consistently structured phases and using an integrative working method. Chapters two to five clarify and explain the four phases, as well as covering some key topics such as basic needs, the therapy environment, the therapeutic relationship and developmental goals.

The text has been livened up as much as possible by describing lots of real-life examples of individual therapy and group schema therapy. Furthermore, each chapter contains individual and group exercises, points of concern and practical tips – all of which are specific to that phase. The final chapter puts some general pitfalls in the spotlight and answers frequently asked questions about working with individual and group schema therapy. Lastly, this chapter focuses on therapist self-care and on applying the phase-oriented method in other settings or with other target groups.

Chapter 1:
Background to the phase-oriented approach

Chapter summary
1.1 The basic principles of schema therapy
1.2 Schema therapy in groups
1.3 Pitfalls in clinical practice
1.4 Guidelines and areas of focus

Chapter summary

This introductory chapter provides an outline of the theoretical frameworks of schema therapy (ST) and group schema therapy (GST), and a brief look at why challenges occur in real life clinical practice. Schema therapy is a complex therapy that consists of a wide range of techniques aimed at a target group with a variety of problems. The task of the schema therapist is to connect with clients, show them what they missed out on in childhood in terms of love, stability and security, and teach them how to put this right. It is an intense form of psychotherapy that may take years to complete, and there are many questions that therapists commonly ask. Where do you start? How do you proceed? When do you finish? How do you achieve depth and efficiency at the same time? How do you take care of yourself? This book seeks to answer these questions and provide further guidance by separating the treatment into a series of phases, each with its own framework, goal, approach and exercises.

1.1 The basic principles of schema therapy

1.1.1 The development of schema therapy

Schema therapy is a form of integrative psychotherapy developed by Jeffrey Young and colleagues and aimed at treating clients with a personality disorder or chronic Axis-I disorder (Young, 1990). Based on the concept of 'limited reparenting', schema therapy integrates cognitive, experiential and behavioural techniques into a systematic and transparent therapeutic approach. Various scientific studies have demonstrated the effectiveness of schema therapy with regard to personality disorders and chronic depression. Schema therapy has its roots in cognitive behavioural therapy (CBT), and combines aspects of CBT, attachment theory, Gestalt therapy, object relations theory, psychoanalysis and psychodrama (Young et al., 2003; Kellogg, 2004). Schema therapy is also sometimes described as a 'third wave cognitive behavioural therapy'.

Arntz & Jacob (2012) describe the differences between schema therapy and cognitive behavioural therapy. Within schema therapy the client's emotions are a core element, more emphasis is placed on biographical aspects, and the therapeutic relationship plays a central role. This relationship is based on the concept of 'limited reparenting' and involves the therapist assuming the role of a surrogate parental figure for the client. Basic needs are an important focus of limited reparenting; indeed, the underlying assumption that every child has the same basic psychological needs is at the heart of schema therapy. If one or more of these basic needs is not met in childhood, or if an individual suffers a traumatic childhood experience, then inflexible, unhelpful 'early maladaptive schemas' may develop which can lead to dysfunctional behaviour in later life (Young et al., 2003). These schemas can be described as fixed frameworks that contain memories, emotions, thoughts and physical sensations. They become a blueprint for the child's world, helping them to survive when their basic needs are not being met. While helpful in childhood, these schemas can cause behavioural problems later in life, as they are rigid and persistent – they don't allow flexibility, and they can overwhelm the adult individual with childlike emotions, thoughts and sensations from the past.

1.1.2 Basic needs

The various books about schema therapy use different lists of basic needs. The basic needs used in this book are based on the lists found in Arntz & van Genderen (2020), Jacob, van Genderen & Seebauer (2014) and Lockwood & Perris (2012).

Basic needs

Safety: For every child it's important that there is sufficient care – that parents understand how much care the child needs and do their best to provide it. This basic need also includes the need for a predictable, comprehensible and reliable environment.

Connection: Children must feel that they are connected to others who show an interest in their experiences and try their best to understand and support them. This is based on the fact that people are social beings who need to feel a sense of belonging and to be part of a group.

Autonomy: It is important for all of us as human beings that we can make individual choices and shape our lives according to our own insights. This need develops at a young age. Alongside a sense of belonging, children also need to make their own decisions and experience things for themselves. →

Self-appreciation: Every child must learn to have self-confidence and to believe in his own abilities. This is essential to be able to function well, not only as a child but also later in life.

Self-expression: Each child is an individual who is influenced by a unique blend of temperament, environmental factors and genetic predispositions. As a consequence, every child and every human being responds to situations with different emotions and perceptions. To be able to experience and express these emotions and perceptions is important for a healthy development.

Realistic limits: In order to live in a society with others and develop into a decent social being, it is necessary for children to learn to take others into account, to develop determination and self-discipline, to learn to tolerate and deal with frustration, and to be able to self-regulate. Children develop these skills in an environment in which realistic limits are the norm. This means that limits are adapted to the child's temperament and stage of development, that they can be explained to the child, and that they take specific circumstances into account.

Play and spontaneity: Every child is born with the ability to learn, to be amazed, to show enthusiasm, to feel emotions and to experience enjoyment. Children must have a safe, secure environment from which to explore and enjoy the world in their own way. They also must be given opportunities to experiment and to learn through trial and error.

1.1.3 Schema domains and schemas

The above list of basic needs relates to five overarching domains (Young et al., 2003). Safety and connection are about attachment, and they relate to the disconnection and rejection domain. Self-appreciation and autonomy relate to the impaired autonomy and impaired performance domain. The basic need for realistic limits is about responsibility and a sense of purpose in the long term, and it is linked with the impaired limits domain. The fourth domain, other directedness, indicates that the person is predominantly focused on other people's needs and feelings and puts his own feelings aside. This relates to a lack of self-appreciation and self-expression. Finally, the over-vigilance and inhibition domain includes a lack of play and spontaneity, which leads to a fear of experiencing spontaneous emotions or needs.

Each of the five domains links to several schemas. Table 1.1 gives an overview of the basic needs, domains and schemas, and how they link together. For more information about these concepts and their definitions, please refer to any of the widely available ST manuals.

Basic need	Domain	Schema
safety and connection	disconnection and rejection	abandonment/instability
		mistrust/abuse
		emotional deprivation
		defectiveness/shame
		social isolation/alienation
self-appreciation autonomy	impaired autonomy and achievement	dependence/incompetence
		vulnerability to illness or harm
		enmeshment/undeveloped self
		failure to achieve
realistic limits	impaired limits	entitlement/grandiosity
		insufficient self-control/self-discipline
self-expression	other-directedness	subjugation
		self-sacrifice
		approval and recognition seeking
play and spontaneity	exaggerated vigilance and inhibition	negativity and pessimism
		emotional inhibition
		unrelenting standards/hyper criticalness
		punitiveness

Table 1.1: Overview of basic needs, domains and schemas

1.1.4 Coping styles

Schema therapy assumes a direct connection between psychological distress in childhood, and problems and dysfunctional behaviour in the present. Environmental influences play a major role in creating distress, but variables like the child's temperament and genetic predispositions are also important. In addition, the way in which a person deals with distress and schemas is a determining factor in the kind of problems and symptoms that may arise for them later in life. In schema therapy we identify three broad coping styles – surrender, overcompensation and avoidance. These can be thought of as approximately matching the human biological response to danger: freeze, fight or flight.

Surrender:
The person gives in to the schema. For example, someone with the abandonment schema gives in if he clings on to his partner in order to avoid being abandoned.

Avoidance:
The person tries to avoid or escape from triggers that may activate the schema or the emotions involved. This includes behaviours such as social withdrawal, procrastination, shying away from confrontation, using drugs or working excessively. For example, someone with the abandonment schema may decide never to be in a relationship again, simply to nullify the risk of abandonment.

Overcompensation:
The person acts as though the opposite of the schema is true. He hides his own weaknesses, insecurities and inabilities by coming across as assertive, dominant and controlling. For example, a client with the abandonment schema tries to dominate his partner, and to give her the impression that he doesn't need her.

Coping styles

Surrender: the person gives in to the dysfunctional schema and behaves accordingly.

Avoidance: the person tries to escape from the emotions that accompany the schema.

Overcompensation: the person thinks and behaves in an opposite way to the schema.

(Van Genderen, Rijkeboer & Arntz, 2012)

Coping styles are not fixed; they can vary across different situations or at different times in a person's life. Most people have a predisposition for a certain style. This depends on their temperament and what they have experienced as a child in their social environment (Bandura, 1986). See Figure 1.1 for a visual representation of the connection between genetics, social influences, coping styles, schemas and symptoms (Arntz & van Genderen, 2020; Faßbinder et al., 2011). As the figure shows, coping styles maintain and can even reinforce schemas. This is because they cause the person never to get what he needs. For example, someone with the abandonment schema will continuously give in to it by choosing unreliable partners. Unfaithful partners will never meet his need for safety and connection, the need will grow, he will become increasingly convinced that he 'will always be alone', and therefore he will begin to feel and behave accordingly.

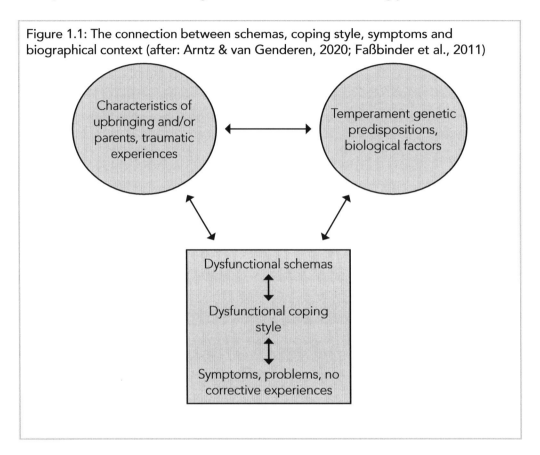

Figure 1.1: The connection between schemas, coping style, symptoms and biographical context (after: Arntz & van Genderen, 2020; Faßbinder et al., 2011)

1.1.5 Schema modes

The final key theoretical concept is the schema mode. This was introduced by Young et al. (2003) to create a better understanding of the complex problems of people with severe personality disorders. Such disorders are characterised by sudden shifts in the person's emotional state of mind, whereby he may experience a certain pattern of feeling, thinking and behaving one minute and a completely different one the next. So many different schemas are present in these patterns of feeling, thinking and behaving that it's difficult for both client and therapist to understand which schema has been triggered when, and which coping style is involved. Young and colleagues also pointed out that the existence of a schema doesn't necessarily mean that it has been triggered. A schema is therefore like a 'trait', a long-term personality characteristic that is usually stable or goes unobserved.

A schema mode revolves around 'the emotional state of mind and coping responses from one moment to another' (Young et al., 2003). It is a mental 'state', in which certain clusters of schemas and coping responses are triggered simultaneously. Triggering one or more schemas at a particular moment of time may go hand in hand with intense emotions. Arntz & van Genderen (2020) define a schema mode as "a set of schemas and processes, which, in certain situations, override the thoughts, feelings and actions of the client at the cost of other schemas."

Four groups of modes have been identified:

Functional modes describe the healthy aspects of a person. These include the Healthy Adult mode and the Happy Child mode. These contribute to a balanced and flexible attitude to life, within which there is room for contentment and happiness. The basic emotion of functional modes is joy.

Maladaptive child modes are innate, universal states of mind, and all children are born with the potential to manifest them. Meeting basic needs can prevent this. The basic emotions of child modes are sadness, fear and anger, and these can be recognized in Vulnerable Child and Angry Child modes. An individual can also act on impulse with a lack of discipline or focus, manifesting an Impulsive or Undisciplined Child mode. If a child mode is triggered, the person overreacts to a given situation and experiences overwhelmingly strong feelings. The overreaction is caused by the fact that the person experienced the same feelings as a child, and wasn't given what he needed at that time.

Dysfunctional parent modes go hand in hand with intense feelings that manifest themselves in self-hatred, shame and guilt, self-blame, pressure to perform and self-criticism. These feelings are not innate but develop as a response to early childhood experiences with important bonding figures, for example parents, grandparents and peers. Children develop ideas and assumptions by reading into the interactions they experience, and they are capable of internalizing and incorporating these ideas and assumptions into their self-image. If they were created in a situation in which basic needs were not met, these internalized ideas and assumptions will be negative. A Punitive Parent mode corresponds to feelings such as self-hatred and self-devaluation, or to strong feelings of guilt, while a Demanding Parent mode corresponds to excessive pressure and high expectations and demands.

Dysfunctional coping modes enable the suppression of intense emotions that originate from the parent and child modes. Like coping styles, they are categorized as surrender, avoidance and overcompensation. Coping modes stem from necessary adaptation to a difficult situation in early childhood. At that time they were helpful way around a problem of unmet basic needs. In present situations too, they may be invaluable for survival as they provide short-term relief and a decrease in strong emotions. However, in the longer term, they only maintain problems; there are no corrective experiences and the underlying basic needs from the child mode are still not being met.

See Tables 1.2a to 1.2d for an overview of schema modes derived from the Schema Mode Inventory or SMI (Lobbestael et al., 2007), along with frequently used alternative terminology. For more in-depth information please refer to Arntz & Jacob (2012).

Table 1.2 Schema modes

Table 1.2a: Maladaptive child modes

Schema mode	SMI terminology	Emotion/feeling	Alternative terminology
child mode	vulnerable child mode	sadness, fear	lonely child
			abused child
			dependent child
	angry child mode	anger	angry child
	enraged child mode	anger, rage	enraged child

Table 1.2b: Dysfunctional parent modes

Schema mode	SMI terminology	Emotion/feeling	Alternative terminology
parent mode	punitive parent mode	self-hatred	punitive parent
		guilt	guilt-inducing parent
	demanding parent mode	pressure, insecurity	demanding parent

Table 1.2c: Dysfunctional coping modes			
Schema mode	SMI terminology	Coping style	Alternative terminology
coping mode	compliant surrenderer	surrender	approval seeker
	detached protector	avoidance	protector
			angry protector
	detached self-soother		soother
	self-aggrandiser	overcompensation	self-aggrandiser
	bully and attack		attacker
			controller
			predator

Table 1.2d: Functional modes			
Schema mode	SMI terminology	Emotion/feeling	Alternative terminology
healthy adult	healthy adult mode	contentment	healthy adult
happy child	happy child mode	joy	contented child

1.1.6 The connection between schema, schema mode and coping style

Recent empirical studies have shown that schemas, modes and coping styles are interconnected in an 'integrated, dimensional model' (Rijkeboer, 2015; Rijkeboer & Lobbestael, 2014). This means that the frequency with which a mode, a schema and a coping style are triggered, the intensity of the accompanying emotions, the credibility of the belief, and the inflexibility of the behaviour are all dimensional. One end of the scale indicates adaptive and healthy behaviour, regardless of whether schemas, modes and coping styles are being triggered. The other end indicates a high degree of dysfunctional behaviour whereby the inflexible patterns are being confirmed over and over again.

To understand the exact meaning of a specific schema mode, we need to ask three questions. First, what is the purpose of the client's behaviour at this moment in time? Second, which coping style is he applying and, third, with respect to which schema? Knowing which schema is present in the background helps to determine which basic need hasn't been met. See Figure 1.2 for a visual representation of the integrated model and the connection between schema, coping style and mode (Rijkeboer, 2015). In this book we build upon this integrative model, whereby a mode consists of one or more schemas that have been triggered in combination with a specific coping style.

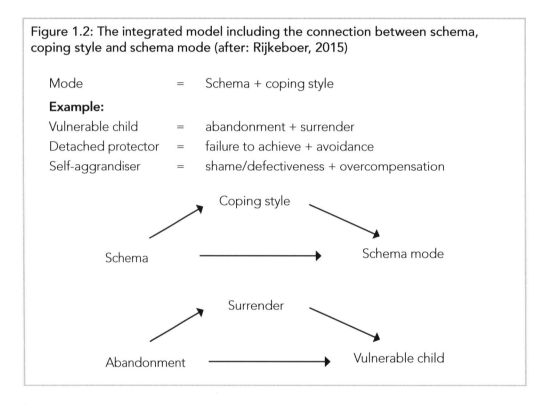

Figure 1.2: The integrated model including the connection between schema, coping style and schema mode (after: Rijkeboer, 2015)

Mode	=	Schema + coping style
Example:		
Vulnerable child	=	abandonment + surrender
Detached protector	=	failure to achieve + avoidance
Self-aggrandiser	=	shame/defectiveness + overcompensation

1.1.7 Treatment approach

Both individual and group schema therapy consist of different components and phases. Along with the general goals of the therapy, these feature in all standard texts on the subject.

Compiling a case conceptualization is always the first step in schema therapy; however, there is no fixed order for the phases that follow. In real-world clinical practice, the phases and goals described below are revisited at various stages. The case conceptualization isn't set in stone either; it is work in progress that is continuously adjusted and refined during treatment. See Figure 1.3 for a summary of the treatment goals associated with each group of modes (Arntz & Jacob, 2012).

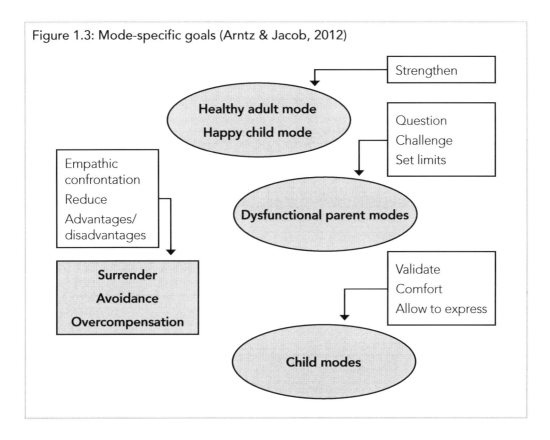

Figure 1.3: Mode-specific goals (Arntz & Jacob, 2012)

Phase 1: Diagnostics, case conceptualization and education

The first phase is primarily aimed at making a diagnosis and providing information. The therapist analyses the schemas and modes that are present, and explores their biographical roots. This leads to a case conceptualization and a mode model that illustrates in a clear manner the connection between symptoms, learning history, schemas and modes. The mode model provides direction when working with people with personality disorders. In that context it serves as an important framework for the entire therapy, and it therefore plays a pivotal role in this book.

See figure 1.4 for an example of a case conceptualization based on a mode model (Faßbinder et al., 2011; Arntz & Jacob, 2012). It gives the therapist and the client a clear overview. Use of the mode model can be regarded as a cognitive technique that helps to focus the mindset.

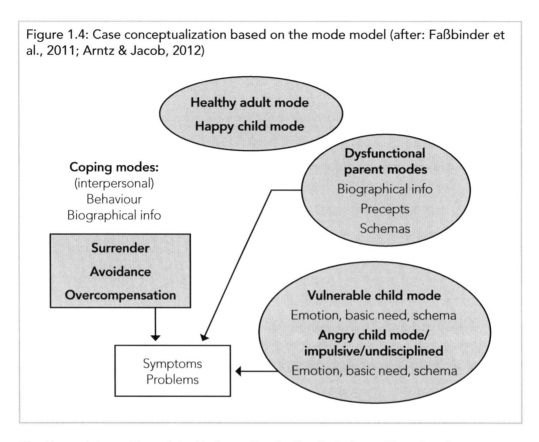

Figure 1.4: Case conceptualization based on the mode model (after: Faßbinder et al., 2011; Arntz & Jacob, 2012)

The therapist provides a lot of information in the first phase. How do schemas develop? What are basic needs? The therapeutic relationship is an area of focus, whereby the therapist aims to create an environment in which the client feels safe and secure. He also explains what the client can expect from the therapy, and what the therapeutic relationship involves. The goals in this first phase are:

- Identifying and labelling schemas and schema modes
- Analysing the origin of schemas and schema modes
- Establishing a link between symptoms, schemas and schema modes

While there is no fixed protocol for how individual schema therapy is structured, in practice this phase usually consists of 3-15 sessions depending on the severity of the problems and disorder. It may also involve treating the clinical condition or drawing up a plan for crisis management (Arntz & van Genderen, 2020).

Phase 2: Transformation phase

In the second phase the client actively works towards breaking away from the inflexible patterns. The therapeutic relationship offers opportunities for the client to connect with his basic needs, and to experience fulfilment of his needs by the therapist. This means that the therapeutic relationship must be secure and focused on the client's most important basic need. For one person this need may be connection, for another autonomy or realistic limits. The therapist will adjust his stance accordingly, and challenge the client's dysfunctional behaviour in a caring and sensitive way. The client will revert to dysfunctional patterns in the therapeutic relationship, often without being aware of it. This gives the therapist an opportunity to draw the client's attention to his dysfunctional behaviour. At the same time the client will be able to connect with underlying feelings and needs and develop adaptive interaction patterns. The goals in this phase are:

- Recognizing the benefits provided by dysfunctional schemas and modes.
- Letting go of these benefits step-by-step.
- Connecting with underlying feelings and basic needs (Vulnerable Child).
- Developing adaptive schemas and modes (Healthy Adult).
- Transforming behaviour patterns, both within and outside therapy.
- Processing traumas, where appropriate.

Phase 3: End phase

Even though they may have been overcome in previous phases, old patterns often flare up in this final phase, in which saying farewell to the therapist and therapy is imminent. Personality disorders are linked with bonding disorders, and many clients have had negative life experiences with loss and having to say goodbye. This phase therefore requires adequate time and attention, whereby the client has sufficient opportunities to prepare him for life after therapy. Generalisation of what has been learnt, as well as exercises aimed at the future, takes place in this phase. The development of the Healthy Adult mode also plays a major role (Claassen & Pol, 2015; Arntz & Jacob, 2012).

1.1.8 Limited reparenting and therapeutic techniques

Throughout all the different phases of schema therapy, the therapeutic relationship is shaped by a key approach known as limited reparenting (Arntz & van Genderen, 2020). Limited reparenting entails providing proper care to the client, which means that the therapist does whatever is necessary to meet the client's previously unmet basic needs. This is a much greater degree of one-to-one involvement than in other forms of psychotherapy, and brings the therapist much closer to the client. It is important for the therapist to be aware of this, and to know his own limits.

Schema therapists provide guidance and are not afraid to offer direct opinions or advice if these are necessary to reduce destructive behaviour or encourage the fulfilment of basic needs. Empathic confrontations and, if necessary, setting limits are other ways in which a schema therapist may use the relationship to guide the client towards a new understanding and, eventually, a transformation. All these techniques are deployed with a view to meeting the basic needs of a specific client, and they feature in targeted interventions.

Schema therapy is an integrative form of therapy, and uses cognitive, behavioural and experiential techniques. To be able to achieve schema therapy goals, it is important that the interventions focus on situations both within and outside the therapeutic relationship, and also on situations from the past, present and future. See table 1.3 for an overview of therapeutic techniques.

Table 1.3 Overview of therapeutic techniques in schema therapy (Arntz & van Genderen, 2020)			
	Feeling	Thinking	Doing
Outside therapy	Roleplaying situation from the present	Socratic dialogue	Behavioural experiments
	Imagination	Schema dialogue	Skills training
	Showing emotions	Flash cards	Problem solving
		Positive logbook	New behaviour
Within therapy	Limited reparenting	Identifying schemas in sessions	Behavioural experiments
	Setting limits	Evaluating ideas about the therapist	Modelling and validating new healthy behaviour
	Switching roles	Self-disclosure	
The past	Imagination with rescripting	Reinterpreting past experiences and integrating them in schemas	Trying new behaviour on important persons
	Roleplaying situation from the past		
	Dialogue using chairs		
	Writing letters		
The future	Imagery or role play	Discussing plans and goals	Trying out new behaviours and activities
	Dialogue using chairs	Anticipating schema activation	Building contacts

1.1.9 The therapist and his schemas

During therapy, schemas and schema modes are triggered not only within the client but also, to a lesser extent, within the therapist. A schema therapist therefore needs to be aware of his own schemas and coping styles (Young et al., 2003). After all, schema therapy is an interpersonal psychotherapy that make use of the therapist's emotions. It is helpful for the therapist to pay deliberate attention to his own thoughts, feelings and behaviour when working with a client.

To be able to deploy all these sources of information in a useful way, it is important to recognize responses which are influenced by the therapist's schemas and to know which coping styles he applies, based on his own learning history and unfulfilled needs. It is also necessary to understand the interaction between the therapist's schemas and the client's schemas. This allows the therapist to filter his responses, and to work with and around his own schemas in the therapeutic relationship. Self-therapy, professional supervision and peer supervision are all helpful for therapists in this regard.

1.2 Schema therapy in groups

Schema therapy also takes place in group settings. Conducting therapy in groups can have significant benefits, not only because it is possible to treat several people at once, but also because a group is more than the sum of its individuals. Participating in a group and watching fellow clients improve can provide hope and support. Being able to identify with others provides relief from feelings of isolation, and the possibility of having a meaningful input that helps other people provides a sense of achievement. These are some of the healing factors as outlined by Yalom (2020), and they have contributed to the development of schema therapy in a group setting.

One group model, developed by Michiel van Vreeswijk and Jenny Broersen, is a short-term treatment outlined in a protocol of 20-40 sessions (Van Vreeswijk & Broersen, 2017). Another, known as group schema therapy, was developed by Joan Farrell and Ida Shaw primarily for people with borderline personality disorder, and it is based on treatment over two years (Farrell & Shaw, 2012; Farrell, Reiss & Shaw, 2014). Both models identify specific phases in the therapy and in the group.

The short-term model describes four phases: 1. A starting phase (3 sessions); 2. An active phase (12 sessions); 3. A concluding phase (3 sessions); and 4. A follow-up phase (2 sessions). The authors give a brief outline of the group dynamics for each phase, the corresponding group standards and the role of the therapists in each phase (Van Vreeswijk & Broersen, 2017).

Group schema therapy combines four phases of a therapy group with the three phases of individual therapy. Farrell and Shaw (2012) argue that the conflict (storming) phase and integration (norming) phase, as they exist in regular group therapy, manifest themselves differently in group schema therapy with clients with borderline personality disorder. They suggest that group therapists have the task of channelling conflicts and actively defining the group standards at the start of therapy. The authors distinguish between a first phase in group schema therapy, in which connection, emotion regulation and safety are key, a second phase focusing on awareness and change, and a third phase aimed at autonomy. Phase one and two each last 6 months, while phase three lasts 12 months. At present this model for group schema therapy is being analysed in an international study (for design see Wetzelaer et al., 2014). For a more detailed description of the group schema therapy model please refer to Farrell & Shaw (2012) and Farrell, Reiss & Shaw (2014).

1.2.1 Group schema therapy for borderline personality disorder

The phases in Farrell and Shaw's model for group schema therapy have been developed on the basis of several goals and components (see table 1.4 for an overview of phases and elements).

The first part of the therapy revolves around creating sufficient connection and safety. The therapists provide emotion regulation by applying strategies and interventions that ensure anxiety levels are manageable. Exercises are aimed at getting to know each other, boosting feelings of safety and connection, increasing awareness and improving recognition of emotions and anxiety build-up. The therapists also give a lot of information about schema therapy, group schema therapy, basic needs and normal development. Clients gradually start to recognize their underlying basic needs, take the first steps towards letting go of their coping styles, and begin to comply with group standards. This creates scope for the group to move towards a change-oriented approach.

In the second phase of the therapy, clients learn to identify their schema modes and to recognize them as egodystonic (i.e. not consistent with their preferred self-image). They also connect with their Vulnerable Child mode and their unmet needs with the aid of various imagination exercises. Initially the therapists take a lead role in fulfilling these basic needs, and focus on providing each of the clients with a sense of connection and security within the group. At a later stage, the group members themselves begin to play an important role in meeting each other's basic needs.

The final part of the therapy is aimed at strengthening and consolidating the Healthy Adult mode, developing an 'own' identity, and behaviour change. Setting up so-called 'mode management plans' and visualising previously gained, positive memories are two examples of working methods in this phase. Throughout the therapy the different modes are dealt with in a fairly structured way, and there are regular homework tasks. There are also plenty of opportunities to have fun and to play in the form of the Happy Child (Farrell & Shaw, 2012; Farrell, Reiss & Shaw, 2014).

Table 1.4 Overview of the phases and elements in GST for clients with BPD (Farrell & Shaw, 2012)	
Phase 1: connection and emotion regulation	
connection and cohesion	recognition, exercises
psychoeducation	in ST, BPD, GST
awareness of emotions	safe place, safety plan, self-monitoring
emotion regulation	circle monitor
Phase 2: transformation phase	
modes in the following order:	**transformation in the following order**
coping mode	1. awareness
Vulnerable Child mode	2. cognitive interventions
Happy Child mode	3. experiential interventions
Angry Child mode	4. behavioural change
Punitive Parent mode	5. integration
Demanding Parent mode	
Healthy Adult mode	
Phase 3: autonomy	
apply, strengthen and consolidate the Healthy Adult mode	
behavioural change now also interpersonal	
an action plan for each mode	
adolescence and development of identity	
farewell, graduation	

1.2.2 Therapeutic style

Group schema therapy relies on a specific therapeutic style based on several key principles. Two co-therapists run the group, doing 'what a good parent would do', anxiety levels are kept to a minimum, and plenty of attention is devoted to providing information about correcting schemas (Farrell & Shaw, 2012; Claassen & Pol, 2015). Breaks, temporisation and exercises to reduce anxiety are used. Awkward silences are prevented as much as possible. Interaction is encouraged, not only by making eye contact, nodding and inviting someone without putting them under pressure, but also by physical contact such as holding someone's little finger, or holding the ends of a piece of fabric together.

The therapists are supportive and active: they validate emotional experiences as well as showing interest and fostering mutual involvement. They divide their attention between group members and adapt their interventions to the client's mode. As a rule of thumb, they deal with the most obvious mode first. Although the sessions are highly structured, there is enough flexibility to address the group's emotional state of being. Last but not least, just as in individual schema therapy, the therapists are role models with regard to healthy functioning. Appropriate self-disclosure, being open about mistakes, encouraging healthy reality checks and focusing on positives are important interventions.

1.2.3 Group schema therapy phenomena

The transformation of schemas and schema modes is always the ultimate goal of individual schema therapy, and this remains true in group settings. The theoretical model of individual therapy likewise acts as a framework for group schema therapy; meeting basic needs and changing inflexible patterns are the main objectives. Interventions consist of experiential, cognitive and behavioural techniques. Group schema therapy also requires the therapists to take account of group dynamics. They must act like parents in charge of a large family and stay aware of the fact that their interventions take place in a social context. Group members will, for example, witness empathic confrontations.

Group schema therapy is aimed at the individual and, simultaneously, the group as a whole, without it being a psychodynamic process (Claassen & Pol, 2015). It is neither individual therapy in a group nor skills training. The interventions are adjusted to the group, and every group member plays a role in the exercises. The therapists are not outsiders; they are coaches who guide the group and aim for more than just sharing knowledge or teaching certain skills. Furthermore, group therapists are required to divide their attention between all clients and to encourage them to join in and to get involved. Inflexible, dysfunctional patterns arise more often and more intensely than in individual therapy. This means that there are more opportunities to practice new behaviour, but also that the therapists must step up their efforts to ensure that the group session is useful for as many clients as possible. The co-therapists must also collaborate well, and be able to rely on each other absolutely.

The degree to which the therapists structure the sessions depends partly on the clients' disorders and the stage the therapy is at. Collectively analysing how certain patterns recur in the interactions between the therapists and the clients is a key element of group schema therapy. This may sometimes conflict with the need for structure and the limited tolerance for anxiety. Anxiety may increase rapidly, especially if the thoughts and feelings that clients bring about in each other are part of the analysis. In such cases, using predefined patterns in terms of modes and schemas can provide support, and help a client to experience and analyse safely the emotions he encounters when interacting with the therapists and group members. The fact that the patterns are predefined helps the client and the group to focus on what is happening in the here and now, and to relate this to previous deficiencies.

The mode model, the use of schema therapy terminology and a customized therapeutic stance provide a framework within which feelings can be analysed in the group, even for very vulnerable clients who can't tolerate much anxiety. Ultimately, it comes down to the therapists utilising the group's developmental stage to adjust their schema therapeutic interventions. They also try to demonstrate and facilitate healthy group standards, just like in a family situation, so that the positive effects of taking part in a group have as much impact as possible on all the clients.

1.2.4 Group standards, cohesion and developmental stages in group schema therapy

Group standards are a prerequisite for a group to be able to function properly, and they are based on the group ethos. They consist of various codes of conduct that control the level of anxiety and the interactions between clients. Standards that are strict and inflexible limit possible interaction patterns, but offer guidance and security; standards that are too flexible (or non-existent) create room for self-expression, but also increase anxiety levels. Group standards fluctuate between these two extremes of freedom versus security. The ideal balance depends on three key factors: the group members, the therapists themselves, and the developmental phase of the group (Hoijtink, 2001).

Group members with borderline personality disorder can't tolerate high levels of anxiety, and the therapists must be sure to take this into account. Standards should gravitate towards the side of security for group schema therapy to be effective

(Claassen, 2012). Security is more important than freedom, as it is necessary to keep anxiety levels to a minimum – especially early in the therapy, before the group enters the active working phase. Farrell & Shaw (2012) confirm this, as they focus on security and emotion regulation in the first phase of their group schema therapy model.

With regard to the therapists, it's essential for them to take a lead role in encouraging clients to interact with each other. They must also actively establish interactions between themselves and the clients, and use verbal and non-verbal communication strategies to maximize feelings of security. This method of being proactive decreases levels of fear and facilitates connection, which is necessary to develop cohesion within the group. The degree of cohesion will impact the extent to which group members enjoy attending therapy, not only because they think the sessions are important but also because they care for the other participants (Hoijtink, 2001). A high level of group cohesion motivates clients to attend the sessions, even if a high level of anxiety is also present.

The group developmental stage is a third factor that impacts client behaviour. Clients behave differently when they have just joined a group, compared to when they have been taking part for some time and are settled. There are various ways of conceptualizing the life cycle of a group. We will use Levine's classification, based on several developmental stages (see Table 1.5 for some features of the different stages). According to this model, transitions from one stage to the next go hand in hand with a crisis – similar to the 'developmental crises' encountered by children. The group and its members must overcome a barrier in order to make progress and evolve to the next stage. This also applies to the development of basic needs: there must be a sufficient level of security before a child is able to achieve some form of self-appreciation.

A well-functioning group moves through these stages in ascending order but, at the same time, they also take on a more fluid form. This means that the classification of group stages is not static; each stage contains elements from a previous stage, in line with the client's level at that moment in time. The same applies to the development of basic needs. They also evolve in ascending order but, at the same time, keep reappearing. For example, a child who is developing a need for autonomy will have to feel safe enough to practice these newfound skills. Moreover, a toddler's ideas about autonomy are very different to a teenager's ideas about autonomy. It is crucial to take the group developmental stages and crises into consideration, as clients and therapists behave differently at each stage. Group therapists who adjust their interventions to the developmental stage of the group are able to create the necessary conditions for growth and development, just as parents do when raising their children.

Table 1.5: Group developmental stages (Levine, 1979; Hoijtink, 2001)

The first column describes the stage and the crisis. The second briefly describes the clients' issues at a certain stage. The third column shows what therapists need to focus on to stimulate development.

	Clients	Therapists
1. Parallel stage	■ what is expected of me? ■ wanting to comply with standards	■ provide maximum reciprocity ■ equal attention for everyone
authority crisis	■ feeling more at ease ■ become more active in influencing the group	■ let the group take on a more influential role ■ do not take criticism personally
2. Integration stage	■ who is in charge? ■ expressing emotions and dealing with conflicts ■ disclosure versus concealment	■ provide room for conflicts ■ encourage clients to express themselves within realistic limits
intimacy crisis	■ content of the standard becomes a driving force ■ feeling responsible	■ encourage empathy and interaction ■ control the pace
3. Reciprocity stage	■ opening up ■ anxieties are not confirmed ■ practicing new behaviour within the group	■ encourage healthy responses ■ ensure the practice environment is the best it can be
separation crisis	■ learn to deal with separation and loss	■ make use of a high level of reciprocity
4. End stage	■ how have you experienced loss?	■ provide opportunities to discuss all possible emotions

1.3 Pitfalls in clinical practice

While the theoretical framework for schema therapy is clear and straightforward, and the language appeals to both therapists and clients because it is user-friendly, it is nevertheless quite complex to use schema therapy in clinical practice at both individual and group levels. In this section we will look at some reasons for this, the problems that can occur, and the ways in which therapists can respond.

1.3.1 Loss of overview and guidance

Both individual and group schema therapy take a significant period of time; a minimum of one year and up to three years for severe disorders (Giessen-Bloo et al., 2006; Farrell & Shaw, 2012). At times, therefore, it can be difficult to keep in mind an overview of the full therapy process. The initial task of compiling a case conceptualization and a mode model is relatively clear – several books describe how the therapist can handle this, and which interventions need to be carried out. These books tend to be ordered in a particular way: based on dealing with a specific mode, schema or therapeutic stance. There are also books that provide a protocol with a list of all the sessions, and books that focus on a certain form or setting (e.g. group: Farrell & Shaw, 2012; clinical: Muste et al., 2009).

So far, so good. In day-to-day practice, however, losing sight of the 'big picture' can easily happen once the case conceptualization is complete. A therapist may begin to wonder: "What exactly am I doing? And why?" Engaging in schema therapy as described by Young et al. (2003) offers the therapist considerable scope and freedom, which can become overwhelming. Clients with a personality disorder have many active schemas and modes, and these can be manipulated using a range of different techniques. In order to simplify this, the therapist may find himself just repeating certain exercises for a specific schema or mode, or resort to following a given protocol like a 'cookbook'.

Using a fixed protocol for sessions and exercises does offer some helpful structure, and it may add value for some therapists. However, a potential disadvantage is that insufficient direct liaison can lead to the therapist losing touch with the client. This may mean that there are still unresolved issues when the therapy is complete. Clients with a personality disorder present with highly complex problems that require the therapeutic process to be continuously adjusted and fine-tuned to their needs. Adopting a structured approach and maintaining an overview are necessary factors for the therapist to keep track of the therapy process, but self-confidence and creativity are just as important.

CASE STUDY

Individual therapy

Linda started schema therapy a year ago, and over the last twelve months she has made some big improvements. By using the mode model, together with her therapist, she has worked hard towards comforting 'lonely and abused Linda'. The therapist has managed to gain Linda's trust by using imagery rescripting exercises, and Linda has experienced that she has a right to feel safe and that she is allowed to have these feelings. She is also aware of her Angry Protector mode, with which she keeps others at a distance and thereby remains lonely. However, in the last few weeks, the therapist →

has noticed that Linda has made very little progress. He feels somewhat frustrated that while Linda appears to have a good understanding of her schema modes within therapy, outside the therapeutic environment she keeps rejecting people. He is starting to wonder: "What else can I do? Repeating the imagery rescripting exercises won't add anything – how much longer does this need to go on?" He believes that he needs to switch to a different approach in order to keep Linda moving forward, but he doesn't quite know which one or how to go about it.

1.3.2 Loss of contact and depth

Therapists are under a great deal of time pressure in current mental healthcare systems. Treatments need to be cost-effective, governments are cutting down on health care expenses and individual practitioners feel pressured to keep therapies as short as possible. These aspects can lead to a lack of depth; pace becomes more important than accuracy.

Someone who is under pressure is also more likely to resort to working methods that feel familiar and safe. After all, every therapist has his own schemas and his own coping styles. Self-sacrifice is a common schema encountered by therapists; they sacrifice their own needs for those of the client, especially if the client appears weaker than they are. For example, a therapist may delay empathic confrontation because the client is already going through a tough time, and a whole session can be spent just talking about a difficult situation instead of analysing it with chairwork.

Resorting to familiar territory can be appealing, in particular if there is little time between sessions or the therapist works with different clients in quick succession. It can also happen that the therapist skips his proper planning and preparation and goes into a session intending to take things as they come and react as necessary. Last but not least, psychotherapists tend to favour verbal skills, as these are what they mainly focus on in training. Implementing a cognitive exercise instead of an experiential exercise is therefore often an easier option.

All of this probably applies even more in a group setting; the focus is on 'surviving' the session and keeping levels of anxiety within the group to a minimum. It is also necessary to avoid exclusion phenomena surrounding coping behaviour, which is regarded as undesirable. This means that individual group members should not be judged on their way of coping. Instead, the therapists need to strategically challenge them with an empathic confrontation and create realistic limits within which there are opportunities to learn.

Depth, experience, experiential techniques and a strong commitment from the therapist are the essential factors for schema therapy to be effective according to Rijkeboer (Hardeman, 2017). Supporting factors are sufficient scope, and confidence and attention for the therapist's own process, as well as knowledge, skills and a good overview of the therapeutic process from beginning to end.

CASE STUDY

Group schema therapy

For the past few weeks, Mark has been taking part in group schema therapy for people with borderline personality disorder. He suffers from a strong sense of shame, and constantly feels as if he is falling short and failing. Overcompensation is his main coping style; within the group he tends to have an "I know best" attitude, and he is usually first in line to confront others and point out their faults. After a few sessions, his peers are so tired of this behaviour that they announce that they don't want to be in a group with him anymore; they find him arrogant and dislike the way he constantly criticizes them yet sees no fault with himself. The co-therapists realize that they've noticed the tension around Mark before, but they haven't done anything about it. One reason for this is that both therapists have other meetings immediately after each session, and therefore they are unable to properly discuss the sessions there and then.

1.3.3 Loss of finiteness and goal

A third pitfall is connected to the difficulties described above. A long, complex therapy, with clients with severe symptoms, putting high demands on the therapist – when is it finished? When have you achieved your full potential? Everything can look equally important in a long-term process with clients with inflexible patterns in various aspects of their lives, and it can sometimes seem that an endless procession of problems needs to be solved. After all, when is a Healthy Adult mode strong enough?

This sometimes starts in the case conceptualization; it can be impossible to jointly agree on the mode model due to the sheer number of problems or additional issues. The therapist may intend to present his client with the final model in the next session, but is confronted with new information or unable to make suggestions due to the client having had a visit from a bailiff because of his debts. Again, there is also the possibility of an interaction with the therapist's own schemas. For example, a therapist with the Unrelenting Standards schema may tend to feel that there is always more change required before he can call the outcome of the therapy truly satisfactory.

Team processes are also influential factors. For example, a therapist may want to work towards the completion of the therapy, whilst other team members may still see opportunities for change. Or one of the team may believe that the therapist hasn't dealt with some important issues. These phenomena occur in group schema therapy too. It is even harder to agree on an action plan if co-therapists develop different points of view. Sometimes, problems like this can be resolved through a more structured therapy process. This involves organising regular reviews based on specific goals, which have been agreed by the therapist and the client as well as the other team members.

> **>> Client:** "I find it difficult not to be in control at all times. I keep thinking about this and trying to find reasons for my feelings. I'm aware of it but can't change my ways. In conversations with my therapist I've realized that I often start my sentences with "I think". We've now agreed that if I want to say something in the session I'll start with "I feel". Hopefully this will help me connect more with my vulnerable side. If I do say "I think", my therapist will point it out. In four weeks we'll review this together. I'm happy with this agreement, as I have something specific to work towards."

1.3.4 Pitfalls in group schema therapy

Group schema therapy also has some specific pitfalls. Many organizations offer therapy in open groups, where clients can join an existing group as soon as a place becomes available. This is to avoid the long waiting lists associated with closed groups. The advantage of an open group is that the waiting list and group dynamics are constantly in motion; a disadvantage is that clients are at different levels and as a result there is a high level of variation in how much anxiety each group member can tolerate. Clients with borderline personality disorder who have only just started group schema therapy benefit from low levels of anxiety and high attention for connection, crisis management and emotion regulation. Connection and safety are key, and the therapist plays an active role in neutralising conflicts and making sure that the group has a healing effect at all times (Claassen, 2012).

Too much cohesion between group members has its own pitfalls, though (Hoijtink, 2001). There is a tendency to smooth over conflicts, and the self-expression of group members is inhibited. This goes against the needs of clients in the working phase, who are ready to process traumas and reconnect and deal with their emotions. Achieving this kind of depth requires a higher level of anxiety, but the group as a whole may repeatedly fall back into the integration phase because of the continuous intake of new clients. At the same time, outflow of clients can cause separation crises that can't be dealt with properly because the group hasn't reached that stage of development yet.

Therefore, in an open group, there is a risk that important topics like interpersonal conflict, trauma processing, individuation, separation and loss aren't adequately addressed, as anxiety regulation must always come first. This may result in group members needing to stay in the group for longer than is desirable, or leaving therapy with unresolved issues. For group therapists it is a constant challenge to maintain an overview and structure, and to simultaneously create depth and ensure an adequate level of anxiety. It does not require much imagination to draw a parallel with a family situation, in which the needs vary depending on a child's level of emotional development.

CASE STUDY

Group schema therapy

Today, two new group members have joined the group. From the mode models it emerges that one of them has a strong Detached Protector and the other an Approval Seeker. It is important to the therapists that the new clients feel comfortable within the group. At the same time, they want to continue with the punisher exercise that they started last week. For other group members it is important to persevere with this, and to be able to experience and deal with their pain. How can the therapists make sure that the levels of anxiety are appropriate for everyone? They opt for a connection exercise and give information about the development of parent modes. Afterwards, they draw the conclusion that the new clients have shared something about themselves with the group, but that unfortunately there was no opportunity for an experiential exercise.

1.3.5 The therapist trapped in his own pitfalls

As we have previously noted, all people have schemas and schema modes. This includes therapists, although theirs tend to be less dysfunctional. Self-sacrifice, unrelenting standards and emotional deprivation are schemas that relate particularly to the skills and abilities of therapists. In some ways they can be useful: a healthy amount of self-sacrifice enables a therapist to put his own feelings to one side and respond empathically to the client; unrelenting standards will drive him to do his job well and get better at it; and experiencing emotional deprivation and overcoming it enables him to better understand the client's experiences and perceptions and compensate for any shortcomings.

On the other hand, these same schemas can also prove to be a therapist's Achilles' heel. Self-sacrifice may make him worry that he is harming a client when challenging unhelpful behaviour, and this in turn may make him prone to delaying confrontations or experiential exercises. Unrelenting standards may lead him to become a perfectionist who is never content with his own achievements and can't see when a client has achieved his full potential. And emotional deprivation may result in him paying insufficient attention to his own needs and feelings, with the result that he holds back and doesn't dig deep enough in empathic confrontation situations.

The therapist having his schemas triggered and applying his own coping style can't be prevented; it's only human. However, if it goes on for a long time, happens a lot or goes hand in hand with intense emotions, then there is a risk of the therapy grinding to a halt, the client experiencing confirmation of his schema or the therapist suffering burnout. Recognizing the dynamics of the relationship, acknowledging the therapist's own schemas in connection with the client, and discussing all this with the client results in a better understanding of how schemas and modes determine certain reactions. A therapist who can carry out self-evaluation and self-disclosure effectively will also be able to provide the client and himself with a schema corrective experience.

> **>> Therapist:** "I find it hard to work with a client with a self-aggrandising overcompensation mode. I seem to get thrown off balance because I think I'm failing and that my efforts aren't good enough. Fortunately, I can discuss this with my peer supervision group. Not long ago, that feeling of self-doubt appeared again and I started to seek approval from a client with a self-aggrandising mode. We did a chair technique in the peer supervision group, after which I felt much stronger and more competent. After all it isn't personal; the client is only repeating her dysfunctional pattern. Now I have the confidence to be myself again in our sessions."

1.4 Guidelines and areas of focus

Clinical experience, in the form of day-to-day confrontations with the pitfalls described above, has enabled the drawing up of a number of guidelines that may provide support to therapists when delivering schema therapy.

Create an overview and structure...

Working with therapeutic phases that are aligned in parallel with the client's developmental phases creates an overview to guide the therapy, as well as increasing scope and confidence. It serves as a framework to helps the therapist better understand what is happening within the therapy, and what is required to go forward. Basic needs are universal for all children, but a baby's main needs are very different from a teenager's (Yperen, 2009). This has consequences for the way in which the parent responds, and the same applies to the therapist and client. A client who has just started therapy has very different needs compared to the same client two years later.

In the complexities of day-to-day clinical practice it may be useful to focus on a specific basic need in each phase and, linked to this, a particular therapeutic stance and style of therapeutic relationship. Without being restrictive, this approach provides an overview and structure because of the developmental goals which are attached to it. The phases follow each other and are connected. The next step can only be taken if the previous one has been completed and, at the same time, the previous stage will continue to grow, just as with the normal development of a child.

...work with the client toward realistic goals and specific agreements...

The overarching goals of schema therapy are built into all phases of the therapy. In addition, each phase is associated with its own developmental goals. As far as possible, these should be Specific, Measurable, Acceptable, Realistic and Timely (SMART - see Table 1.6), as this helps the therapist to manage the depth and duration of the therapy process. Working together when setting goals lets the client connect fully with them, and understand better what is expected of him. Similarly, building in a timeframe helps to monitor progress; the client follows the programme rather than vice versa.

Having agreed goals and a clear timeframe means that if a client is making insufficient progress then the therapist can address this within therapy. He can discuss his observations and link these with the case conceptualization and mode model ("I've noticed that you still use your protector mode quite a lot, which may be preventing you from having many schema corrective experiences"). He might use an exercise ("Let's do an imagery rescripting to give that little one what he needs"), or suggest specific actions to get the client back on track ("This week I want you to list the pros and cons of your protector, so that next time we can discuss what you want to get out of therapy").

Table 1.6: SMART goals	
Specific	Is the goal well-defined and unambiguous? Does the client understand it?
Measurable	Under which observable or measurable conditions will the goal be achieved? Has the client been included in this?
Acceptable	Is the goal acceptable for the client? Does he agree?
Realistic	Is the goal achievable? Does it fit in with the client's developmental stage?
Timely	When (in time) should the goal be achieved?

...be aware of an intense change in all areas...

A third area of focus is the importance of ST as an integrative therapy which combines, in a logical manner, ideas and working methods drawn from a variety of existing psychotherapeutic frameworks. This integrative nature provides a foundation for creating depth and experience through therapeutic exercises (see Table 1.3). In collaboration with drama therapists, numerous additional exercises have been developed in clinical practice by integrating thinking, feeling and doing and using basic needs as starting points. The exercises reflect the different developmental phases; they simultaneously affect different levels and different channels and therefore they are multidimensional.

The case conceptualization and the mode model always form the basis of the rationale. They act as a framework enabling the therapist to understand complex problems and are therefore continuously present, cognitive components of the therapy. They also form the context within which thoughts, feelings and actions are transformed. For schema therapy to be effective there must be a focus on emotional perceptions. Collaborating with other professionals can be particularly helpful when using experiential techniques; for example, drawing inspiration from elements of (psycho)drama therapy can have a direct effect on maximising value and client gains during experiential exercises (see box).

Elements of psychodrama that can help clients to physically undergo an experience

Role reversal: The client switches roles with someone else. For example, the therapist sits in the client's chair and pretends to be the client, whilst the client takes the therapist's chair and pretends to be a neutral receiver. This allows the client to see the situation and himself through someone else's eyes, which in turn enables him to empathize with another side of the story and experience the effects of his behaviour on other people.

Mirroring: Someone else takes on the client's role or copies his verbal and non-verbal behaviour. The client becomes the observer and looks in the 'mirror' from a short distance away. The aim is to confront him with his own situation and allow him to witness his own reactions. It's as if the client is looking at himself via someone else in order to get a better understanding of himself.

Doubling: Someone else adopts the client's behaviour and movements, echoing any feelings and thoughts that he believes to be characteristic of the client whilst staying connected with his own emotions. This helps the client to connect more with his emotions, including subconscious emotions, and with the issues that are really important.

(Van Dun, 2015; Lafeber, 2013).

…and definitely don't forget your own needs.

Schema therapy is a complex therapy that places high demands on both therapist and client. Both individual and group schema therapy require effort and commitment from the therapist, along with the ability to balance distance and closeness. Furthermore, the therapist's own schemas are triggered within therapy, which can have a range of consequences. It is therefore vital that sufficient time is set aside for peer supervision and discussions about cases and clients. Peer supervision gives the therapist the opportunity to process his own emotions: "Which feelings, thoughts and behaviours do I encounter in my contact with this client?" Similarly, discussion about clients offers an opportunity to review a client's process: "How is this client's development unfolding within the therapy?"

This applies even more in a group setting, as the co-therapists go through various emotions and experiences with each other and depend on each other in sessions (Arntz & van Genderen, 2020). It is essential that group co-therapists use peer supervision sessions on a structured and regular basis in order to review their relationship and collaboration. The prompt identification of group dynamics, as well as identification of the therapists' own strengths, weaknesses and particular pitfalls to avoid, is beneficial to the group and thus also to each individual client's therapeutic process.

Chapter 2:
Phase 1 – Safety first

Chapter summary
2.1 Basic needs
2.2 The therapy environment
2.3 Goals in this phase by schema mode
2.4 The therapeutic relationship
2.5 Exercises
2.6 Areas of focus and tips

Chapter summary

In the first phase of schema therapy, the client learns to recognize the relationship between his problems and his life history. He takes the first few steps towards a happier life, learns to comply with the therapy, and experiences how this benefits him. Safety and connection, the basic needs that he missed out on earlier in life, play a major role. The therapist must regulate anxiety levels within both the individual and the group, while simultaneously increasing the pressure applied to clients to let go of their acquired coping styles. To balance these tasks, the therapist is required to take on an active, corrective and committed role. Alongside information about the framework and the therapeutic relationship, this chapter also outlines specific goals, based on the different schema modes, for this phase. Exercises consisting of experiential, cognitive and behavioural elements and aimed at achieving these goals are explained. Finally, a few important focal points are highlighted.

2.1 Basic needs

2.1.1 Safety and connection

Safety and connection are the basic needs that play a major role in the first phase. A child can only learn and develop when he or she feels sufficiently safe. Unfortunately, for many clients this need for safety wasn't fulfilled when they were young, inhibiting their development. The aim of schema therapy is to restart this development, and therefore safety comes first. Routine, firm agreements, openness, transparency and collaboration all contribute to a sense of safety (see table 2.1).

> **>> Client:** "At first I found it really scary to go to therapy. I really had to drag myself to the meetings. I didn't want to be there, and on a few occasions I actually didn't go. Or I acted very stubbornly. I noticed that my therapist understood how I felt. She didn't get angry or reject me; instead, she discussed it with me. Together we looked for underlying childhood experiences that could explain these patterns of behaviour. Gradually, I began to feel safer and calmer."

Speaking the same language and sharing a vision creates safety and connection. The case conceptualization and the mode model are therefore invaluable. In collaboration with the client, the therapist tries to achieve a shared understanding of the problems and underlying patterns. Offering support, sympathy and compassion, as well as acknowledging feelings, contributes towards a sense of security. The client develops a feeling of "it's OK to be me with all my good and bad sides" and learns to feel safer and more connected. He also experiences that needs such as safety and connection aren't 'all-or-nothing' – they are dimensional, and he can influence them. For example, a client will learn that he feels somewhat safer with the therapist after he has talked about his difficult childhood and noticed that the therapist responds in a supportive, empathic way.

2.1.2 The language of schema therapy

The importance of safety and connection is also reflected in the shared use of 'schema therapy language'. Speaking the same language creates understanding and provides a solid framework. It helps clients to talk about their feelings and basic needs in an efficient, powerful way. The therapist can support clients in this by explaining the terminology, and by asking reinforcing questions such as: "What do we call that again in schema therapy? Could this be your demanding parent mode?" Or, in a group schema therapy session: "Could this be her demanding parent mode, what do you all think?" Translating how people speak or behave into basic needs is also part of this. For example, if one group member says to another "How annoying that you're not taking part in the exercise!", the therapist can translate this into "Do you mean that you would like to connect more with her?"

Safety and connection are conditions that must be met to a sufficient level before other basic needs can be fulfilled. Attending meetings, joining in with exercises, looking at the past, receiving support, being challenged about subconscious but undesirable behaviour, thinking about patterns, focusing on feelings and complying with the therapy framework are some of the factors that indicate whether these conditions are being met. Setting realistic limits, from the beginning of therapy to the end, is vital too: it provides a framework and creates a sense of safety, routine and predictability. The client is introduced to the experience of realistic limits as a condition of being able to grow further, and comes to understand that such limits are an expression of therapeutic care, not punishment.

Table 2.1: Overview of the components of phase 1	
Theme:	Safety first
Basic need:	Safety, connection
Limited reparenting:	Baby and toddler
Overall goal:	A platform for change
Important exercises:	Experiential case conceptualization; basic modes
Empathic confrontation:	High
Group development phase:	Parallel phase
Mode model:	Basic
Role of the therapist:	Creating favourable conditions

2.2 The therapy environment

2.2.1 Creating favourable conditions

Given that safety and connection are the most important basic needs, it follows that the therapeutic environment should be secure, warm and supportive with a focus on small steps that enable clients to experience success. This phase creates the necessary conditions but is therefore also limiting. The therapist is not afraid to challenge, but he monitors safety as well. He empathizes with the client, but also wants him to experience what it means to be in therapy and to understand that there are painful and negative emotions and beliefs hidden behind his coping style. After all, schema therapy is a long, intense and difficult process; it is important that the client knows what's ahead and how this can benefit him in the end. In this way he can make an informed decision about whether or not to go through with it and, as it were, 'surrender' himself to the therapy with an open mind.

> **>> Therapist:** "In the start phase of therapy I want my client to begin to feel emotions and to experience success in doing so. When I prepare a session, I say to myself "Keep it small and simple." This helps me to avoid becoming too demanding, towards myself or the client, and instead to focus on small victories and mini-moments in which the client feels something."

2.2.2 Anxiety regulation

In the start phase the client gets to know the therapist, the working methods of schema therapy and, in case of group schema therapy, his peers. He also gets to know himself in a different way. He gains an insight into his feelings, thoughts and behaviour in the present, and learns how these are related to experiences and feelings from the past.

Analysing the relationship between symptoms/feelings in the present and experiences in the past is a key element of this phase. It is all about learning to see and feel the connection between then and now. This encounter enables a change in the existing pattern, but inevitably causes some anxiety for both client and therapist. Managing an ideal level of anxiety is thereby essential.

Clients with a borderline personality disorder often cannot tolerate much anxiety. In many cases, exposure to unsafe situations in their childhood has prevented them building up inner stability. Attachment relationships haven't really developed, and therefore they perceive others as a threat. Anxiety levels may rise too quickly, overwhelming them, or remain too low due to them seeking to maintain stability by avoiding emotions altogether. In such situations it is difficult to learn anything, there is a risk of schema-affirming experiences, and worst of all the client does not feel safe.

In this phase it is the task of the therapist to achieve a balanced level of anxiety: an environment within which the client feels safe enough to interact with others and learn about himself. The client cannot achieve this for himself, because he hasn't learnt how to do it in childhood. Empathizing and connecting with the client are methods that the therapist may use, as well as alternating between concealing and revealing interventions. Another useful technique is accelerating by zooming in on an emotion, or by shifting the focus to another topic – for example, switching from the inner to the outer world or from the past to the present. The opposite is also possible: decelerating by taking small steps within a chosen subject area. In this way and using these tools, the therapist can balance anxiety and security, and maintain a suitable connection with the individual client.

2.2.3 Everything is fine

When a client begins therapy it is important that, from the very first moment, he has different experiences to the ones he has had in his past. This is because schema corrective experiences must begin as soon as possible. The foundation is a relationship in which anything can be said and any emotion is allowed, providing it's respectful. The therapist gives the client compliments and takes a positive stance towards any form of progress, no matter how small. He lets the client experience how important it is to express himself, and he models how to handle this in a respectful manner.

This also applies to group schema therapy (Farrell & Shaw, 2012). The motto is: "Everyone is different, everyone is allowed to be themselves, but at the same time we also form a group and we respect each other for who we are." Group therapists look for recognition within clients, and they use exercises to create an open but respectful and safe group standard with a high level of cohesion. Another essential group standard is a high level of reciprocity: "Everyone joins in and gets an equal amount of attention." The therapists manage this by organizing time slots for example, so everyone gets a turn. Verbal and non-verbal reciprocity are encouraged. Therapists ask their clients to make eye contact with each other, nod their head or share something with the group. By doing so, they show that every client is expected to join in and to express himself, no matter how little or how briefly, appropriate to his abilities and level at that moment in time.

CASE STUDY

Group schema therapy: Positive reinforcement of input

In her second meeting Anna explains:

>> **Anna:** "I was really affected by all the stories other people shared in our last meeting. I haven't been able to sleep properly since."

>> **Therapist 1:** "How brave of you to tell us! It's important to say if things have had an impact on you. So, how did you feel in our last session? Were you mainly scared, angry, happy or sad?"

>> **Anna:** "Oh I'm not sure… I have enough problems of my own, maybe other people's problems just confuse me."

>> **Therapist 1:** "Yes, I understand. It sounds as though maybe you felt slightly overwhelmed, so you got scared that you might not be able to handle it. Is that right?"

>> **Anna:** "Yes, I think so."

>> **Therapist 1:** "Well done for expressing your feelings." (to the group): 'Who recognizes this, that you feel overwhelmed and get scared that you won't be able to handle it?" (to Anna): "Look around, I see quite a few people nodding. You see, you're not the only one who gets scared by this."

>> **Therapist 2:** "This is an important topic, and also a point of focus for our next exercise in which we'll discuss the question: What are the advantages and disadvantages of feeling emotions?"

2.2.4 The environment for group schema therapy

In the start phase of group schema therapy, the new group goes through the parallel development phase. This requires the therapists to manage reciprocity to achieve an ideal level of anxiety; they focus on safety, emotion regulation and connection (Farrell & Shaw, 2012). Visualising a safe place at the start of a session is an example of this.

At the same time, this phase does contain moments when anxiety levels increase, for example when there are conflicts surrounding authority. Clients may experience resistance to attachment, and surrender to childhood experiences in which they have developed a fear of contact with others. The tension between the client's simultaneous need for contact and fear of others may manifest itself in the form of destructive behaviour, possibly arising from a coping mode, as in most cases clients haven't learnt how to express their desires in an appropriate way.

The level of anxiety also rises when new clients join the group, or when existing members leave. With each new encounter the fear of connection flares up again, and with each goodbye there is the possibility of a separation crisis as clients realize that they have formed an attachment despite their initial sense of resistance. In group sessions the therapists use the mode model and basic needs terminology to 'subtitle' all these emotions and the way they are displayed by the group members. This helps to control anxiety. In addition, reverting to a joint framework and making connections between emotions, behaviour and cognitions and between past and present provides consistency.

2.3 Goals in this phase by schema mode

2.3.1 Overall goal: A platform for change

By the end of the start phase it should be clear if a client is suitable and motivated to continue with therapy. This will only be the case if he is compliant with the therapy and therapist, acknowledges and can roughly explain his mode model at cognitive, behavioural and experiential levels, and understands why he has become the way he is. He will know his own emotional world in the light of the four basic emotions (fear, anger, sorrow and joy) and, with support, be able to talk about it. He will be aware of the dynamics between his modes and understand that his modes affect others. With help, he can see things from another person's point of view. He is aware that his internal emotions are not always congruent with the behaviour he displays on the outside and, again, with support, he can see things from both sides. In group schema therapy, clients will have learned that it's fine to dislike certain things about someone else and still get along in a respectful manner.

2.3.2 Child mode: "What do I feel?"

The client should come to realize that he has child modes, which go hand in hand with intense emotions, unfulfilled basic needs and childhood memories. He experiences the differences between the vulnerable child, the angry child and the happy child, and he connects with all these modes. This also applies to group schema therapy. He is aware of his unmet basic needs, and he knows which biographical events and carers' characteristics have contributed to this. He has also gained greater insight into his own temperament and strengths. By the end of the start phase he recognizes the primary schemas that are triggered in the vulnerable child mode, and is aware of how this feels and how it affects his behaviour and thoughts. He is able to express this within therapy. He is not afraid to show his child mode to the therapist (and also to his peers, in the case of group therapy).

2.3.3 Coping mode: From "My coping style rules me" to "I rule my coping style"

In the start phase the client gains insight into his coping mode. He knows what his main coping style is and why and when he developed it. The sub-categorization into avoidance, surrender and overcompensation is therefore very important. He is aware of the advantages and disadvantages of his coping mode, and wants to learn to cope with emotions in a different way. He has experienced that, within the therapeutic environment, he can feel reasonably safe without his coping mode. He allows the therapist to challenge his coping, accepts empathic confrontation and shows willingness to break away from his coping. Based on all this, both therapist and client gain sufficient confidence in the ability of the client to make even more progress in the remainder of the therapy.

2.3.4 Parent mode: From "Huh? Punitive parent, is that a mode?" to "Oh, that's my punitive parent mode again!"

By the end of the start phase the client is aware of the existence of a parent mode. He knows how this mode was created and what impact it has on his life. He understands that this mode isn't innate but rather internalized by external influences. It's all about the difference between knowing and feeling; he knows he has a parent mode, but doesn't necessarily see it as one of his states yet. The parent mode is still egosyntonic, or consistent with self-image. The client has experienced the effects of the parent mode on the feelings of the vulnerable child. He is in a position where he can allow the therapist and his peers to challenge this mode and experience how this feels for the vulnerable child.

2.3.5 Healthy adult mode and happy child mode: "What would a good parent say or do?"

Towards the end of the start phase the client's healthy adult mode has become stronger. He has practiced observing, identifying and acknowledging his emotions. He knows and feels the link between these emotions and his unmet basic need, for example: "I'm feeling very sad so I need contact." He has also practiced imagining what a good parent would say or do, and he has encountered the happy child within himself.

CASE STUDY

Individual therapy: Growing awareness

Linda mainly shows her protector mode. The therapist makes use of a multiple chair technique for himself and Linda, in order to get a better understanding of the protector, its survival value, its forms of expression and its characteristics. In this mode, which Linda calls 'the mask', she keeps others and her own feelings at a distance to enable her to keep functioning as a mother. She developed this mask as a child, when she was on the streets with a group of older boys and had to be untouchable and invulnerable to avoid being perceived as a burden. By using the multiple chair technique, the therapist helps Linda to see and experience the disadvantages of the mask; it's a lonely and unsafe place, she doesn't get the support and warmth that she needs, and she doesn't feel secure or connected. Gradually, Linda comes to recognize more often when the mask is triggered during therapy, and she is able to let 'little Linda' speak when the therapist asks her to. She has also told her partner about this side of her personality and how and why it came about.

2.3.6 Simplified mode model used in this phase

Using a simplified version of the mode model prevents excessively rationalising and analysing experiences. It also contributes to an efficient use of language and helps to connect emotions, thoughts and behaviour. The simplified mode model consists of five basic modes. See figure 2.1 for an illustration of this basic mode model (after: Arntz & Bögels, 2000; Arntz & Jacob, 2012).

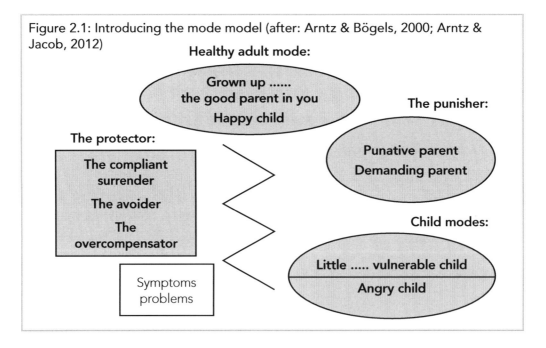

Figure 2.1: Introducing the mode model (after: Arntz & Bögels, 2000; Arntz & Jacob, 2012)

Healthy adult mode:

Grown up ......
the good parent in you
Happy child

The punisher:

Punative parent
Demanding parent

The protector:

The compliant surrender

The avoider

The overcompensator

Symptoms problems

Child modes:

Little ..... vulnerable child

Angry child

Parent modes: The general term used to refer to the parent mode in the start phase is 'the punisher.' The client learns about the difference between the punitive parent mode and the demanding parent mode on the basis of the kind of ideas and assumptions that have been internalized, but he is not required to choose between the two just yet.

Vulnerable child mode: This is often addressed with 'little … (client's name)' and the main basic emotion and basic need arising from the primary schema (little scared Emma wants to feel safe).

Angry child mode: This is also addressed as directly as possible and linked with a basic need (little angry Emma wants to be taken seriously).

Coping mode: This is often referred to as 'the protector'. As therapy progresses, the client will be able to distinguish between 'the approval seeker' (surrender), 'the avoider' (avoidance) and 'the fighter' (overcompensation), and he will choose the coping mode that is the most common or causes the most suffering. In rare instances where the client really struggles to make a choice, it is possible to choose two or more coping modes.

Healthy adult mode and happy child mode: The healthy adult mode is referred to as 'the good parent in you.' From the start of the therapy, the therapist looks for healthy behaviour in his clients: 'What would a good parent do? What would you want for your own child?' Focusing the therapy on moments in which the client feels content and comfortable shapes the happy child mode.

The core problems that are the reason why a client is in therapy become part of the mode model by linking them to specific modes. For example, drug abuse might be an aspect of 'the avoider.' This can be illustrated by drawing an arrow in the mode model from the avoider to the problem.

2.4 The therapeutic relationship

2.4.1 Limited reparenting

In the start phase of schema therapy, the therapist takes a lead role in establishing the therapeutic relationship. He provides fulfilment of unmet basic needs and creates an ideal level of anxiety. After all, the client's healthy adult mode is usually still underdeveloped. The therapist empathizes with the client; he takes him by the hand and does what a good parent should do, within the professional and ethical boundaries of the therapeutic relationship.

Arntz & Jacob (2012) combine this limited reparenting with 'extra reparenting'. This means that the therapist makes sure that he becomes a key person in his client's life. He is less distant; in fact, he should be really close and involved. He puts in extra effort to provide care, to guide the client in his life and behaviour, and to create conditions under which the client can flourish – just as the parent of a young child would do. It's hard work; the relationship is very intense, and it requires the therapist to take on a proactive, committed attitude. He provides safety and connection, but he also encourages acts of self-expression and self-appreciation, no matter how small. This can include non-verbal signals. For example: "I noticed you looked away as if something shocked you. What was it?"; or "I see you're sitting up straight. Is that because you want to show us you're part of the conversation?"

Complimenting to each demonstration of self-expression reinforces the behaviour and boosts self-appreciation: "I hear you say that you find it stupid, well done for expressing your opinion!" Explaining this therapeutic attitude beforehand may contribute to the client's sense of safety: "I'm going to shake things up a bit here and there and sometimes I might get under your skin – not to annoy you, but to really understand you and help you connect with what is important to you".

2.4.2 Limited reparenting in a group setting

In group schema therapy, limited reparenting is even more difficult. Group therapists, in a sense, are the parents of a large step-family, and they are connected with all the family members. Whilst caring for one child, they must keep an eye on the others and on the family as a whole. Another way to think of them is as the conductors of an orchestra full of anxiety-sensitive musicians (Farrell et al., 2016). The basic needs of the group are crucial in this first phase, and safety and connection again take priority. The group cannot tolerate a high level of anxiety, and anxiety and fear are contagious – if one member feels too anxious or scared, then others will start to feel unsafe as well. For that reason, it is critical to choose an approach that is manageable for the entire group. Adjusting an exercise spontaneously, as well as giving a group member extra support or a little time out, helps to regulate levels of anxiety. This enables all members to fully join in and to go home with the same experience. Individual attention might consist of the therapists pointing out a client's non-verbal behaviour, their efforts to join in and their reactions to others. The core message is always "You are important."

> **>> Client:** "Last week we worked with the punisher. For me it was the first time. I found it very scary. I had to draw something on a card, a symbol for what I say to myself, or what I think of myself when I feel angry with myself. I wrote it down quickly and struggled to even look at it. I was glad that one of the therapists glanced at me and winked, it made me feel a bit more at ease. I also liked it that we could hand in the cards straight away and we got a card back with a lovely message on it. Mine said 'little steps are still steps.' I try to read it every day."

This also means that attention is focused first and foremost on the needs of the whole group at any specific moment in time, even when an intervention is aimed at an individual member. Having two therapists means that one can keep an eye on the group whilst the other continues his intervention with the individual (Farrell & Shaw, 2012). Individual interventions don't last longer than absolutely necessary, so that the rest of the group can be involved as quickly as possible: "You say that you often feel sad. It's really brave of you to express these feelings. Let's have a look. Who else in the group recognizes this?" When some of the other group members nod, the second therapist asks one of them: "Can you tell us to what extent you recognize this?" It is then considered how making use of the wider group can benefit individual clients.

Applying structural elements based on group dynamics is another way of managing anxiety levels (Hoijtink, 2001). The Dutch having a saying that babies and toddlers need three R's (rust, regelmaat, reinheid – rest, regularity and cleanliness), and this is that motto transposed to a group therapy context. The therapists take a leading role in embedding these structural elements. They monitor the balance between freedom and safety for the group as well as for the individuals within it. This means that the behavioural repertoire of group members may be quite restricted in this phase, so as to achieve an ideal level of anxiety and maximum safety. Reciprocity, cohesion and self-expression are encouraged, so that differences and conflicts can be expressed. However, at the same time they are limited by the anxiety level that the group can tolerate. The therapists take a proactive, guiding role, and are prepared to use themselves as a resource. An example of this is the 'group thermostat' (Hoijtink, 2001), where one of the therapists says: "Just wait a minute, I've noticed that my colleague is wiggling her foot. I know she is someone who can really sense an increase in levels of anxiety." (To colleague): "Is that right? Can you tell us what you've noticed?" This kind of intervention can also be done using a group member, if there is an adequate balance between safety and freedom.

2.4.3 Empathic confrontation

Empathic confrontation and limited reparenting together form the core of the therapeutic relationship in schema therapy. In order to help the client change his schemas, it's essential for the therapist to take an empathic but confronting stance whereby he can put pressure on schema-controlled behaviour in a caring way – just like parents who set limits for their child in a caring and loving manner. For clients, this means that they get to experience the difference between unhealthy and healthy pressure. Many of them experienced unhealthy pressure in their childhood and have internalized it as a demanding parent mode. In the therapy they get to experience healthy pressure resulting from realistic limits and the desire to grow and develop themselves. There are differences in emphasis in the substance of empathic confrontations based on the various coping styles.

Elements of Empathic Confrontation

Several manuals outline the basics of empathic confrontation (e.g. Young et al., 2003, Arntz & Jacob, 2012). It includes the following components:

- The therapist states that he wants contact.
- He points out which behaviours and modes might hinder contact. He does this in a personalised manner, describing them as characteristics of the client.
- He emphasises that he says these things because he wants to stay connected with the client and understand what he really needs, and this is impossible if the client doesn't express himself.
- He validates why the behaviour was necessary for the client in the past.
- He explains the effect of the behaviour on himself and possibly also on others.
- He asks for a connection with the vulnerable child whilst monitoring emotions that are evoked.
- He gives the client the opportunity to respond to the empathic confrontation.

An empathic confrontation takes time as typically the client hasn't yet developed awareness of his modes and behaviour patterns and requires guidance. In a group setting, however, an empathic confrontation should be brief to aid the group process. The therapists do need to explain that all group members will learn to talk about the emotion or memory that their coping is trying to avoid.

At the beginning of therapy the therapist needs to show lots of empathy in order to enable the client to tolerate the anxiety caused by the confrontation. Moreover, an empathic confrontation must be repeated over and over again; after all, the patterns of thinking and behaviour are inflexible and persistent. As the therapy progresses, a word or a gesture on its own might be sufficient to repeat the empathic confrontation. See Chapter 3 for the differences in empathic confrontation by phase.

Empathic confrontation of the overcompensator

Empathic confrontation of overcompensation takes the highest priority. At the same time, for therapists who the self-sacrifice schema, it can be a pitfall to be impressed by this behaviour and subsequently ignore it. However, behaviour that is part of an overcompensating coping mode quickly leads to insecurity. In individual therapy this tends to lead to the therapist 'walking on eggshells' so as not to make mistakes. In a group setting, clients with this behaviour may be popular with other group members to begin with, but the atmosphere soon becomes insecure with a risk of schema-affirming exclusion and it is therefore important for the therapists to challenge this behaviour at an early stage. It is the only way to protect themselves and the client, as well as the group and its other individual members, against the long-term consequences of this behaviour.

Empathic confrontation of overcompensation starts with the therapist reminding the client of limits and describing the behaviour in question. He makes eye contact and matching arm movements: "Just stop for a minute. You're talking really loudly and you're not listening to what I'm saying. Your fighter is taking over. That's what you learned in the past, when you had to be strong as a child. We know that your fighter can say things in a harsh or rude way, and that you regret this later. I don't want that to happen."

After this, the therapist describes the effect of the client's behaviour on himself: "I get scared and I feel like keeping my distance when you talk that way and look so angry. That's not what I want. I'd rather stay connected with you." In the case of group schema therapy, he describes the effect of the client's behaviour on the group: "If I was one of the group members, I would probably think that you find me ridiculous because you're talking to me in a really harsh voice. I would maybe back off. Is that what you're trying to achieve?"

Finally, he addresses the child mode: "I'd like to know how you're feeling. I know that behind the fighter, there is a sad little girl who has been affected by everything that has happened to her. Try to connect with that little girl. How does she feel?" Negotiating can also be part of this: "Can you tell me how you feel on the inside? It would help me understand you and you wouldn't feel so lonely." Or "Maybe you'd like to count to ten and then I'll come back so you can tell me how you're feeling?"

>> **Therapist:** "A while ago I noticed that I was feeling very nervous about going into the group. I felt unsure; I was scared to make a mistake and be criticised for it. I discussed this with my co-therapist. She felt the same. We analysed the reasons for it, and we discovered that it was linked to strong overcompensating coping. We came to the conclusion that this has been going on for a while, but we ignored it because we didn't really know how to deal with it. In the next session, we discussed this behaviour with the use of an empathic confrontation. That was quite challenging, but we had practiced and were prepared for it. Afterwards we noticed that there was less anxiety in the group."

Empathic confrontation of the avoider

In the short term, emotional avoidance behaviour is often less challenging than overcompensation, but it still creates insecurity in the long run. In individual therapy it can lead to a lack of connection between therapist and client, making it is difficult for the therapist to assess exactly how dangerous the client's destructive behaviour actually is. In a group setting, emotionally avoidant clients can seem more like spectators than participants. The fact that they are relatively 'unreadable' to others causes anxiety levels in the group to increase. This triggers schemas, which then pave the way for schema congruent interpretations of other people's intentions.

Once again, the therapist starts by describing what he can see and what the effects are. A limit is not necessary because the behaviour isn't immediately dangerous: "I can see that you're not making eye contact. What are you thinking? Am I right to say that this is your avoidant side? I understand that you're tempted to distance yourself from others as that's what helped you in the past. Withdrawing was the only way to stay safe at home. However, here and now it means I can't make contact with you. You're keeping me at a distance, and I don't want that because I don't want you to be alone." Then he addresses the client directly: "What is it that you need to help you not withdraw yourself?" and encourages him to connect with his feelings: "Go on, try the best you can and tell us what your vulnerable side is feeling at the moment." Again, negotiation is an option as well, for example in a group session: "It's always scary if you've only just joined a new group. For now, we ask that you try your best to use your vulnerable side to observe what we're doing. We'll teach you step-by-step how to slowly come out of your coping mode."

Empathic confrontation of the approval seeker

In the start phase of therapy, the approval seeking coping style will generally cause least trouble and stand out less than other styles. And therein lies the key problem for these clients – they are used to not standing up for themselves, so they risk going unnoticed and staying on the sidelines. It is even possible that a therapist will actually appreciate a client's approval seeking behaviour, especially if they are occupied with the 'difficult' behaviour of other clients individually or in a group. Because of this, the approval seeking client doesn't get what he needs; he doesn't really learn to express himself, and he doesn't get enough attention for his feelings and his basic needs. The result is that the coping style is reinforced, and the client doesn't experience its disadvantages.

It is therefore crucial that the approval seeking coping style is noticed, and met with an empathic confrontation, early on in therapy. It allows the therapist to check how the client reacts: "I hear that you agree with my suggestion, but your response makes me wonder – is that your compliant surrender side or is that really how you feel? I think it might be your compliant surrender side that you developed because you often had to take care of your sick mother when you were a child. Now, however, this approval seeking behaviour causes you to be disconnected from your feelings and, therefore, from me. It is important for me to hear what you're thinking and feeling, so I'd like you to try your best to connect with your vulnerable side and tell me what you're feeling now."

CASE STUDY

Individual therapy: Confront more directly

Becoming aware of schema-controlled behaviour and modes is an important goal in this phase, and therefore it is necessary to frequently engage in an empathic confrontation. In addition, it's important to directly address negative behaviour and link it to the basic needs. For example:

Linda rolls her eyes as she tells the therapist that her partner asked her for a hug.

>> Therapist: "When you roll your eyes like that whilst telling me about that hug, it appears to me that you disapprove of what your boyfriend asked for. Is that how you want to come across?"

>> Linda: "No, not at all, it makes me happy when he hugs me."

>> Therapist: "Did you realize that that's how you come across?"

>> Linda: "Oh, no, I didn't... I think I do it a lot, subconsciously."

>> Therapist: "Does it sound familiar to you, that people don't understand your needs when you respond like that? That they think it's something you don't want, when you, on the inside, maybe actually do want it?"

>> Linda: "Yes, that happens. I often feel misunderstood."

>> Therapist: "Yes, I understand. I'm a therapist, so I can ask you if your feelings on the inside are different from what you're showing on the outside. However, other people might not check this. Your partner will see you roll your eyes and think 'Oh, Linda thinks a hug is silly.' He'll then turn away, when you actually want a hug."

In a group setting it's easy to involve the other group members in this: Therapist 2 can ask the other participants: "Was it clear to you that Linda felt the need for contact with her partner when she rolled her eyes?", "What do you feel when Linda rolls her eyes and what does it make you think?" or "Do you recognize this in yourself?"

2.4.4 The therapist's perspective

The start phase also means the beginning of something new for the therapist. He doesn't know the client well, so it's difficult to assess the purpose of his specific behaviour. He also hasn't established an attachment relationship or bond of trust yet. Some clients may have pinned all their hopes on this treatment; others are demoralised and see it as a last resort. Some have developed mistrust towards the professional care system as a result of past experiences. For as long as clients don't learn to deal with these and other feelings in a healthier way at the beginning of therapy, there will be a lot of dysfunctional behaviour. For example, clients may show off to camouflage their insecurities; or they may be introverted, clingy or rebellious, or seek refuge in drug use, self-harm or gaming.

Even though the therapist is more or less prepared for this behaviour, it can still be overwhelming. There is a lot to analyse and discover in the interactions with the client and, at the same time, the therapist is expected to be firm and thorough as well as kind. In a situation like this, the therapist is put to the test. His schemas and coping style will be triggered – he may, for example, suffer from a sense of insecurity or perfectionism: "Are my feelings about this correct? Am I in a position to say something about it? Something is wrong but I can't put my finger on it. What if I'm wrong about what I think I saw or heard?" He may also experience feelings of irritability ("When will that coping style go away?"), sadness ("This client has such a tough life"), impatience ("When will you reveal that vulnerable child?"), disgust ("That memory she shared was horrendous") or fear ("I'm harming the client with this treatment"). Further, clients regularly express their needs in non-verbal ways, for example by looking at the therapist with piercing eyes or by drawing attention to themselves in another way. In group schema therapy it may be the case that several clients simultaneously make implicit appeals for help from the therapist. As a result, the therapist may feel overburdened.

It takes time and effort for a therapist and client to find and understand each other, just as the parents of a new-born baby need time to adjust to their child and grow into their role. The therapist can only meet the client's need for safety and connection if he himself feels safe and connected. This requires time and attention, as the therapist must deal with a lot of different feelings in this phase. Client discussions and peer coaching are vital for him to analyse his own experiences and responses: What belongs to the client and what belongs to the therapist? How is the therapist personally affected? What does he need to enable him to work with this client or group of clients? To what extent are colleagues or a co-therapist able to support him with this?

If the therapist learns to listen carefully to his own needs, he can set an example for the client. By showing that he knows what he needs and can stand up for himself, he teaches the client to do the same.

Transference: The therapist's feelings as a sign

Transference is a key principle of therapy. During their lives, clients have usually had little or no help with understanding specific feelings or interactions. In the start phase, the coping style leads the way and feelings are suppressed and 'outsourced' to the therapist (projective identification). As a result, the therapist's feelings can give an indication of, or 'point towards', the client's feelings. For example, a client appears impassive when he talks about a situation in which he was treated unfairly. The therapist notices a sense of anger, and wonders if this is the anger the client is unable to feel right now. Or, the client reveals something hurtful from his past but the therapist feels little compassion. This too could point to something; perhaps the client is sharing his experiences not from the perspective of the vulnerable child but instead through his coping style. In both cases, it is important that the therapist shares his observation and discusses it with the client.

2.4.5 Thinking, feeling and doing

Providing structure and psychoeducation and discussing the mode model are examples of cognitive tasks in the start phase. The therapist does a lot of explaining: How do children learn? What do they need? What rights does a child have? Why are children so vulnerable? What makes a person scared, angry, sad or happy? What is the purpose of emotions? What is the difference between a desire and a need? Why are children loyal to their parents? Why can a child never be held responsible?

Many clients have gained very little knowledge about these areas as a child; they probably didn't get any explanations, and they weren't taught how to verbalise their body and feelings. To initiate this process, it is advisable to use the four basic emotions: scared, angry, sad and happy, and to link these with body signals: What do you notice inside your body? How do you feel that? Where do you feel that? What kind of sensation is that? This prevents the client from searching in his head for 'pseudo-manifestations of feelings', and it helps him to connect his thoughts and his feelings with each other. This exploratory approach enhances the client's awareness.

Step by step

If the therapist notices that a client is struggling to express himself in a concise manner, he intervenes and gently diverts attention back to the topic of discussion. For example: "We were talking about connection as a basic need. Is what you're telling me now related to that?" Or: "I've noticed that there is a lot you want to tell me about this topic or situation, perhaps because it creates strong feelings inside you? However, in this therapy we work step-by-step towards dealing with problems. Today I want to particularly focus on your avoidant reaction. We can talk about other things another time. How can I help you to tell me, in five minutes' time, something about…?"

In this way the client learns that therapy isn't just talking, but also doing and feeling. He practices this healthy way of making serious and emotional statements in a concise manner. He also practices focusing attention on his basic emotions and on what he needs to deal with certain situations. New members of a group learn this as they go along. They find that there are circle discussions in almost every session, whereby clients are asked to say something about a particular theme. The available time is shared equally between the clients to make sure everybody gets a turn and, preferably, one of the clients keeps track of things with a timer. To begin with this may feel somewhat awkward for the therapists; however, experience shows that it provides clarity and the group gets used to a form of conversation whereby everybody is guaranteed the chance to speak.

Role reversals

Multiple chair techniques and imagery are important methods to make contact with underlying emotions. By using these techniques consistently, the client learns that his therapy is invariably about connecting with the emotion and the basic need so that this can be fulfilled. Role reversals, whereby the therapist (or a group member) interprets and depicts a particular side of the client, help the client to become aware of his patterns. When the client takes on someone else's role, for example in a group session, he learns something about himself as well by seeing things from another person's point of view. This method of 'stepping in and out' of the emotion not only helps to increase awareness, but it also helps the client learn how to regulate his feelings.

2.5 Exercises

The exercises below are aimed at discovering and exploring the various modes and schemas, and they can be used alongside the regular exercises found in schema therapy manuals. They can be divided into three categories:

1. **Safety and connection:** these exercises are particularly suitable for the start of therapy or with a new intake in a group, where members are finding their way and learning how to share.
2. **Discovering modes:** exercises to become aware of modes and explore connections between past and present. These exercises mark the start of the therapy proper.
3. **Impact of modes:** exercises exploring how modes impact each other and other people. These can be used when a sense of safety is established, and the client can tolerate more anxiety.

2.5.1 Exercises concerning safety and connection

Exercise 2.1: Over the line	
Goal:	To get to know each other, and to learn that sharing thoughts and feelings is an essential element of therapy.
Category:	1: Safety and connection.
Preparation:	The group members stand in a circle. The therapists join in. Therapist 1 explains the exercise and the goal, then models the task by being the first to have a go.
Instructions:	Clients take turns to step into the middle of the circle and share something about themselves. In the first round this can be something superficial.
Step 1:	The therapist who is modelling (or the client who is taking over) steps forward and shares something about a hobby or an interest (e.g. I love rock music). →

Step 2:	The other group members are asked to step towards the middle of the circle as well, matching the extent to which they agree with what the person in the centre has said. The nearness to the middle reflects the degree of recognition (e.g. clients who also love rock music would stand in the middle as well).
Step 3:	The client is asked to have a look around ("See, you're not the only one").
Step 4:	Everyone steps back to their place in the outer circle. The next person has a turn.
Step 5:	After a few goes, it's time for the second round in which clients are asked to share something more personal, for example a feeling ("I often feel lonely"). The round then proceeds in exactly the same way as the first round.
Notes:	■ The exercise can be extended with an extra round to express doubts or vulnerabilities ("I'm not sure if... [I will ever be happy]") or a round to express something important ("it is important for other people to know that I... [can act really tough when I feel insecure]"). ■ The therapists begin each new round with an example to make the goal very clear. They also join in in showing the degree of recognition. ■ To keep anxiety levels manageable, it's important to keep up the momentum and maintain some spontaneity. If necessary, the therapists can take the lead more often, bring in an example or invite specific group members to contribute. ■ Everybody should be given a turn; people may have more than one turn.

Exercise 2.2: Portraying the coping mode	
Goal:	To create openness and connection, and to practice expressing thoughts and feelings. To learn to recognize the coping mode and what's behind it.
Category:	1: Safety and connection.
Preparation:	The group stands in a circle. The therapist explains the exercise and has the first go.
Instructions:	→

Step 1:	The central question is: "How do you respond to anxiety or stress?" After the therapist has modelled his reaction, Client 1 steps into the circle and acts out in a non-verbal way what he does when he feels anxious or stressed. His posture, facial expressions and gestures portray his 'outside'.
Step 2:	He steps back to the outer group member circle.
Step 3:	Client 2, who is standing to the left of Client 1, steps forward and mirrors the outside of Client 1; he copies him in as much detail as possible.
Step 4:	Client 2 steps back to the outer circle and takes a moment to connect with his own behaviour when he feels anxious or stressed.
Step 5:	Client 2 steps forward again and acts out in a non-verbal way what he does when he feels anxious or stressed.
Step 6:	Client 2 steps back to the outer circle.
Step 7:	Client 3, who is to the left of Client 2, steps forward and mirrors his outside. And so it continues so that everyone gets a turn to portray and mirror the outside.
Step 8:	Start the second round when everyone has had a turn. The task is now to portray what you actually feel on the inside, again in a non-verbal way, by using facial expressions, gestures and posture. The therapist again models the task once.
Step 9:	Client 1 steps forward and shows his 'inside' in posture, facial expression and gesture.
Step 10:	Client 1 steps back to the outer circle.
Step 11:	Client 2, who is to the left of Client 1, steps forward and mirrors the inside of Client 1. He copies him in as much detail as possible.
Step 12:	Client 2 steps back to the outer circle and takes a moment to connect with his own inside. He then steps forward again and portrays this. The exercise continues in this manner until everyone has had their turn.
Step 13:	Debrief: What is the difference between the inside and outside? How does an outside like that develop? What reactions are evoked when watching others?
Notes:	■ The therapists actively coach the clients to express themselves ("Go ahead and show us… it's good to exaggerate a bit") and they praise every attempt a client makes to show something ("Well done! Very brave!"). ➜

<table>
<tr><td></td><td>
■ This exercise can also be done within individual therapy. The therapist models his own coping behaviour when feeling anxious, then asks the client to mirror it. Then the roles are reversed. The inside is repeated in the same way.

■ A variation on this exercise is for the clients to introduce themselves in the first round in the style of their coping – for example, Amber says "I'm Amber" while avoiding eye contact and turning away from those being addressed.

■ A third round can be added where clients express and mirror basic needs.

■ The therapists can join in with the whole exercise if it helps to lower the barriers for anxious clients and increases their willingness to engage.
</td></tr>
</table>

Exercise 2.3: The introductory interview	
Goal:	To get to know each other. To learn to listen, summarise and share.
Category:	1: Safety and connection.
Preparation:	Think beforehand about the questions you want to ask the group.
Instructions:	
Step 1:	The group divides into pairs, preferably combinations of old and new members.
Step 2:	The therapists formulate a few questions for the group members to ask each other, such as: "Why am I attending the therapy?", "What do I want to change with the help of this therapy?", "What is it important to know about me?"
Step 3:	The pairs have ten minutes to interview each other in this way.
Step 4:	The participants return to the group. The interviewer tells the group about the interviewee. The therapists help the interviewers to keep the information brief and to the point.
Notes:	■ The same questions are suitable for individual therapy. The client can even think about this as a self-interview, possibly in the form of a homework task. ■ In between the presentations, the therapists can ask the other group members for recognition ("Just put your hand up if you recognize this…"). →

> - This kind of interview is also useful at other moments in therapy, for example to evaluate the goals or to find out about each other's mode model. Possible questions thereby are: "What does your punisher systematically say?", "What do you tend to do when you're feeling sad?", "What have you achieved since you started the therapy?", or "What is your biggest fear?"

2.5.2 Exercises to discover modes and explore connections between past and present

Exercise 2.4: Experiential case conceptualization	
Goal:	To gain insight into feelings, sensations, cognitions and basic needs, and to link these with the client's own personal history.
Category:	2: Discovering modes.
Preparation:	The therapist needs a box with props such as cuddly toys, old toys, a pair of sunglasses, cans, a light and a scarf.
Instructions:	This exercise covers four sessions in the following order:
	1. Child mode
	2. What is your bond with your mother like?
	3. What is your bond with your father like?
	4. What were your family's rules of behaviour when you were growing up?
SESSION 1: CHILD MODE	
Step 1:	The client is asked to close his eyes and picture himself when he was a small child (approximately 6 years old).
Step 2:	The therapist asks: "What kind of a child do you see? Just watch him, what does he look like? What does he reflect? Try and put yourself in his shoes. What kind of character does he have?" The therapist provides suggestions such as: "Does he like to play with others or on his own? Is he happy to make himself heard? How does he ask for attention from the people around him? Is he a dreamer, a thinker or a doer?" The therapist also asks: "How does little (client's name) feel? Can you feel a connection with him?"
Step 3:	The client may open his eyes and choose a prop from the box that symbolises the child in the imaginary picture. →

Step 4:	The client puts the chosen prop between himself and the therapist.
Step 5:	The therapist asks the client to present the prop through the following questions, aimed at gaining insight into temperament: "What did you choose and why? Tell me something about that little one. What did you see when you pictured him? What kind of child was he? What was his character like? What about his temper? What did or didn't he like?"
Step 6:	The link to the present is made by questions such as: "Do you still recognize that little one's character? How does it manifest itself now? What do you miss about little (client's name)? What would you like to get back?"

SESSION 2 and 3: WHAT IS THE BOND WITH YOUR MOTHER/FATHER LIKE?

Step 1:	The client is asked to close his eyes and picture himself when he was a small child (approximately 6 years old).
Step 2:	The therapist says: "Focus on an image that is typical of the relationship between you and your father/mother. What do you see? How does your father/mother look at you? What kind of expression or posture does he/she have? How does that make you feel as a child?"
Step 3:	The client may open his eyes and choose a prop from the box that symbolises that image of his father/mother.
Step 4:	The client puts the chosen prop between himself and the therapist.
Step 5:	The therapist asks the client to present the prop through the following questions, aimed at gaining insight into the bond between the client and his father/mother: "What did you choose and why? Tell me something about that image; what did you see and how did you feel? What does this say about your father/mother?" The therapist also asks: "What was missing for you as a child in this image?"
Step 6:	The link to the present is made by questions such as: "What message did you take from this? How does this still affect you now?" The therapist also asks: "What do you want to do with this prop and the image it represents; put it away or keep it with you? Go ahead and do it."
Notes:	It may happen that the client only focuses on pleasant images of his parents to avoid negative feelings and memories. If this is the case, it is possible for the therapist to tell him directly that must concentrate on a less pleasant image of his father or mother.

SESSION 4: WHAT WERE YOUR FAMILY'S RULES OF BEHAVIOUR WHEN YOU WERE GROWING UP?	
Step 1:	The client is asked to close his eyes and picture himself when he was a small child (approximately 6 years old).
Step 2:	The therapist says: "Try to focus on a typical atmosphere at home. You walk along your old road. You can see your house and you walk in through the front door. What situation do you find yourself in? What can you see? Who is there? Who isn't there? How does it feel to be in this house? How does the little one feel?"
Step 3:	The client may open his eyes and try to represent this image in the present, using himself and the therapist to capture the atmosphere of the image.
Step 4:	Together with the therapist, the client reflects on what this means and decides on a suitable caption, for example: In this home there is no laughter, or: In this home it is not safe.
Step 5:	The link to the present is made by questions such as: "Does this message still play a part in your life? How does a message like this make you feel about yourself? What does it make you think about yourself? What does it make you do?"
Notes:	■ This is an excellent group exercise. The group members conduct the imagery together and they simultaneously each choose a prop. Then they take it in turns to present their own stories. Group interaction is encouraged with questions such as: "Who recognizes this?"; "How does this make you feel?"; and "Which basic need wasn't met, having a father like that?"
	■ With regard to the family's rules, the group members are deployed to portray the image and atmosphere. The client and therapist don't play an active role in the image itself; they look at the complete picture and devise a caption.
	■ The information that arises from these exercises can be added to the mode model. For example, the image of a father with a disapproving expression on his face continues to exist in the form of the punisher.
	■ Other props can be used such as animals or glove puppets.
	■ Use your imagination to think of variations on this exercise. For example with regard to coping, with the client choosing a prop that symbolises his coping.

Exercise 2.5: Mode flipping	
Goal:	To become aware of different modes.
Category:	2: Discovering modes.
Preparation:	The therapist puts a few chairs out: one for the parent mode, one for the coping mode and one for the child mode.
Instructions:	
Step 1:	The therapist shows which chair represents which mode.
Step 2:	The client talks about a situation, preferably from the past week, in which he felt uncomfortable and stressed.
Step 3:	When the client is done, the therapist sits, one by one, in the mode-chairs. On each chair, he gives a verbal and non-verbal reaction (posture, facial expression, use of his voice) from the perspective of the specific mode that the chair represents. For example, on the first chair, the therapist shows how the parent mode comes across in the client's story.
Step 4:	The therapist asks the client to indicate what he does and doesn't recognize in the demonstration of that mode.
Step 5:	The therapist moves onto the second and third chairs and repeats the process.
Step 6:	In the follow-up the therapist asks about feelings with questions such as: "How does this punitive mode impact on your feelings? Is that familiar to you in real life?" The therapist also asks about schemas, for example: "Are you particularly scared to be abandoned?"
Step 7:	The therapist can add extra chairs as he gets to know the client better.
Notes:	▪ In this exercise it is important to maintain momentum in order to keep levels of anxiety under control. ▪ This exercise is good for groups; different members can sit on the different mode-chairs. As they get to know each other better, they feel more comfortable responding to each other spontaneously. They can add chairs themselves to represent extra modes. It's also possible for 'the modes' to respond to each other in a second round. ▪ Instead of taking turns voluntarily, the group members can swap seats in a certain order. For example, all clients can move up one chair to the left when Client 1 has finished. By doing things this way, all the clients know in advance that they will get a turn and when it is going to be their turn.

Make it experiential

Schema therapy incorporates experiential techniques. The therapist can enhance the experiential learning by focusing on non-verbal expression of schemas, for example by drawing attention to or demonstrating:

- Facial expressions
- Posture and gestures
- Tone of voice

Exercise 2.6: Basic modes

Goal:	To clarify the mode model.
Category:	2: Discovering modes.
Preparation:	Get four chairs ready. Take a ball with you.
Instructions:	
Step 1:	There are four rounds. In each round the therapist and client brainstorm about one of the four basic modes by discussing word associations, i.e.: "What do you associate the word 'child' with?"; "What do you associate the word 'punisher' with?" "What do you associate the word 'protector' with?"; "What do you associate the phrase 'healthy parent' with?" In each round they throw the ball to each other several times to come up with ideas.
Step 2:	The translation to the individual. There are four chairs ready. The therapist explains that each chair represents a specific mode: vulnerable child, punisher, protector and healthy adult.
Step 3:	The client sits on the vulnerable child chair and answers the following question: "What is little (client's name)'s biggest uncertainty or fear?" The therapist supports the client with his verbal and non-verbal expression (posture, facial expression, use of voice).
Step 4:	The client sits on the parent mode chair and answers the following question: "What does the mean (critical) voice inside me sound like?" The therapist supports the client with his verbal and non-verbal expression.
Step 5:	The client sits on the coping mode chair and answers the following question: "How do I keep my feelings away?" The therapist supports the client with his verbal and non-verbal expression.
Step 6:	The client sits on the healthy adult chair and answers the following question: "What have I achieved already that makes me feel better about myself?" The therapist supports the client with his verbal and non-verbal expression. →

Notes:	■ This exercise can be used several times; round 1 can be skipped on subsequent occasions.
	■ In a group context it's important for everyone to get a turn, so it's essential to keep the momentum up. Using hoops instead of chairs increases the pace. It's also possible to prepare the questions in pairs then present them to the group. Lastly, the therapist can ask if other clients recognize what's being said: "Just put your hand up if you're familiar with this."
	■ In an individual session there is scope to expand a little on the questions – asking about feelings in question 1, for example, or relating certain answers to a schema ("Alright then, your biggest fear is that you will always be alone. I sense the schema abandonment in those words").

Exercise 2.7: Awareness of child modes

Goal:	To become aware of the different child modes, along with when they are triggered and what they need.
Category:	2: Discovering modes.
Preparation:	Put an extra chair out.
Instructions:	
Step 1:	The therapist and client take turns to portray various child modes: the happy child, angry child, undisciplined child, rebellious child, stubborn child and impulsive child. They do this in verbal and non-verbal ways. The therapist supports the client when it is his turn to portray a child mode: "Show me, what does this kind of child look like? How does a child like that feel?"
Step 2:	One person portrays, the other observes the child mode and practices portraying a good parent, the healthy adult. The therapist supports the client when it is his turn to portray the adult: "You are the good parent who is watching this child. How does a good parent position himself? What is his posture like? What about his expression? And his appearance?"
Step 3:	The therapist puts a chair out and asks the client to portray one specific child mode that he is familiar with (for example undisciplined child). The therapist asks questions to explore this mode, such as: "In what kind of situation do you forget to behave yourself? When does that mainly happen? How do you feel in those situations? Which basic need plays a role in those moments?" →

Step 4:	Afterwards information is added to the mode model, if necessary.
Step 5:	A possible next step can be to consider together which healthy behaviour could meet the basic need and replace the dysfunctional behaviour related to the child mode. Another option is to make a flashcard in response to this exercise.
Notes:	■ This is an excellent group exercise as clients can take turns to zoom in on the child mode that they are most familiar with. ■ This exercise can be followed by psychoeducation about the different feelings children may experience, and how these can translate into modes.

2.5.3 Exercises exploring the impact of modes on each other and on other people.

Exercise 2.8: Coping mode association exercise	
Goal:	To learn to recognize a coping mode and its impact on others.
Category:	3: Impact of modes.
Preparation:	Take a ball. Make tickets with the names of the group members written on them.
Instructions:	
Step 1:	The group members and the therapists throw the ball to each other and answer the following question: "What are the disadvantages of having emotions?"
Step 2:	The group members and the therapists throw the ball to each other and answer the following question: "What are the advantages of having emotions?"
Step 3:	The group members each take a ticket with the name of a participant on it.
Step 4:	One group member portrays the coping of the person whose name is on his ticket. This may be exaggerated to make it obvious what the coping style is. →

Step 5:	Another group member explains the impact of the coping by answering the therapist's questions, for example: "Does this behaviour create a specific feeling inside you? If so, what kind of feeling? Do you have a connection with that person? What are you tempted to do in response to this kind of behaviour?"
Step 6:	The group member who portrayed the coping reveals whose name was on the ticket. This person is now asked: "Do you recognize this?"
Step 7:	It's the turn of the next group member to take a ticket.
Step 8:	These steps are followed by a group discussion about coping, the impact of the coping behaviour on the client himself and its potential impact on others.
Notes:	■ In individual therapy the therapist can portray the client's coping. In this case the tickets can state various forms of coping rather than people's names. ■ Towards the end of phase 1, an extra chair may be added to represent the authentic part of the coping. "Which part of this behaviour is really yours, and fits with your temperament? Which part of this authentic behaviour veers towards coping because it occurs too often or it becomes too rigid or strict?" The client can sit on the chair and portray what this behaviour looks like if it's authentic.

Exercise 2.9: Implicit parental messages	
Goal:	To become aware of the parent mode and to excuse the child.
Category:	3: Impact of modes.
Preparation:	
Instructions:	
Step 1:	The therapist and client act out a scene about an implicit parental message. For example, a child arrives home from school feeling enthusiastic and keen to tell his mother about his day. His mother gives the impression that she is too busy to listen to him. The therapist acts as the mother, the client as the child.
Step 2:	The therapist asks the client, who is still acting as the child: "How do you feel? What's your reaction? What do you think?"
Step 3:	The therapist describes how he experienced his role as the mother: "How did I feel? What did I think or experience? Did I see the child? What did I think of him?" →

Step 4:	The client and therapist come out of their roles and review the exercise: "What impact do implicit messages have on a child? How does a child interpret a message like that? What kind of self-image will the child develop?"
Notes:	■ In a group session, the group members can act out the parts so the therapist doesn't have an active role to play. The group can also provide feedback: "What do you see? How will this child feel and think about himself?"
	■ If the level of anxiety is manageable, the client can contribute examples from his own childhood – in other words he can play himself. Or he can act as the director, looking at images of his own life from a distance.
	■ This exercise corresponds with the first phase of a role play of a situation from the past (Arntz & van Genderen, 2020).

Exercise 2.10: Parent mode chair technique

Goal:	To become aware of the impact of punitive or demanding messages on the vulnerable child, and the difference made by positive parental messages.
Category:	3: Impact of modes.
Preparation:	Get extra chairs ready: one for the vulnerable child and one for the parent mode.
Instructions:	
Step 1:	The client sits on the parent mode's chair and explains, in a few brief sentences, the key message of his parent mode.
Step 2:	The client sits on the vulnerable child's chair.
Step 3:	The therapist sits on parent mode's chair and repeats a sentence from the message in step 1. He then returns to his own seat.
Step 4:	The therapist asks the client how he feels about that parental message. What kind of emotions and physical sensations does he experience?
Step 5:	The client returns to his own chair and, together with the therapist, reflects on events. "What would a good parent say or do to oppose this parent mode? What would a good parent say or do to support this vulnerable child?" These messages are written on a card; the messages to oppose the parent mode on one side and the messages to support the child mode on the other.

2.6 Areas of focus and tips

2.6.1 Areas of focus

Working from our original description of the start phase, in which safety comes first, the following areas of focus can be distilled in order to provide the therapist with support and guidance:

- Be predictable. Being punctual at the start, setting homework and ending sessions on time all increase predictability. It also helps to use the same terminology, to regularly repeat information and to make sure that each session has a set structure (see Table 2.2 for an example of a set session structure).

- Make the client feel that he is important. This can take many different forms. Be warm in your role as the therapist but don't ignore important things that need a more confrontational approach. Discuss destructive behaviour and explain that you do this out of concern for the client. Link it to the mode model and guide the client towards healthier solutions. Express your appreciation for every small step in the right direction.

- Use your own emotional perceptions to empathize with the client and help him experience that he is able to tolerate feelings. Adjust levels of anxiety by speeding up or slowing down, increasing the pressure or being more laidback instead. Use humour and spontaneity to trigger the happy child mode.

- Switching between experiencing an emotion and looking at an emotion gives the client a sense of control and prevents him from becoming overwhelmed by emotions. Alternating between experiential and cognitive techniques is part of this, as well as using symbolic props and role switching with the therapist or another group member for example. This enables the client to connect with his perceptions and, at the same time, maintain some distance.

- Keep in mind that, at the beginning, the client's dysfunctional pattern is something that he feels he can rely on, and he depends on the therapist for information about other ways of dealing with situations. Take the client by his hand and guide him by providing step-by-step explanations, by doing brief imagery exercises with suggestions for the interpretation of the image, and by modelling different, healthier reactions.

- Empathic confrontations help the client to step-by-step gain insights into his coping mode and underlying basic needs. The more he realizes how his dysfunctional pattern affects his life, the better he will be equipped to decide whether or not to take part in the therapy.

- In group schema therapy, it is important that each group member leaves the sessions with a similar experience and that all clients participate in an exercise in one way or another. The group's interest comes first. Make sure there is always a sense of safety and connection underlying mutual cooperation and within the group as a whole.

Table 2.2 Example of a set session structure	
Individual session (60 minutes)	**Group session (90 minutes)**
1. Starter: how do you feel?	1. Starter: safe place exercise
2. Analyse which mode takes priority	2. Warm-up: brief exercise or explanation, introduce the topic
3. Exercise: choose an exercise appropriate for the mode, with the aim of connecting with the vulnerable child so that needs can be met by providing support, comfort and explanations	3. Exercise: devise an exercise appropriate for the topic, with the aim of connecting with the vulnerable child so that needs can be met by providing support, comfort and explanations
4. Follow-up: reflect on changes in schemas, feelings, thoughts to strengthen the healthy adult	4. Break: if necessary, for regulation purposes
5. Plenary: finish with homework and possibly a happy child exercise	5. Follow-up: create an overview by repeating steps, reflect on changes
	6. Plenary: finish with homework and possibly a happy child exercise

2.6.2 Tips

Everything is therapy for the client…

The more natural it becomes to perceive everything that happens during sessions and interactions as therapy, the easier it becomes to raise difficult issues. Adopting this mentality allows the therapist to view things more objectively. For the client it's reassuring if the therapist doesn't avoid difficult subjects, but instead – just like a good parent with his child – shows that he takes them and the client seriously without always having a readymade solution. The following questions can be a useful resource: "What is the client's underlying need?"; "What feelings does this subject create in him and what thoughts does it provoke?"; What is it important for him to experience?" The therapist can use these questions to prepare himself for a session in which he wants to discuss the client's behaviour. It is also possible to address these questions together with the client during the session.

CASE STUDY

Individual therapy: Ignore nothing

For the third time in a row, Linda is five minutes late for her session. The first time the therapist said: "Great that you're here! Let's start quickly as we're running late." The second time he looked at his watch, frowned and said: "Come on, let's start quickly again." Today he takes this approach:

>> Therapist: "Hey Linda, today is the third time in a row that you've arrived five minutes late and I'd just like to briefly talk about that."

>> Linda: "Oh okay, well, that can happen, can't it?"

>> Therapist: "Yes of course, but I'd still like to discuss it. I wonder if something is wrong."

>> Linda: "No, not at all, there's nothing wrong. It just happened accidentally. Can we start now?"

>> Therapist: "I think this an important subject to talk about, so actually I think we've already started. I know you take this therapy seriously, but I also know that you sometimes find it difficult to do the things that are good for you – especially when you don't feel great. Now that this has happened three times, I worry that maybe there's something going on in your life that affects your mental wellbeing and makes you struggle to stick to agreements. I'm not angry, I'd just like to know if that's the case or not. So please tell me, is there anything the matter?"

>> Linda: "Well, I haven't slept very well for a few weeks because I'm worried about my little dog. He's a bit poorly."

>> Therapist: "Oh dear, how awful for you. That's good to know though!"

Then Linda talks about her fear of losing her dog. The therapist responds in an understanding and supportive way. Together they make a list of things that may help Linda to get a better night's sleep.

…for the group…

Difficult situations are also most definitely part of the therapeutic process in group schema therapy. Clients will keep repeating their patterns after all, even in a group. Discussing this is important, not only for a client himself but also for his peers. They will feel irritated or agitated by another person's negative behaviour, often before the therapists do. Sensing that the therapists find their irritation or agitation important adds to their feeling that they're being taken seriously. It also means that the clients have a healthy role model: emotions should be taken seriously and discussed, in order to enable you to get what you need. In doing so, a schema corrective experience is provided.

Giving clients shared responsibility for the successful functioning of the group, right from the start, is another example of 'everything-is-therapy'. For example, clients who have been part of the group for a while are given the task of welcoming new members, sharing information about the atmosphere in the group and describing ways of interacting with each other. Or, by being put in charge of the stopwatch, clients can help to keep track of the schedule and make sure that the available time is shared equally between the group's members. Having such responsibilities enables clients to experience for themselves that they play an important role in the effective functioning of the group. At the same time, it gives them opportunities to practice healthy adult behaviours such as maintaining control, sharing and caring for each other.

Lengthy stories in the group

The therapist needs to intervene if a client takes a long time to tell his story. Gently guiding the client back to the subject is one way of doing this: "We were talking about connection. I've noticed that you've got a lot to say about this. Maybe it creates strong feelings inside you? However, in this therapy we use a step-by-step approach to learn how to deal with problems. Today we focus on this part of the topic, and other things will be addressed at another time. How can I help you to say something about (topic) in the five minutes we have available?" If the therapist sees that this causes a feeling of discomfort for the client, he can choose to make this a topic of conversation too: "Tell me, what is happening now? What do you feel? What do you need?"

...for the therapist...

Applying this form of treatment is only endurable if the therapist is permitted to make mistakes too. He doesn't always have to be super alert, and he doesn't need to constantly check on everything. In other words, the therapist must also have a lenient and tolerant attitude toward himself – one that allows him to be properly connected with his own basic needs. This prevents him from triggering his own schemas and helps him set a good example for clients. It also prevents him from lapsing into his coping mode. Doing this is not only bad for him personally, but sensitive clients will also detect it and react in line with their schemas. To be able to take himself seriously, it is important for the therapist to acknowledge and analyse his own feelings by asking himself questions like: "What is happening now? What does it say about me? What does it say about the client? What is necessary now?"

The therapist's own needs

It has been a tough morning for the therapist, He has had to deal with a difficult situation at home and take part in a work meeting about moving the department. He has noticed that he's feeling really restless and tense. However, his next client is already waiting for him. Still, the therapist doesn't feel ready yet to open up to the feelings and needs of the client. He feels he needs some time to put the morning behind him. He puts his feeling of guilt to one side and walks towards the client in the waiting room. He tells the client that he has had a hectic morning and that he needs a ten-minute break before starting the session a little bit later. The client agrees to this. The therapist goes outside for a bit and does a breathing exercise. Once the session gets underway, the client is given time to say how this made him feel, and to gain a better understanding of why some things trigger him. Towards the end of the session, the therapist and the client discuss with each other the degree of connection they've experienced in the session; both are satisfied with this.

...and for the team.

In group schema therapy, the principle of 'everything-is-therapy' also applies to the cooperation between the therapists. In a new group for clients with personality disorder, collaborating therapists won't be able to avoid having their own schemas triggered and reacting to each other in ways based on old patterns. Differences in reference frameworks may create extra challenges when therapists of various professional disciplines work together, for example when a psychotherapist collaborates with a drama therapist. To prevent this from jeopardizing the collaboration and seeping through to the cooperation with clients, it is essential that the therapists don't ignore these feelings towards each other but openly discuss them instead. Not for every therapist it will feel comfortable putting himself in a vulnerable position in front of a colleague. However, the co-therapists must agree on the importance of it – like a prenuptial agreement – for this form of collaboration to be successful.

>> **Therapist:** "I've been working with my colleague for some time now. After a while I realized that she gets nervous if a client reacts in an angry protector mode. She then veers towards an angry protector mode herself: 'attack is the best form of defence'. The first few times her behaviour shocked me. I tried to overrule her and to take control myself. My colleague didn't like this – she felt like I was trying tried to overrule or discredit her. This caused stress and both of us started to walk on eggshells. In the end we picked a moment to discuss this 'clash of schemas' between us. We also both talked about the history of our own patterns. We understand each other much better now, and we are more able to support each other when we're being triggered.

2.6.3 When is it time for the next phase?

When should a client move into the second phase of treatment? When will he have achieved the goals that make him ready? Assuming that the entire therapy process takes two years (Wetzelaar et al., 2014), each phase should take six months and the client should move into the next phase after that period of time. Based on clinical experience, it is useful to keep this six-month period as a guideline. It puts time pressure on the therapy and encourages the therapist and client to make firm agreements that help to achieve the goals within the schedule. It also guides specific interventions.

The following checklist can be used to help determine whether a client is ready for the second phase:

- He agrees with the mode model and he is willing, step-by-step, to let go of his coping and replace this with healthy behaviour with which he is able to meet his own basic needs.

- Both therapist and client are sufficiently confident that the client's healthy adult mode can develop further during the remainder of the therapy process.

- The client has been able to put himself in a vulnerable position in his contact with the therapist or group and he has been able to tolerate his primary schema becoming visible and tangible.

Chapter 3:
Phase 2 – Express yourself

Chapter summary
3.1 Basic needs
3.2 The therapy environment
3.3 Goals in this phase by schema mode
3.4 The therapeutic relationship
3.5 Exercises
3.6 Areas of focus and tips

Chapter summary

In the second phase of therapy, the client re-experiences the pain of his life and learns that it is up to him to either resign himself to it or work towards a solution. The expression of needs, emotions and wishes is central to this phase, as well as negotiating the conflicts that are created by doing so. The therapist monitors the balance between self-expression and preserving the connection that has been established up to this point. This requires the therapist to facilitate and to show understanding, but also to set limits and confront where appropriate. Just as in the start phase, the link between past and present is critical; however, the pressure to 'do things differently' within the safe environment of therapy is intensified. For this reason, there are specific goals and exercises for each schema mode.

3.1 Basic needs

3.1.1 Self-expression

In the start phase, the client learned about the link between his intense emotions in the present and his unfulfilled basic needs of his childhood past. He can now identify how this feels in his body, and he knows what kind of negative beliefs he has developed. He can look at his own dysfunctional thinking patterns from a greater distance and acknowledge when they are triggered. With support, he will allow the therapist to ignore his coping mode and challenge his parent mode. In short, he feels safe and emotionally supported enough to show vulnerability. He has developed a connection with the therapy and the therapist, and he has progressed into phase 2 – a phase of development in which there is more scope for improving his own competencies (Meij, 2011) (table 3.1).

Self-expression plays a key role in phase 2. This puts pressure on the safety and connection that was established in phase 1, as many clients have had little experience with expressing themselves and their own preferences. In childhood, they had parents who were preoccupied with their own needs, or who punished them if they tried to express their feelings. Think of a toddler who wants to play a favourite game with a friend, but who hasn't yet learned to play with others and therefore acts in a stubborn or aggressive way leading to arguments and conflict. In many clients, normal healthy childhood forms of self-expression like this were buried away and replaced with dysfunctional coping strategies, while spontaneous and/or authentic reactions were (and are) repressed or distorted.

Outwardly a client may seem compliant; or he may overcompensate for his deficiencies and seem demanding. He may even try to rationalize things to check if his feelings are 'correct'. These coping behaviours cause emotions to build up, and every now and then they will 'explode'. In such moments the client is overwhelmed, and he expresses his feelings and needs in a childish, dysfunctional and uncontrolled way. Spontaneity is necessary to reconnect with the authentic self, and the client is expressing that basic need. Therefore, setting realistic limits on destructive and dysfunctional behaviour is important, to enable the client to practice self-expression and standing up for himself while at the same time experiencing that safety and connection are retained or even strengthened.

> **>> Client:** "Recently, I got angry with my therapist. She postponed our appointments a few times because she was poorly. It wasn't her fault, but I did find it annoying. I thought: 'There you go, another person who just isn't interested in me, I'm sure she doesn't do that to other clients.' On top of that, my children were being difficult just before I left to go to therapy, so I'd really had enough. I was snappy and grumpy in the session. My therapist wanted to know what was wrong and kept asking questions. So, I told her how I felt about everything. I found it scary and thought: 'Now she definitely won't want anything to do with me anymore.' But she stayed calm and said she was happy that I'd told her. I found that hard to believe, but I still felt less anxious."

Table 3.1: Overview of the components of phase 2

Theme:	Express yourself
Basic need:	Self-expression
Limited reparenting:	School child
Overall goal:	Recognizing the pattern
Important exercises:	Mirror exercise; strengthen the healthy adult

Empathic confrontation:	High
Group development phase:	Intake phase
Mode model:	Scope for differences in modes
Role of the therapist:	Encourage authenticity

3.2 The therapy environment

3.2.1 Towards self-discovery

In phase 1, the client experienced what it was like to focus attention on feelings rather than just talking about things that have happened. He also experienced the therapist reacting in a responsive and sensitive way, just as a good parent would. He is now ready to practice expressing himself, and to work out what suits him and what doesn't. It is important that the therapist provides opportunities and reinforces this behaviour; at the same time, he also needs to monitor the structure and limits.

3.2.2 Anxiety regulation

Now that the client has an adequate sense of safety and connection, he will be able to surrender himself more to the therapist and show his vulnerability. He has a clearer understanding of his underlying schemas, he has better insight into his maladaptive thinking patterns, and he is more aware of the impact his coping has on his current life.

However, for the moment the client is caught between two opposing forces. He is willing to give up the advantages of his dysfunctional coping, but he is stuck in behaviour patterns that are influenced by his schemas and which extend across all areas of his life. He wants to change, but he doesn't yet know how to do so and his dysfunctional behaviour is familiar. And he wants to rid himself of these unpleasant feelings, but as yet he has little realistic hope for a different and more positive future.

These feelings, in combination with a feeling of powerlessness, create constant anxiety. When anxiety levels rise, dysfunctional modes are triggered. Therefore, this phase of therapy is tough and strenuous, and anxiety regulation is vital. The client's own communication and emotion regulation skills are often insufficiently developed to cope with this increasing anxiety, and consequently it frequently happens that clients go into crisis and rely enormously upon the therapist.

Anxiety regulation first and foremost consists of the therapist being present and available. He acknowledges, supports and cares for the vulnerable child. The therapist helps the client to tolerate and overcome these feelings, just as parents of small children do when they are scared to go to sleep because of the monster under the bed. Giving hope for the future and tackling old beliefs also help to manage anxiety. The therapist sends a punisher away, just as a mother chases the monster under the bed away, and he expresses his confidence in the client and the client's abilities.

A further element of anxiety regulation is gaining the client's trust. The therapist takes him by the hand and provides him with opportunities to practice regulation skills for himself. Working on a safety plan is part of this. The client does not yet need to be able to successfully regulate anxieties all by himself; he may still rely on the therapist for help. However, it is important that he tries things out, practices and perseveres. By doing so, whilst encouraged and supported by the therapist, he can expand his repertoire and strengthen his ability to tolerate frustration. After all, a mother might also say to her child "Do you want to chase off the monster too? Come on, let's do it together."

CASE STUDY

Individual therapy: Anxiety regulation through the therapist

Linda feels confident enough to talk about her memories during the sessions. However, she tends to dismiss her feelings as 'nonsense'. The therapist points out the punitive message in this and asks for little Linda. This helps Linda to show more of her feelings.

>> **Linda:** "I'm just really scared that it will never get better!"

>> **Therapist:** (leans a little towards Linda, talks in a soft voice and makes eye contact) "I can see that you're really scared. Please tell me about it."

>> **Linda:** "There's always something! Every time I think 'I've been through the worst now', there's always something else. Things will never work out for me. I was born to fail.

The therapist identifies this as Linda's punitive parent mode. With the aid of a two-chair technique he sends this mode away, so that he can support little Linda. Then he records some comforting words for her to listen to at home when she's feeling desperate and downhearted. He also tells her that she can email him if she ever finds that she is really struggling.

The ability to put things into perspective, to use self-mockery and humour or to engage in physical exercise, is a fourth way of managing anxieties and softening a serious, laborious atmosphere. Ridiculing dysfunctional modes in an appropriate manner or simply getting up to loosen the limbs can relieve the pressure. Stepping in and out of the emotion enables the client to experience that he is in control of his feelings: "I can be feeling really sad, but then laugh again afterwards."

Here too, a parallel may be drawn with a good parent. When a mother and her child have chased off the monster, they might make a joke or sing a song about how silly monsters are. Humour may at first glance seem inappropriate to the serious matter of anxiety, so it calls for an explanation. A jolly, cheerful exercise is in no way intended to trivialise feelings: it is undertaken because it is important for the client to discover that there are different ways to influence his anxiety levels, and to experience that a healthy balance between tension and relaxation is a key precondition for growth.

Last but by no means least, psychoeducation is a key factor in regulating anxieties. As we have discussed, the client is caught between forces in this phase. He is in transition – aware of the old but incompetent in the new. The therapist can provide him with a framework to better understand the world and himself by repeatedly providing a running commentary of the client's interactions with others, and by being open about the feelings he experiences himself in his contact with the client.

3.2.3 Increasing the pressure

In phase 1, the client learned that everything is therapy and the therapist won't ignore important issues. These schema therapy frameworks are retained in the second phase, in which the therapist perseveres in his efforts to challenge the coping and help the client display healthier behaviour. The therapy is very much at a transitional stage, and it is important now to make contact with the vulnerable child and his needs (Young et al., 2003).

To begin with, this increases anxiety. The client experiences high emotions and will tend to fall back on the coping he's familiar with. The therapist puts pressure on the client to put his coping aside and instead express his feelings. The client may experience this as negative, and a violation of his autonomy: "You're going too far in being so insistent!" This is because for him, in the past, pressure went hand in hand with negative feelings such as the need to prove himself, punishment and rejection if he didn't succeed, or the loss of space for his own needs and wishes. The therapist is able to explain this: 'I know that you see pressure as something negative, and it's normal to want to keep away from painful emotions. However, in the end that won't help you. Children do need a healthy amount of pressure, a stimulus to develop themselves. And that is what I want to provide for you."

The therapist who perseveres, explains his interventions and rationalizes his behaviour will enable his client to experience that pressure can also be healthy and a positive force for growth. "I do this because I want to make contact with you, not because I want to dominate you. Your little self won't get what he needs if you cling on to your coping." The therapist actively tries to find ways to make contact with the client's emotion and, if necessary, he negotiates: "Come and sit in my chair and pretend you're the therapist. What would you say to the avoider from that position?" The client experiences that it is possible for him to comply with someone else's guidance and remain true to himself. He also finds that pressure isn't always negative: it can also be a positive sign of commitment. "The therapist wants to be there for my vulnerable child."

CASE STUDY

Individual therapy: Healthy pressure

In the time between sessions, Linda has listened several times to the recording of comforting words that the therapist made for her. Today, she tells him she feels very sad when she listens to it.

>> **Linda:** "You see, that doesn't help either. I'd be better off doing some extra cleaning – at least it would stop me thinking about it all."

>> **Therapist:** Well done for telling me honestly that my words made you sad. It isn't nice to feel sad, and I definitely understand that you're tempted by your old ways of avoiding feelings. That's part of this phase and it really isn't a problem that you can't always resist the temptation. But you've noticed it, and that's already really good. At the same time, it's important that we focus on those feelings in our sessions, so I can help you tolerate them and get what you really need."

>> **Linda:** "I don't know, it's all so tough. "

>> **Therapist:** (in a soft, warm voice) "Yes, I understand… little Linda's old feeling that she will never be good enough has been deeply triggered. I can feel it now as well, here in the session. It feels like a weight or a burden. Is that right?"

>> **Linda:** "Yes. "

>> **Therapist:** "You're right, it's tough and it's a long and difficult road, but it's also the road to something better. You will feel happier, honestly (tries to make eye contact). I suggest we do an imagery exercise in which I can help little Linda, so that she gets the support she needs. Okay? Close your eyes and go back to the moment you were listening to my recording and feeling sad…"

The rest of the session consists of an imagery rescripting exercise. In a discussion at the end, the therapist and Linda agree that the burden has gone, and that Linda feels somewhat relieved.

3.2.4 The environment of group schema therapy

In group schema therapy it is possibly even more important that the therapists manage anxiety levels in order to protect the safety and connection of group members. However, they also need to increase the pressure to enable clients to discover new feelings. This is because all the clients in the group are scared to feel. If one client manages to 'get away with it' (i.e. avoid exploring new feelings) then it reinforces the coping behaviour for the whole group: "You see, it's better not to feel."

After all, clients in a group learn partly through each other. If, on the other hand, the group members see that coping isn't simply accepted without question, and that other group members are encouraged to express themselves, then they will feel inspired to explore and discover too.

To stimulate this self-expression, the therapists provide a running commentary of what they're doing and why they're doing it: "We think it is important that we treat each other in this way, so that you are able to experience that things can be done differently from how they were done at home in the past. There are no taboos. You are allowed to give each other feedback. Anything can be said, as long as it's respectful. We'll help you with this."

The clients feel comfortable with each other and are happy to have found people in similar situations to themselves. At the same time, because of their past negative experiences with pressure and authority, they no longer always accept the guidance of the therapists without question and so the group enters an authority crisis. If the therapists stimulate and manage this development by showing the clients that they are pleased with any expression of emotion, even negative, then the group will move into the integration phase. The clients experience support from each other and want to keep it that way; however, contrasts and differences also come to light because individual clients feel more and struggle with their coping. This causes anxiety in the group as well, and it's natural for group members to sometimes choose to push feelings away and rely on the coping they're familiar with.

In this development phase, clients aren't yet able to distinguish between someone's opinion or behaviour and their personality (Hoijtink, 2001). They take a black-and-white approach, like a child: "you're either my friend or my enemy." Moreover, their response is driven by a fear of conflict. Often, experiences in the past have led clients to believe that a conflict will end in a destructive break-up. They want to keep things friendly and maintain the safety and connection they got used to in the start phase. It is the task of the group therapists to take on a regulating role by focusing on the necessary level of safety and connection (Farrell & Shaw, 2012).

At the same time, as we have said, the therapists must increase the pressure and actively encourage clients to express themselves. After all, it is important that they move forward with the work of therapy, however difficult that may be and no matter how small the steps are. Ultimately, schema corrective experiences are the only way of reducing inner tension. If a client expresses himself under the supervision of the therapists, he will experience the absence of a schema-affirming response: "I'm not being rejected when I talk about how I feel." At a later stage he may perhaps even start to feel better: "Actually, talking about how I feel leads to more contact… I feel noticed."

>> **Therapist:** "The clients are more capable of experiencing emotions and more aware of their own needs. They feel safer and more open with each other. The tension that can be sensed in the group is the same as the tension they felt in their childhood, when showing emotions would lead to cutting off contact or getting into arguments with accusations flying back and forth. As they care about each other and the group, they get worried that things will fall apart, just as happened in their childhood. Being able to express themselves and still carrying on as a group, is a corrective experience for the clients. It is our task as therapists to facilitate this experience."

CASE STUDY

Group schema therapy: Healthy pressure

Today the therapists want to focus on instances in the past week when the vulnerable child was triggered.

>> **Nico:** "I'm not joining in with that exercise and there's no need for you to push me."

>> **Therapist 1:** "It sounds as if you're angry? Maybe it's because you think we won't accept you saying 'no' and try to force you to join in, is that right?"

>> **Nico:** "Yes, exactly. That's why I'm telling you in advance."

>> **Therapist 1:** "Well, I think it's really good of you to express your opinion. I know that, as a child, you were often forced to listen to your parents. So my taking the lead in this session and possibly asking you for input makes you feel like I might want to dominate you. Do you recognize that?"

>> **Nico:** "Yes. I just don't feel like it, so I don't want to do it."

>> **Therapist 1:** "It's good that you can recognize this, and I understand that you don't want to do things you're not in the mood for. But tell me please, how does it feel when you think I want to dominate you by taking the lead?"

>> **Amber:** (interrupts Therapist 1) "I think you're being very pushy now. You can see that you're crossing his limit, can't you?"

>> **Therapist 2:** "Wow Amber, I can tell you're trying to support Nico. That's really kind! However, I think that this a limit set by Nico's protector, with which he's trying to keep people away from little Nico. If that's the case, then going along with it means we're doing the opposite of helping Nico. It means we're leaving little Nico all by himself."

(Looks around the group)

"Is that a possibility? You all know Nico and his protector very well."

(Some of the group members nod)   →

> **>> Therapist 1:** (to Nico) "It isn't my intention to cross your limit. If that's how you feel, then I understand your angry reaction. At the same time, I can imagine that it might make you feel scared to think that your limit is being disregarded again, just like it was when you were a child?"
>
> **>> Nico:** (Nods in agreement)
>
> **>> Therapist 1:** "Well done for expressing this. I understand that these feelings can make you react in a way that can seem somewhat stubborn and uncompromising. After all, you haven't had many positive experiences of being able to be yourself under the direction of someone else. So, it's only natural that you'd rather not be directed at all. We're going to keep practicing this though, as it's important for you to learn. At your own pace."
>
> **>> Therapist 2:** (Looks around the group and asks) "Will you all help us and Nico to make sure we aren't crossing his limit, like Amber just did? But also make sure that Nico's reactions aren't too uncompromising, as that may be part of his coping? (To Nico) "Is that alright with you?"
>
> (Nico nods in agreement)

3.3 Goals in this phase by schema mode

The start phase has its own specific goals, that have been achieved when the transition into phase 2 takes place. The second phase also has several goals for each schema mode, that fit in with the basic needs and the therapy environment.

3.3.1 Overall goal: Recognizing the pattern

Towards the end of this phase the client is able to recognize retrospectively when he has gone off-track into a dysfunctional mode or schema. He knows his own modes and schemas in terms of behaviour, feelings, thoughts and interdynamics. With help, he can substitute one mode for another. He can distinguish himself from other people, and he can connect with his own and other people's basic needs. He has practiced tolerating conflicts and frustrations. In group schema therapy, the client can stay true to himself and his own needs without losing connection with his peers. He can accept that everyone is different and, with support, he is able to fix a broken relationship.

3.3.2 Child mode: "Oh dear, I feel!"

The client has connected with his vulnerable child mode, and experienced that his basic needs are being met in the therapy. He has been able to allow the therapist to provide him with good care and, if necessary, he has started trauma counselling. All this has made the vulnerable mode with its accompanying schemas less overwhelming. The client has also connected with his angry child mode. He knows how this mode feels and what he needs in this mode. Finally, he is aware of the presence of modes like the impulsive child and the undisciplined child and their respective needs.

3.3.3 Coping mode: "Thanks but I don't need you anymore…"

The coping mode is egodystonic at the end of this phase. The client knows when he goes into his coping mode, what the pros and cons of this are for himself and for others, and what his vulnerable child then actually needs. He knows how his coping mode was created and, with support, he can look at it in a compassionate and understanding way. More and more often he is able to choose to put his coping aside. There is also greater differentiation in the various coping modes. For example, overcompensation may be more specified as a perfectionist controller while avoidance may manifest itself primarily as soothing behaviour in the form of gaming.

3.3.4 Parent mode: 'Go away, you're not helping!'

The parent mode is more egodystonic. The client recognizes the feeling he gets when the parent mode has been triggered, and he is aware of the impact this mode has on the vulnerable child. With the therapist's support he can challenge this mode, and he has an expanding verbal and nonverbal repertoire of techniques to fight against it. The client has also made progress towards being able to specify the parent mode. He knows the difference between a punishing and a demanding parent, although as yet he isn't always capable of recognizing these in himself.

3.3.5 Healthy adult mode and happy child mode: "I'm here too and I'm learning…"

The healthy adult mode is more developed towards the end of this phase. The client is more hopeful and confident that things will get easier, and that he can be happy. He is also more capable of refining things. He can link his feelings to his thoughts and express what is going on inside him. He has practiced how to respond in a healthy, step-by-step way to negative feelings and conflicts. He has experienced that others are willing and able to meet his needs. He also has some experience in meeting his own needs by himself. He has learned to request time and attention for himself to enable him to meet is own needs. He has also further explored his spontaneous, happy child and he knows what this child needs to be able to be there.

3.3.6 Mode model in this phase

As shown by the mode goals, there is now more scope for refinement and differentiation. This is also evident in the mode model. Important modes are added, such as an impulsive child mode alongside the vulnerable and angry child modes.

Identifying specific schemas ensures that the nature of the modes is more apparent. At the same time as adding refinements, it is vital that the model remains clear and uncluttered, with a maximum of only six or seven modes. Furthermore, the modes are always personalized with a familiar name and specific information about the biographical context. The use of specific names for modes will gradually replace the general terminology from the start phase. See figure 3.1 for an example (after: Faßbinder et al., 2011; Arntz & Jacob, 2012).

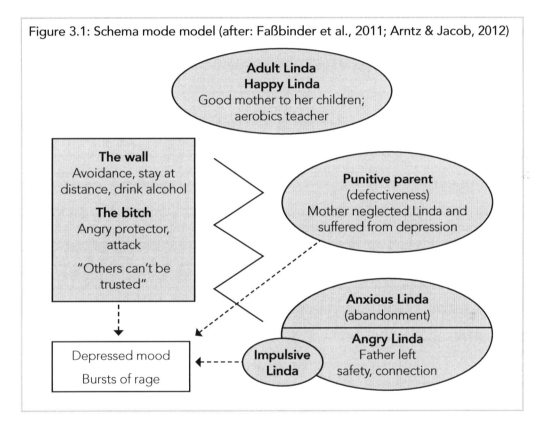

Figure 3.1: Schema mode model (after: Faßbinder et al., 2011; Arntz & Jacob, 2012)

Parent mode: Important historical contexts and precepts are now linked to this mode. If possible, an image is added of how the internalized message originated, for example the mother's voice. If the client knows the difference between his punishing and demanding parent mode, this is added too.

Child mode: This is also differentiated, if necessary, into the vulnerable child, the angry child, the impulsive child and the undisciplined child. If further refinement is helpful to connect with this mode, then this is included. For example, the stubborn child may be an elaboration of the angry child.

Coping mode: Here too, refinement and a personal link are sought, with the aim of helping the client understand himself and his inner dynamics. A client who overcompensates for fear with a paranoid controller and bullying mindset may, with therapist agreement, choose the name 'the Watchtower'.

Healthy adult mode and happy child mode: Both these modes have further developed during this phase and are given greater prominence in the model. The client is able to see himself as someone with healthy adult characteristics. 'Big (own name)' and 'happy (own name)' are now used most.

3.4 The therapeutic relationship

3.4.1 Limited reparenting

Clients are now more in touch with their past deprivations and, to begin with, they project this onto the therapist. He must try to compensate for these deficiencies, especially now there is a connection and attachment. However, he invariably fails to succeed in this as the deficiencies are so significant. Primary schemas such as emotional neglect, social isolation and feelings of inferiority or shame are triggered and ready to be played out again. The client keeps a watchful eye on the therapist: "Is he doing it right?", "Is she actually paying attention?", "Is he taking good care of me?" or "Does she think I'm stupid too?" Anger over the deprivations is also slowly surfacing. This places another burden on the therapist, in the form of defiance against the therapy and the therapist himself.

These feelings are often confusing for the client, and can lead to 'mode flipping': the client jumps from the angry child into the demanding parent, then into the detached protector and eventually into the distress of the vulnerable child. The sessions are characterized by frequent conflict and high levels of anxiety. The therapist offers safety, guidance and security and, by doing so, he shows the client: "I can handle this and I'm staying with you". This in itself is a schema corrective experience.

Providing a running commentary of what's happening is important; it provides a clear overview, acknowledgement and hope. If the client complains about progress, the therapist can respond by saying: "In this phase you are 'consciously incompetent'. That can be very frustrating: having a clear understanding but not knowing how to do things differently. There's no getting around it, you must go through this to develop. Plodding along and fiddling around is part of it, but you've never had a chance to learn to do that. Trust me, it will be fine. Just look at the steps you've already made!"

3.4.2 Limited reparenting in a group setting

Just as in the start phase, the therapists have to work hard in the second phase. It won't be just one client who has doubts about the therapy; a whole group of them may project their deprivations. They may do this in a passive aggressive way ("no-one understands me"), they may fall silent and not express themselves ("I just don't know"), or they may actively demand from the therapist that he fulfils their needs ("you have to do it for me"). The fact that clients are able to express themselves like this, is actually a positive sign, as it shows that they feel safe enough to share their emotional deprivations. However, for the therapists it's tough. They can feel overburdened, inadequate or even scared. Therefore, it's vital to have a healthy sense of perspective, a sound working relationship with the co-therapist and support from a colleague or a team. In this phase, a group therapist really needs his co-therapist, just as two parents consult one another in difficult situations.

Within the group, the clients become more and more aware of the fact that they differ from one another and, at the same time, they find this harder and harder to tolerate. They aren't yet ready to be separated and prefer to do everything together. These feelings manifest themselves in group rebellion: an authority crisis whereby the rules are put up for discussion yet again. Here too, it's important that the therapists recognize the projection of these feelings. This allows them to respond in their role as good parents, reinforce self-expression and show understanding for all the different emotions. To present themselves as healthy human beings and role models, it is also important for the therapists to be transparent about their own feelings and needs. They need to express what their priorities are for the group and explain what kind of atmosphere they want to create. The therapists aren't hovering outside the group; they are part of it, just as parents are part of a family.

Finally, the therapists provide guidance by linking the clients' experiences to the mode model and making them the subject of the therapy: "Everything is therapy. Let's investigate which mode is talking and what your actual need is when you say: 'you have to do it for me'."

3.4.3 Empathic confrontation and limit setting

Alongside the soft component of limited reparenting, it's important that the therapist prevents the recurrence of schema directed experiences by using empathic confrontations. In this phase, the therapist ups the ante with regard to the client's coping. He simply won't let the client get away with it; he addresses everything that could possibly be the result of coping. The therapist also puts himself 'in the relationship': he refers to his own feelings, thoughts and reactions. Focused self-disclosure of feelings evoked in the therapist by the client is an important tool in this phase; both parties express themselves, and the therapist does everything possible to connect with the vulnerable child mode.

CASE STUDY

Individual therapy: Making an empathic confrontation personal

The therapist would like to do an exercise, but Linda refuses and shuts herself off. The therapist hears himself explain for the third time why the exercise is so important.

>> **Therapist:** "Just wait a minute, this isn't going well... I'm nagging you and I can see that you're distancing yourself."

(Linda frowns and nods)

>> **Therapist:** "I'm trying to persuade you, I think. I know I tend to do that when I'm frustrated because I can't feel a connection. I want to make contact, so I nag. But my nagging is annoying you so you're shutting yourself off."

>> **Linda:** "Yes, I do find it annoying. "

>> **Therapist:** "I think this means we're repeating something. How it used to be at home – your mother was so persuasive that you could only do things your way in secret. Does that sound familiar?"

>> **Linda:** "Yes, my mother was very pushy. It didn't matter what I wanted. So, I just let her preach and meanwhile I'd be thinking about other things."

>> **Therapist:** "Just like now really. And what did you actually need, back then as a child?"

>> **Linda:** "Well, it would have been nice if she'd taken me seriously and asked me what I wanted."

>> **Therapist:** "So you actually wanted to make contact, just like I do. Now that we're talking about it, I can already feel more of a connection. Can you?"

(Linda nods)

>> **Therapist:** "I'm also more aware of what happened to me earlier. I know now, for example, that I feel quite worried when you shut yourself off – because I'm not sure how you feel then, I can't work you out. At the same time, I also feel a bit annoyed with your protector guarding little Linda and her needs, because I know that you feel lonely again then."

(short silence; Linda looks at the therapist).

>> **Therapist:** "And you know, Linda, that's not what I want. I don't want you to feel lonely behind that protector. And it's not necessary anymore, because you know now that I'm here for you.'

(Linda nods)

Four levels of empathic confrontation

The empathic confrontation is an essential part of limited reparenting, and a recurring element of the therapy process from start to finish. Sometimes an empathic confrontation is short, because the client's schemas have developed and are healthier. At other times it may be necessary to extend an empathic confrontation and specify a limit in order to motivate the client to adapt his behaviour. It is important that the therapist is able to apply the full range of different levels, and that he makes optimal use of his knowledge of the client along with his modes and schemas.

Using the case conceptualization as a roadmap, the therapist will know when to show empathy and when to set limits. Besides this knowledge, his own instinct can help him respond as authentically and spontaneously as possible in his contact with the client. It can also help him decide which of his own feelings towards the client are important enough to share with him. It may be useful here to categorize the empathic confrontation into four different styles (also see table 3.2).

Minimal: This empathic confrontation consists of a wink, raising an eyebrow, clearing the throat or other similar signs. It is a playful, light-hearted intervention, used by the therapist when he wants to make the client aware of the fact that he has noticed that his coping is directing his responses. This type of intervention is suitable when both therapist and client know all too well what has triggered the coping, and when the client can easily switch to more adaptive behaviour. This is the case when the therapist has already applied the other empathic confrontations on a number of occasions.

Low: The therapist just needs to say one or two sentences to indicate that the client's coping has been triggered and to encourage him to show his true feelings. "Hey, come on, we know this coping now. Push it aside and show me how you're actually feeling." There is more emphasis on the confrontation and less on the empathy. This intervention can only be used if the therapist has previously devoted extensive attention to the empathic confrontation of coping behaviour, and if the client has been able to switch to more functional behaviour after these in-depth confrontations.

Standard: This refers to the conventional empathic confrontation as outlined in other manuals (Young et al., 2003; Arntz & Jacob, 2012) and described in Chapter 2. The therapist describes the behaviour, its function, the historical background and how it affects himself and the client. The empathic component and the confronting component are equally important. This approach is vital at the start of the therapy but continues to play a role throughout the whole process.

High: The empathic confrontation is extended with a limit. This is necessary if the other styles of empathic confrontations have insufficient impact and the client persists in dysfunctional coping that leads to a stagnation in the therapeutic process. For example, imagine that in the last three consecutive sessions the therapist has applied the different forms of the empathic confrontation in an effort to encourage the client to behave less arrogantly. If the client continues to roll his eyes and speak in a disdainful way about the therapist in the following session, then the therapist will adopt a different strategy. He will explain to the client that they need to discuss the client's behaviour and come to an agreement over it before they can move on and talk about any other issues.

Table 3.2 Four levels of empathic confrontation		
Empathic confrontation (EC)	Content	When to use
Minimal	Non-verbal, playful, light-hearted	Previous ECs were successful; client can easily switch
Low	More confrontation than empathy, short	Previous ECs were successful; client needs help to switch
Standard	Conventional EC	Early stages of the therapy but also continuous
High	EC extended with a limit	Previous ECs have been unsuccessful

Empathic confrontation in a group setting

In group schema therapy, the second phase often brings a high level of anxiety. This makes it necessary for the therapists to use empathic confrontations not only to address individual clients' coping behaviour, but also to address the coping behaviour of the group as a whole. After all, their goal is for clients to connect with the feelings that are hidden behind the coping. As soon as the therapists notice that several clients are being led by their coping, they put the group interaction on hold. Signs for this may be a seemingly unproductive and sluggish atmosphere, a participant who is holding everyone up, or clients who seem to treat their therapy as if it were a laughing matter.

Firstly, the therapists point out how they perceive the situation. "Let's just stop what we're doing. You're not taking this seriously enough, which makes it difficult for us to stick to the subject. Do you recognize that? Laughter can be a way of avoiding other feelings – do you think that might be true for you? And can you see that your behaviour is causing a lot of coping in the group?" Then the therapists continue to ask questions until they connect with the vulnerable child: "We know that coping means that there are a lot of feelings present. Just tell us, what's the matter? What do you really feel? Let's take a moment and deal with this steadily, step by step." The therapists make it clear that the clients' feelings are important to them, and that expressing yourself is a positive thing.

In a defiant or passive-aggressive group, the therapists explain that there is a big difference between saying "no" as part of coping behaviour and defiance led by autonomy. The first is a way of avoiding feelings, the second a way of voicing a need: "Perhaps you're trying to tell us that we're going too fast for you? Or that we haven't shown enough consideration for your needs?" Furthermore, it's important to point out the difference between coercion and direction, as these are often perceived as synonymous by clients: "We definitely don't want to force you, your opinion matters to us and we want you to understand why we're doing this. However, we're going to take the lead as we know how important it is for you to have these new experiences to meet your needs."

In this way, the therapists clarify the importance of the therapy and the ways in which it is implemented. They provide explanations, are open to feedback and allow room for negotiation with clients, but they also keep moving forward with the exercise: "We know it's difficult and you're not used to it, and we do think it's very important that you continue to express yourselves, but now we're going to get on with the exercise again. Join in as much as you can."

If these interventions don't lead to a greater presence of the vulnerable child and a lesser presence of coping in the group, then the therapists can extend the empathic confrontation with a limit. For example, they may use a time-out for one of the participants – or even for the whole group.

CASE STUDY
Group schema therapy: High level empathic confrontation

The therapists have noticed that several clients systematically make negative comments about another group member. This has been pointed out and discussed before, the group rules have been restated and the importance of respect and security has been explained. Unfortunately, nothing has changed.

For today's session, the therapists want to increase the sense of security by putting the coping modes to one side and connecting with the vulnerable child modes. To achieve this, they have come up with an exercise whereby everybody says something about their feelings, the mode that has been triggered and a relevant experience from their childhood. →

Soon after starting the exercise, there is a tense atmosphere in the group again. The reactions of some clients are led by their overcompensating coping, and they aren't managing to replace this with functional behaviour. The therapists look at each other:

>> Therapist 1: "We're not getting through this. The atmosphere is still tense and insecure. Shall we have a time-out?"

>> Therapist 2: "Yes, I think that's a good idea."

(They involve the group again)

>> Therapist 1: "We're going to have a time-out. We're stopping the session because we're not able to create a safe and respectful atmosphere at the moment.

>> Therapist 2: "If we were to continue now, then that would lead to a replay of what you know from your past and that's not what we want. That wouldn't do anybody any good."

>> Therapist 1: "We want you to go home now and not to have any further contact with each other today, so that you're all able to cool down and relax. We'll get in touch with you later to discuss how we're going to shape the next session."

Later that day, the therapists call the clients and ask them to answer a few questions in preparation for the next session: How did you feel during the session? Which mode got triggered? What do you need to feel safe? What can you do to contribute to a sense of safety for everyone? They discuss this task in the next session and come to an agreement on how to increase the feeling of security.

3.4.4 The therapist's perspective

This phase involves many ambivalent feelings that the client wants the therapist to fix. While this 'dependency' is appropriate in schema therapy (Arntz & Jacob, 2012), it also triggers feelings and schemas in the therapist. It makes many therapists insecure to see a client struggle or fall into a crisis, or they may be alarmed by the client's level of dependency. The empathy for the client's urgent need may result in a lack of professional distance. A schema like 'failing' can lead to daunting thoughts such as: "I'll never be able to help this client." 'Self-sacrifice' can lead to the therapist trying to be available for the client at all times and stepping over his own limits in the process, and 'high demands' may result in the therapist going along with the client's wish to solve all his problems.

>> **Therapist:** "My clients are really struggling in this phase! They see the misery in their lives, but they can't see many positives. They understand a lot, and they're more aware of the role their childhood and their own behaviour has played. They reveal beliefs such as "I'll never get what I need" or "I'll always be a loser" and they're convinced that these are true. I find that difficult myself, and their desperation triggers my own fears. I feel like I'm failing them, and I want to try harder. It helps then if I say to myself that I'm doing my best. I explain to the client that this is part of this phase, that he's going through different emotions, that it's scary but not dangerous and that it will get better. We also look at specific things he's already doing differently, for example, the fact that he can tell me how he's really feeling or that he can look at me when I support him."

The tense, stressful atmosphere of this phase requires on the one hand a confrontational stance, and on the other a more laidback, playful and light-hearted approach. The therapist requires spontaneity to maintain his unbiased manner among all the highly charged schemas. Therefore, it's important that he has the skills to handle difficult topics by normalizing them and putting them into perspective. A certain degree of self-mockery and an awareness of his own pitfalls are also essential. Furthermore, the ability to turn negatives into positives and to focus on small achievements contributes to a tolerable level of tension. For example, the therapist can say to a complaining client: "You're having a go at expressing yourself, well done!" Or he can say to a client who's overwhelmed by emotions: "There's a rush of emotions going through you right now. That's awful, but it will pass. Emotions are like waves; they fade away again."

>> **Therapist:** "Unfortunately, I know all about having a pretty demanding personality. Luckily, I'm now quite aware of the fact that I've got those traits and I've managed to overcome quite a few of my issues. It helps me to make fun of that part of myself, and I sometimes use sarcasm to break the tension in a session. For example, a little while ago I noticed that my client was stuck in self-reproach. So, I said: "It's definitely a good idea to dwell on everything that goes wrong – that will make you really happy and guarantee you success in wanting to try new things!" The client looked at me, saw the grin on my face, and burst out laughing. "You're right," he said, "it's the demanding side of my personality again!" Sometimes, though, I completely miss the mark with my humour. Then the client feels misunderstood. When that happens, I apologize and I explain that it wasn't my intention to make fun of him but to make fun of that demanding personality trait. I also praise the client for the fact that he had the courage to say that he felt misunderstood."

A therapist who allows himself to make mistakes and doesn't feel the need to be perfect has more leeway and freedom of action. He also provides the client with a more realistic image of human nature: we're only human, and none of us is perfect.

Learning is a matter of trial and error for all concerned. A therapist who loses sight of what's going on in a two-or-more-chair technique can say something like: "I've lost the thread now. Can we get back to where we were?" Sometimes this will prove impossible, and the therapist will be sucked into a desperate, negative sense of conscious incompetence, often partly triggered by his own schemas. This can't be prevented and it's important to use it as a sign. Emotions and schemas have been triggered, which means there's also a need at work. The therapist can continue by analysing the client's pattern and need as well as his own reactions. This will allow him to choose interventions in line with the need that is at risk. Starting with himself can be a good approach; the continuous parallel processes and the feelings that are passed from to client to therapist offer clues as to what kind of challenges the client is facing. The sooner the therapist is aware of his own reactions, the sooner he will know what the client needs.

CASE STUDY

Group schema therapy: Discussing and using the therapist's feelings

The therapists have noticed that, in the last few weeks, there has been a tense and highly charged atmosphere in the group sessions. They're both having to work hard to keep things on track. By adopting a proactive attitude, they're trying to encourage the clients to express themselves. At the end of the session they discuss this recurring pattern.

>> **Therapist 1:** "It strikes me that we seem to be working really hard in the sessions. I'm exhausted."

>> **Therapist 2:** "Yes, me too. I've noticed that we're both trying really hard. Shall we try to analyse the situation?"

>> **Therapist 1:** "Yes, I think we should. Let's look at our own pattern first."

>> **Therapist 2:** "I start to work really hard when I believe I'm failing. When the group is quiet, it makes me think I'm doing something wrong. It makes me feel insecure and I become demanding."

>> **Therapist 1:** "Okay! That's what happens with you. I start to feel insecure when I see you working hard. It makes me think: 'Oh no, I'm leaving her to it. So then I start working harder as well."

>> **Therapist 2:** "So both our schemas are being triggered! That's good to know. I'm also aware that there is no point in me working harder when I feel insecure."

>> **Therapist 1:** "Do you know what you need in those situations?"

>> **Therapist 2:** "To accept in myself that I sometimes have to fiddle around a bit, that the therapy doesn't always have to be perfect. I'm trying my best and that's good enough. Just hearing myself saying this out loud makes me feel calmer."

>> **Therapist 1:** "That sounds good! I feel more relaxed already too."   →

>> **Therapist 2:** "Do you think maybe the group faces the same issue? They're struggling, they're scared that it will never get any better and they focus on everything that goes wrong. That triggers their demanding personality traits and, as a result, they shut themselves off. They don't feel their pain, but it's passed on to us so we get double the amount."

>> **Therapist 1:** "It's not impossible that we feel our own deficiencies as well as theirs."

>> **Therapist 2:** "And just like you feel better when you're not under so much pressure and you know that it's fine to do things your way, the clients feel better too. When you're feeling scared, you need support and encouraging words to enable you to face your challenges. You don't need anyone to raise the bar."

>> **Therapist 1:** "Let's see if they recognize that their pattern has been triggered and that they're trying to avoid their feelings. Anything they reveal related to this deserves a compliment."

3.4.5 Thinking, feeling and doing

This phase focuses on changing the client's pattern by having schema corrective experiences through experiential exercises. Imagery rescripting and two-or-more-chair techniques are key interventions. The cognitive framework also remains important in linking the experiences of the exercises to schemas and modes. For example, after an imagery rescripting exercise, the therapist and client can discuss what was most helpful in the exercise, what it physically did to the client and what that means in terms of his fear of the vulnerable child being abandoned. The experiential exercises are mainly aimed at connecting with the vulnerable child mode and aiding the healing process of the primary schemas; feelings of sadness and fear are worked on in particular.

Anger

Anger is another subject that requires attention. This is a targeted emotion: the client must try to connect with it, whilst simultaneously the therapist provides information about anger and its different forms. The first form is the client being angry with himself, which is expressed by the parent mode and goes hand in hand with self-reproach, self-criticism or feelings of guilt. In the second form the anger is aimed at others, in order to keep them at a distance, and it is linked with a coping mode such as an angry protector. The third form is connected with the angry child and his emotions; the client is angry because his basic need is violated.

Being angry is a way of standing up for one's rights, and it is a healthy and helpful emotion. Unfortunately, many clients express their anger inappropriately as they have never learned a more effective way. Providing information and explanations, and analysing which form of anger is present and when, will enable the client to understand and tolerate this overwhelming emotion. This is a vital step for the next therapy phase, in which the development of a fourth form of anger takes place: the healthy adult who takes his emotions seriously and uses them to meet his basic needs as best he can.

Reality check

The reality check is a cognitive technique that provides schema corrective experiences. The therapist asks the client to express his fear and then check whether it actually becomes reality. For example, one of the participants confides that she is dreading the other group members' reaction to her recounting of a bad experience she had in her childhood. She fears that they will reject her, so she turns away and keeps her eyes fixed on the floor. The therapist notices that the other group members are touched by her story and show empathy. Therefore, he asks the client to look up: "Just look around you and see the compassion in everyone's eyes. Can you see any sign of rejection?"

Practicing new, healthier behaviours is another way of gaining schema corrective experiences. The therapist increases pressure on the client to step out of his comfort zone within sessions. To achieve progress it is important to experiment and try things out, even if it makes the client uneasy or he finds it difficult and awkward. He doesn't necessarily have to succeed first time, but it is vital for him to explore new and different ways of behaving. Every small step counts. For example, with regard to the vulnerable child, he must learn how to receive recognition, disempower his childhood beliefs and experience hope (Van der Wijngaart, 2015). For the parent mode, he must practice setting a firm limit: there is no room for negotiation, stop means stop. The coping mode actually requires a softer limit due to its functional, protective elements; this too the client must practice in order to make progress.

3.5 Exercises

In this phase all the interventions that are described in schema therapy manuals are revisited (see table 1.3 for an overview). The exercises outlined below are either an addition to or a variation on these, and they can be divided into three categories:

1. **Mode dynamics:** exercises to be able to understand and regulate mode dynamics, suitable at the start of phase 2.

2. **Strengthening the healthy adult:** exercises to explicitly strengthen the healthy adult mode and to change underlying schemas. These are ideal exercises for when the client is mid-way through the second phase, as they make use of mode dynamics.

3. **Anger management:** anger can be manipulated later in this phase, and these exercises mark the transition into the next phase.

3.5.1 Mode dynamics exercises

Exercise 3.1: Mode regulation mirror exercise	
Goal:	To connect with primary schemas and recognize inner reactions.
Category:	1: Mode dynamics
Preparation:	Share the tasks between the co-therapists. Re-read the mode model in an individual setting.
Instructions:	
Step 1:	Therapist 1 asks the clients to close their eyes and think of an event from the last week that touched them. He asks which basic emotion they experience: "Are you scared, angry or sad? Where in your body can you feel this?" He also asks about their schema level: "In what way is this feeling part of your life? What are you really scared, angry or sad about? Take time to think about it, then open your eyes."
Step 2:	The clients form a circle. The therapists take the lead and model the exercise as an example. They don't take any further part, but they remain active and supportive.
Step 3:	Client 1 and his neighbour, client 2, stand opposite each other. Client 1 tells client 2 about the emotion of his vulnerable child mode ("I'm really scared that I'm not good enough and that I'll be rejected"). Therapist 1 checks to make sure that client 1 is connecting with his emotions: "Can you feel it? Where in your body?"
Step 4:	Client 1 returns to a more neutral position. Therapist 1 might say something like: "Keep that feeling with you, as if it's inside a balloon that you're holding on to with a piece of string. Relax your posture, put your feet hip-width apart and look at your neighbour. Now we're going to analyse your first urge, your first reaction to this emotion, within yourself."
Step 5:	Meanwhile, client 2 has been watching client 1. He now puts himself in client 1's shoes and mirrors client 1's vulnerable child mode by portraying it in as much detail as possible, both verbally and non-verbally. Therapist 2 supports him in this.
Step 6:	Whilst client 2 is mirroring, client 1 tries to capture his first internal reaction, both verbally and non-verbally. Therapist 1 supports him.
Step 7:	The other group members are now asked to provide feedback on their observation of client 1's reaction: "What is happening with client 1? How does he look? How does he move? What does he say? What sound does he make?"

Step 8:	Together, the whole group focuses on the following: "What characteristic of client 1 is this? Is it a punisher, a coping mode, or maybe a healthy adult?"
Step 9:	Therapist 1 asks client 1: "Do you recognize this in yourself (that your first reaction is to withdraw when you're feeling scared)?"
Step 10:	Therapist 2 asks client 2: "What does client 1's first reaction do to you? Does it help you with your vulnerability, or does it do the opposite? Is that unpleasant feeling getting worse or better?"
Step 11:	The exercise continues with the next client. Client 2 expresses his vulnerable child mode to his neighbour, client 3. Therapist 1 checks to make sure that client 2 is connecting with his emotions.
Step 12:	Client 2 returns to a neutral position and keeps the emotion with him, inside a balloon. He is now going to analyse his first reaction to this emotion.
Step 13:	In the meantime, client 3 has been watching client 2 and he now has a go at mirroring his vulnerable child mode. Therapist 2 supports him in doing this.
Step 14:	Whilst client 3 is mirroring, client 2 tries to observe and capture his first internal reaction. Therapist 1 supports him.
Step 15:	The other group members provide feedback. Together they explore: "What characteristic of client 2 is this?" Therapist 1 checks whether client 2 recognizes it.
Step 16:	The exercise continues until everyone has had their turn.
Notes:	■ This exercise can also be used with an individual client, with the therapist mirroring the vulnerable child mode. This requires the therapist to keep swapping roles, as he must also support the client in connecting with his emotions and capturing his first reaction. ■ It is important for the client to feel his vulnerable child mode and for the therapist to get a clear picture of the client's primary schema. Therefore, the therapist will keep asking "What do you feel? Are you mainly angry, scared or sad?" and 'What are you really scared of? What does that mean to you?" He will continue to do this until the schema becomes visible (Socratic dialogue). ■ Initially, this exercise can be difficult for clients; it isn't easy for them to change between personality traits within themselves, let alone to swap roles with someone else. It is useful to keep repeating this exercise for a few weeks, to enable each client to gain a tighter grip on and better insight into his internal mode and mood fluctuations. →

	■ In the exercise the clients learn to perceive the mode that is being triggered and they practice letting it go again. Apart from that, nothing else is done with the mode. However, it is possible to follow up this exercise with a chair technique in which the activated schema can be manipulated.

Exercise 3.2: Spontaneity in mode regulation	
Goal:	To learn how to regulate modes.
Category:	1: Mode dynamics
Preparation:	Get three chairs ready: one for the vulnerable child mode, one for the first reaction to this mode and one for the healthy adult mode.
Instructions:	
Step 1:	Client 1 sits on the chairs one at a time and briefly repeats what these modes express. He begins with the vulnerable child mode (for example, the emotion in the balloon of the mirror exercise). Then he moves to his first reaction (coping, parent, child or healthy adult mode), and finally he takes the healthy adult chair.
Step 2:	Client 2 sits on the vulnerable child chair and mirrors client 1's child mode.
Step 3:	Client 1, on the healthy adult chair, experiences his reaction to the child mode. Therapist 1 supports him by asking questions such as: "What do you feel? What do you notice?"
Step 4:	Client 3 takes the first reaction chair and mirrors client 1's first reaction.
Step 5:	Client 1 remains on the healthy adult chair to experience his mirrored reaction to the mirrored urge. Therapist 1 supports him by asking questions such as: "What do you feel? What do you notice?"
Step 6:	Next, client 1 has a go at responding in a spontaneous but functional way. The therapist can provide pointers, for example: "What does your heart tell you to say or do? With regard to the child? With regard to the urge? What is your first instinct, verbal or non-verbal?" The other group members help the client with this by taking it in turns to show their own healthy, spontaneous reactions.
Step 7:	Where appropriate, client 2 and client 3 may be asked how it feels to receive this healthy, spontaneous reaction from the healthy adult. →

Notes:	■ In individual therapy, the therapist mirrors the child mode and the first reaction. He then supports the client in finding a healthier way to respond.
	■ Clients often need help when learning how to respond in a spontaneous and healthy way. Practice is important; every little gesture or expression means progress. It's also fine to copy another group member's reaction.
	■ It's possible to make this exercise more difficult by letting the modes – directed by the schema - 'respond' to the healthy, spontaneous reaction (for example: "you can say that now but you don't really believe it").
	■ It's also possible for the client to practice a healthy adult response to his own spontaneous reaction: encouragement, praise, support and so on. By doing so, he will learn how to strengthen his own healthy adult mode.

3.5.2 Exercises to strengthen the healthy adult

Exercise 3.3: Discussing and creating group rules	
Goal:	Moving on from old, negative experiences to new, positive experiences.
Category:	2: Strengthening the healthy adult
Preparation:	
Instructions:	When the safety or atmosphere within the therapy comes under pressure, the therapist explains that the client is repeating old family habits. For example, if the client is disrespectful towards the therapist, this gives him the opportunity to replace the old family code of conduct with a new, functional code of conduct.
Step 1:	The therapist asks the client to return to his childhood home in a brief imagery exercise: "Watch yourself walking towards your house. You can see the colour of the door, the street. You go inside like you always do. What do you find? What's the atmosphere like? How do people treat one another here? How does that make you feel? What would you like to be different? What do you miss? What do you need? What kind of atmosphere would help you to meet your needs? In what way would you like people to interact with each other?" ➔

Step 2:	The client opens his eyes. Together, therapist and client talk through the imagery exercise. The therapist focuses on a healthy atmosphere and functional manners.
Step 3:	The therapist also states what is important to him with regard to the client's behaviour and code of conduct: "It's important to me that there is an effective two-way communication between us, and that we take each other seriously."
Step 4:	The therapist checks the client's commitment by asking: "Can we agree then, that from now on, you will try to… ?"
Notes:	■ In a group setting, each client will get to discuss his family code of conduct, need and commitment. The co-therapists will each explain what kind of behaviour and manners they personally find important. ■ If necessary, for example in cases where old and dysfunctional family codes of conduct recur problematically, the new behaviour rules can be set down in writing and signed like a contract by both client and therapist.

Steps in empathizing with the coping mode

1. Set a gentle limit for the coping behaviour
2. Validate its protective function
3. Disempower its protective function
4. Provide hope in the form of a feasible pledge

Exercise 3.4: Empathic confrontation of the coping mode (see also figure 3.2)

Goal:	Practicing empathic confrontation of the coping mode.
Category:	2: Strengthening the healthy adult
Preparation:	Get five chairs ready: one for the coping mode (protector) and four for the steps of the healthy adult. Perhaps put sheets with the various elements written on them in front of the chairs, as guidance for the client.
Instructions:	See figure 3.2 for a visual representation of the exercise.
Step 1:	The therapist asks the client to sit on the protector's chair and briefly talk about a situation in which his coping mode was triggered ("there I go again"). The client successively sits down on the individual chairs and reads the corresponding messages out loud. →

Step 2:	The first part of the healthy reaction is setting a gentle limit for the protector: "Just stop for now...."
Step 3:	The second part is showing appreciation for the protective function: "Thank you for being there for little (Nico). Without you he might not have survived. You were vital for little (Nico) to be able to face up to his challenges...", etc.
Step 4:	The third part is imposing a limit on the dysfunctional behaviour in the present, by establishing a connection between the protector, the symptoms and the basic need: "But if you stay, you will keep everyone away and little (Nico) will never learn how to develop close relationships. This means he won't be able to overcome his loneliness."
Step 5:	The fourth part is the healthy adult taking over and making a pledge that corresponds with what's achievable at the moment: "I'm here now. I can help (Nico) to do things differently so that he will get the connection he needs. I may not always know how, but I promise to persevere until I've found a way."
Step 6:	Follow-up: What did the client think of the exercise? Which part touched him the most?
Notes:	■ This exercise is easy to apply in a group setting. Client 1 remains seated on chair 1 whilst other group members sit on chairs 2, 3, 4 and 5. This enables client 1 to experience how it feels to receive a healthy adult reaction. When the exercise has been done several times, client 1 can also take a turn sitting on chairs 2, 3, 4 and 5. ■ An extra step can be added where the client is asked what gesture his healthy adult wants to make (e.g. turn away, pull shoulders back, walk forwards). ■ It's possible to link the exercise with a homework task: "What do you intend to do in response to this exercise?" ■ It is important for the client to understand that the exercise consists of distinct steps. The therapist must provide the client with guidance, especially the first time the exercise is used. For example, he might model a specific step in terms of facial expressions, body language, tone of voice and repertoire. Or he might sit next to the client and give him instructions. It's also important for the client to practice a healthy posture: making eye contact, projecting his voice, standing or sitting straight and so on. ■ Switching roles can also be useful in enabling the client to 'look at himself' and review his own reactions to each step. →

- If there aren't enough chairs, the exercise can be done whilst standing.
- This exercise may trigger the parent mode ("You will never succeed!"); it is important to anticipate this and provide an explanation for it. It is also advisable to provide information about the various forms of coping and their value for survival.
- Lastly, the exercise can be repeated to firmly embed the individual parts.

Figure 3.2: 'Empathic confrontation of the coping mode' exercise

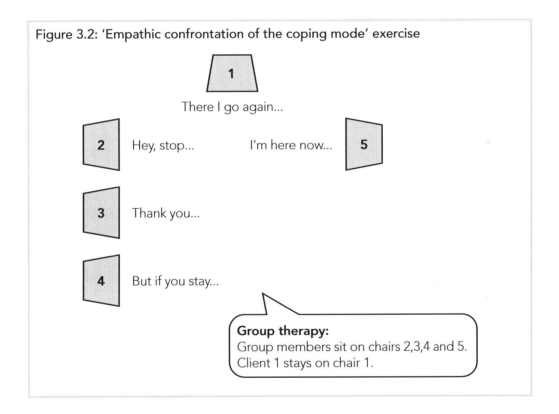

Steps in empathizing with the vulnerable child mode
1. Acknowledge the emotion
2. Disempower the negative belief
3. Provide hope for the future

Exercise 3.5: Empathizing with the vulnerable child mode (see also figure 3.3)	
Goal:	To practice self-regulation of the child mode.
Category:	2: Strengthening the healthy adult
Preparation:	Get four chairs ready: one for the child mode and three for the steps of the healthy adult. Perhaps put sheets with the various elements written on them in front of the chairs, as guidance for the client.
Instructions:	See figure 3.3 for a visual representation of the exercise.
Step 1:	A brief imagery exercise whereby the client connects with a recent situation in which he felt off balance, insecure or sad, caused by a primary schema. Support the client with this by zooming in on sensory information.
Step 2:	The client sits on the vulnerable child chair. He opens up about what his trigger is and how it makes him feel by answering questions such as: "Which schema does this relate to? What does it make you think of? In what way have you become familiar with this in your life?"
Step 3:	The first part of the healthy reaction is acknowledging and validating the emotion towards the child mode. This can be done in three ways: with a physical gesture (supportive look, raised eyebrows, gentle smile, hand on shoulder), with a sound (pfff, oooh) and with words ("I can see that…", "I can tell from your voice that…").
Step 4:	The second part of the healthy reaction is disempowering the negative inner belief. This starts with: "it's not true that…", or: "it's not right that…", along with information that is known about the client. What has he managed to overcome already? What progress has he made in terms of healthy behaviour? For example: "It's not true that no one likes you. I like you a lot. Your jokes often make me laugh." If nothing comes to mind, there's always the option to refer to the fact that the client is attending the therapy: "It's not true that you will never succeed. After all, you've started therapy and you're going to learn a lot from it."
Step 5:	The third part of the healthy reaction is giving hope for the future. This starts with saying things like: "I know for sure that you'll succeed in…", or: "I truly believe that you…", along with encouraging facts linked to the basic need. It's also possible to draw on universal norms and values, such as: "I know for sure that you'll manage to feel less lonely. Every human being is capable of enjoying the nice things in life as well as getting through the not so nice things. And so are you. I can see you gradually opening up and letting me get to know you. That will really help you." →

Step 6:	Follow-up: What did the client feel at each individual step? What does he want to do with this information? Is he able to set himself another target? Does he want to try out different behaviours?
Notes:	■ In a group setting, the group members can execute the individual steps. ■ If it's the first time the exercise has been used, the therapist may model it and demonstrate what kind of messages can be given to the client. ■ The client needs support to enable him to display a healthy adult attitude, reflecting the different steps. The therapist can set him a task to prepare or practice this at home. It's possible to practice the different steps separately. ■ The exercise can be extended by the client returning to the vulnerable child chair after each step to express how it felt to receive that particular message. Of course, it's also possible to review the client's feelings at the end. ■ This exercise is an alternative to one outlined by Van Vreeswijk & Broersen (2017). It puts more emphasis on a healthy adult treatment of the vulnerable child, with regard to body posture, facial expressions and use of language.

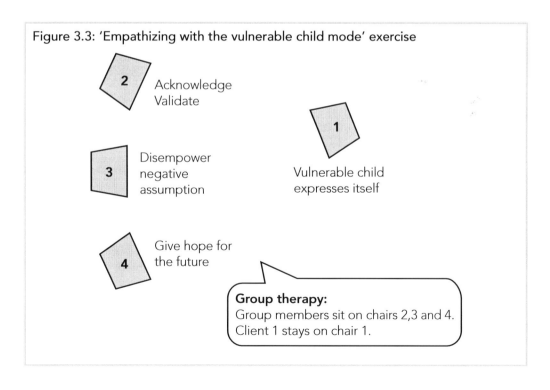

Figure 3.3: 'Empathizing with the vulnerable child mode' exercise

2 — Acknowledge Validate

1

3 — Disempower negative assumption

Vulnerable child expresses itself

4 — Give hope for the future

Group therapy:
Group members sit on chairs 2,3 and 4.
Client 1 stays on chair 1.

Exercise 3.6: Setting firm limits	
Goal:	To increase the repertoire for setting limits.
Category:	2: Strengthening the healthy adult
Preparation:	Have a soft fabric ball ready.
Instructions:	
Step 1:	Often, the client hasn't got much of a repertoire or lacks the skills to be able to set limits in an appropriate way. Therefore, to begin, it's necessary to practice expressing firm limits. In the first round the therapists asks: "What can you say if you want to make it clear that there's something you don't want anymore?"
Step 2:	The client and the therapist (or the group members, if it's a group setting) throw the ball at each other whilst calling out examples ("Stop!"; "Back off!"; "Quit!"). The therapist makes sure that tone of voice, facial expressions and body posture are more or less consistent with what's being said.
Step 3:	In the second round one person calls out a limit (e.g. "Stop! I've had enough!"), after which the other person repeats his words but in an 'exaggerated' way, both verbally and non-verbally (for example, by talking louder, taking a bigger step forwards or looking particularly angry).
Notes:	■ This exercise can easily be done in a group. ■ In a group setting, the therapist may ask the participants to repeat client 1's limit, all together and at the same time. For example all the group members could simultaneously step forward and shout "Back off!" ■ Clients can also practice expressing limits with regard to demanding beliefs. ■ This exercise is an essential prerequisite for successful implementation of the next exercise, 'Blocking the parent mode'. Without it, the client doesn't have the repertoire or skills needed to enable him to block the parent mode.

Exercise 3.7: Blocking the parent mode	
Goal:	To practice setting a firm limit against something destructive.
Category:	2: Strengthening the healthy adult
Preparation:	Have a soft fabric ball ready. Warm up with Exercise 3.6: Setting firm limits. →

Instructions:	Before starting, the therapist gives a brief explanation of the exercise.
Step 1:	This exercise consists of two rounds. In the first round, the client expresses in a few words or a sentence at most the central message of his parent mode (e.g. "Loser!"). It doesn't matter whether the message is demanding or punishing.
Step 2:	The client throws the ball to the therapist. The therapist catches or takes the ball and expresses his first spontaneous reaction to this message ("Whoa!", flinches).
Step 3:	The therapist and client swap roles. This time the therapist voices a parent mode message and the client tries to react spontaneously. The therapist helps with this.
Step 4:	In the second round, the client voices the destructive message again ("Loser!") and throws the ball to the therapist.
Step 5:	The therapist takes the ball and sets a firm limit for the parent mode message, for example: "Stop!" (and turns away), or: "Back off!" (and looks angry). He makes sure that this firm limit goes hand in hand with appropriate non-verbal facial expressions and body language (for example, standing upright, making eye-contact, keeping an impassive face). If he wants to check how convincing he is, the therapist can ask the client: "Do you believe me? Would you stop?"
Step 6:	The therapist and client swap roles. The therapist voices a parent mode message and the client sets a firm limit. The therapist helps him with this. If appropriate the therapist may also point out whether he finds the client credible or not.
Notes:	■ This exercise can be used when the client has experienced resistance and defiance against the parent mode in previous sessions. ■ It can easily be used in a group setting. The group members throw the ball to each other; one person voices the destructive message and throws, another person catches and reacts. In a group it's even more important to make sure that the firm limit goes hand in hand with appropriate non-verbal behaviour and that it comes across as serious and believable. Everyone has a turn. ■ When using this exercise for the first time, it's fine to mix the punishing and demanding parent modes and the reactions to them. As the therapy progresses, the messages should be split into punishing or demanding so that the client learns the difference with regard to the firm limit required.

Exercise 3.8: Using spontaneity in imagery rescripting	
Goal:	To strengthen healthy schemas by changing underlying schemas.
Category:	2: Strengthening the healthy adult
Preparation:	Perhaps an exercise like 3.2 Spontaneity in mode regulation or 3.6 Setting firm limits.
Instructions:	This in an exercise in imagery rescripting, a key technique in schema therapy. The client's first, authentic reaction is used as this often has healthy elements. Teaching the client how to utilise these will help increase his self-confidence.
Step 1:	The therapist asks the client to close his eyes and to return to an unpleasant situation from his childhood in which his needs weren't met. The client describes the image from his perspective as a child, along with his feelings and his needs.
Step 2:	The therapist steps into the image, together with the client's healthy adult. Through questions and comments, he encourages the client to react as authentically and spontaneously as possible, led by his healthy adult mode. For example: "Have a look at the situation. You know what you feel. Often you have the answer already, you just have to find it. Go on, let it out. I'll help you. How does it affect you when you see the little one like that? What does it prompt you to do or say? What's your first urge? What comes into your mind to say to the parents? What impact does it have on you when you see this? What would you do if this was the little girl next door? What would you say to her? What would you say to her parents?" The therapist also helps the client to express himself in a healthy adult way with regard to tone of voice, posture and facial expressions.
Step 3:	If necessary, the rescripting is briefly extended before its completion. In the follow-up the therapist asks the client to reflect on the exercise, led by his child mode: How did it feel to hear big [client's name] react so spontaneously?
Notes:	■ Imagery rescripting can also be done in a group setting. In this version all the group members step into the image of the client who is the point of focus, and they all contribute by expressing their first, spontaneous, authentic reaction. The therapists reinforce these reactions.

3.5.3 Anger management exercises

Exercise 3.9: Angry child mode warm-up	
Goal:	To introduce the experiencing and expression of anger.
Category:	3: Anger management
Preparation:	Take a ball. Make sure there is plenty of space. The exercise is done standing up.
Instructions:	
Step 1:	The therapist briefly explains the exercise and outlines its importance: "Anger is an important emotion but not easy to feel. As a child, you learned to hide your frustrations. In this exercise we're going to practice reconnecting with them in a safe way. The aim is to say in one sentence what you're fed up with, then throw the ball. Then the other person takes the ball and repeats what you've said."
Step 2:	The therapist models the exercise by standing up with the ball in his hands. He takes a moment to connect with his own frustrations, then he says for example: "I'm fed up with… [a frustration]." Then he throws the ball on the floor.
Step 3:	The client takes the ball and repeats what the therapist said ("You're fed up with…)"
Step 4:	The client has his turn. The therapist helps him put his own anger into words. He also checks the client's non-verbal expression and, if necessary, guides him through this. He asks the client to focus on his physical sensations: "What can you feel inside your body? I see you smiling, what does that mean?"
Step 5:	The client throws the ball. The therapist picks it up and repeats what the client said.
Notes:	■ This exercise can be used when the therapist has explained the different forms of anger. ■ It can easily be used in a group setting, with the clients all taking turns. ■ Clients often have a lot of anger piled up inside, and this exercise is a safe way to let it out. It may therefore be necessary to have multiple rounds of this exercise; with an individual client there is plenty of time for this. ■ As a follow-up, the experiences can be related to a cognitive framework by explaining the natural course of anger as an emotion. For example: "You've noticed that a few minutes ago you felt wound up, then you felt relieved and now you can feel yourself calming down again."

Exercise 3.10: Empathizing with the angry child mode	
Goal:	To experience what a healthy adult reaction to anger feels like.
Category:	3: Anger management
Preparation:	Provide two extra chairs for the angry child and the vulnerable child. Perform exercise 3.9: Angry child mode warm-up.
Instructions:	
Step 1:	In a brief imagery exercise the client connects with a recent situation in which he felt angry with someone else. The therapist may ask questions such as: "Can you describe the situation? Who is involved? How do you know that you're feeling angry? What do you feel inside your body? What is it that you're actually angry about? What has triggered your anger?"
Step 2:	The client sits on the angry child chair and expresses this mode; there is no need for him to be subtle. The therapist guides the client through his reaction, to make sure it is the expression of a child, not a coping mode.
Step 3:	The therapist responds to the mode as a healthy adult; he asks in a soft and neutral voice if there is anything else the client is angry about.
Step 4:	When the angry child mode has finished raging, the therapist acknowledges the anger and the importance of it. He praises the client for expressing his feelings and asks him how it feels for the angry child be acknowledged and understood.
Step 5:	The therapist asks the client to sit on the vulnerable child chair. He then asks questions like: "What is it that you really need? What do you miss? What do you need more of?" He lets the client express himself.
Step 6:	The therapist responds to the vulnerable child mode as a healthy adult and shows acknowledgement.
Step 7:	The therapist and client swap roles. The client sits on the healthy adult chair and practices responding to the angry child as a healthy adult. The therapist actively supports him in this by asking questions such as: "How do you position yourself? How do you look? What tone of voice do you use?" The therapist reminds the client of his own interventions in the previous steps and encourages the client to try these out. He also gives feedback on the client's messages from his current perspective in the role of client.
Step 8:	The client and therapist together think of a phrase with which the healthy adult can stay in touch with or defend the angry child. ➡

Notes:	■ In a group setting, the clients take turns to sit on the healthy adult chair to acknowledge anger and encourage its expression. The client who is expressing his angry child mode stays seated on that chair. One of the therapists supports the angry child mode and asks the client how this makes him feel. The other therapist supports the healthy adult mode. As a follow-up, the whole group can work together to identify a phrase that the healthy adult mode may say to the angry child.
	■ It is important that the client really connects with his emotions in this exercise, and that the therapist helps him with this. He may, for example, re-enact the situation in a role play. Or he may sit next to the client and mirror the angry child mode in terms of posture, facial expressions, tone of voice and choice of words, then ask the client to copy him.
	■ Role switching may also be helpful: the therapist asks to sit on the angry child chair for a minute. He then portrays the angry child mode as authentically as possible and asks the client if he recognizes it and if the image is correct. The client then returns to the angry child chair and portrays it in his own way.

3.6 Areas of focus and tips

3.6.1 Areas of focus

Keep in mind the following areas of focus during phase 2, with its emphasis on 'Express yourself':

■ The therapeutic relationship is the force for change. Ensure the relationship is reciprocal and personal and use healthy interactions, imagery rescripting and chair techniques to enable the client to achieve his full potential.

■ Raise the level of authenticity and spontaneity both within yourself and within the client; you often already have the solution and just need to find it. Make room for humour and light-heartedness. Support the client by modelling step-by-step what you're aiming for and providing a running commentary for every step ('sculpting'). This enables the client to copy and internalize the expected behaviour.

■ If there is a parent mode present, then there is also a lot of vulnerability. Help the client to connect with this: what kind of fear or desire is hiding behind this parental message? The focus is always on the connection with the vulnerable child, no matter what gets in the way.

■ Plan and shape each session in a way that provides the client with opportunities to learn to tolerate emotions. Start with a warm-up or introductory conversation, then focus on the underlying schemas. Every session has an experiential exercise. Imageries are followed up with a happy child moment. By doing this, without realizing it, the client will gain more control over his levels of anxiety.

■ In a group setting, not everyone gets a turn in this phase. Therefore, the client must learn to ask for attention and to recognize himself by looking at others. He will also learn that he is responsible for his own process of transformation and, at the same time, his ability to manage frustrations will be improved.

■ Increase the pressure; schemas will only heal through new experiences. Show empathy but challenge the client too. Discuss problem behaviours frequently and set limits, including consequences such as a time-out. Do this from the start so the client has opportunities to learn.

■ Use the frequent parallel processes and exchange between therapist and client to better understand the client. Colleagues often have different ideas about a client, which may emerge in a client discussion and can also be used to better understand the client or group's dynamics.

■ Don't avoid tensions and take irritations, impatience or other feelings seriously. Clients experience these feelings even more in a group setting. They depend on the therapist to show them that negative feelings aren't necessarily destructive and can even be productive.

■ A standard phrase to approach a difficult situation can be helpful when starting a discussion, for example: "I feel tension – that must mean something", or: "Good! You're expressing yourself. What does that mean?" This makes it easier to then really tackle the issue.

■ Having a peer support group and paying attention to his own feelings are both vital for a therapist to be able to practice interventions and stay connected with his instincts.

■ In Group schema therapy there often is a higher level of anxiety as clients reinforce one another. It is therefore even more important for the therapists to have as little tension as possible in their working relationship, and for both therapists to feel comfortable enough to, for example, consult each other during a session if any unexpected situations occur.

3.6.2 Tips

Stand strong in the storm...

Crises and difficult behaviour are inherent features of this phase. The client is struggling with himself and is self-centred. He depends on the therapist to provide schema corrective experiences and help him manage his anxieties. Sometimes, his behaviour can be so destructive that the client puts himself in danger. In such situations, once again it's safety first. Safeguarding responsibility lies with the therapist and, if necessary, he must intervene and set a limit. This requires perfect timing: not too early, but not too late either. An early reaction prevents the client from further risk and also provides scope for him to learn from the situation. Intervening too early, however, can create too much pressure. After all, the problem behaviour is often linked to schemas and, for that reason, it deserves sympathy and empathy. Responding too late, on the other hand, may lead to exasperation and overreaction. It must always be clear which behaviour the therapist wants to address and why; after all, he needs the client to be on his side eventually for him to be able to make any progress.

In this phase, problem behaviour in a group setting often consists of conflicts. For example, the clients are so self-centred that they don't feel like helping each other. They also notice each other's peculiarities, but don't yet have the ability to express this in a constructive way. In such situations, it's important for the co-therapists to form a strong team, to stop any destructive interactions and to guide the clients step-by-step through a more constructive approach.

A step-by-step approach to supporting clients in expressing interpersonal conflicts

When there's a conflict between group members, it is important that the accompanying emotions are expressed. This can be done safely by following these steps:

1. The client who needs to express himself first describes the behaviour in other person that triggered his schema-directed reaction. He also describes the effect of the behaviour on him: "When you do or say... I interpret it as..."
2. Next, he explains his trigger and his urge: "That makes me think of... and I get the urge to ...
3. He also reflects on his schema-directed behaviour and his dysfunctional modes: "The thing I did that wasn't very good was that I..."
4. Finally, he explains which dysfunctional mode he finds difficult to deal with in the other person: "What I find difficult with you is... [for example: that your angry protector appears when I'm trying to be nice]."
5. Afterwards, the receiver can respond by answering the following questions: "What can you hear him say? How does that make you feel?" If necessary, the receiver can follow the same steps and talk about his own reaction led by the dysfunctional mode.

...react early...

Timing is key when responding to undesirable behaviour. This should be done as early as possible, and the behaviour should be described precisely. It enables the client to become aware of what he's doing and the impact this has on others. After all, in most cases the client doesn't realize that his behaviour is causing issues. Delaying the intervention only makes things more and more difficult for the therapist. The tension rises, frustrations increase, and it becomes more and more likely that the therapist's own schemas will be triggered. Allowing problem behaviour to persist before intervening also gives the client the impression that double standards are applied; first it was fine, then suddenly it wasn't. When the therapist eventually does intervene, it will be more difficult for him to explain the reasons why. Depending on the type of behaviour, there is then room for negotiation to meet the client's need for autonomy. The more destructive and dangerous the behaviour, the less room there is and the greater the need for the therapist to set limits. It is important that the therapist is willing to take a firm lead in this: he needs to provide the client with guidance, use his own instincts to decide what is healthy and what isn't, and attach consequences to the limits he sets.

...increase the pressure...

If the client is aware of his destructive behaviour but not changing, the therapist may increase the pressure to motivate him to let go of it. The therapist who drew up a crisis or safety plan in phase 1 can remind the client of this and ask him to follow it through. It's also possible to repeat empathic confrontations, to re-analyse the pros and cons of the coping behaviour, or to recap the rules. Starting every session with a conversation about the behaviour can help put pressure on the client to change, and a time-out can be appropriate if the client still fails to make progress. Time-outs can be used in a range of helpful ways. In individual therapy, a time-out may involve the client not seeing the therapist for a week, the client having to attend a meeting with one of the therapist's colleagues, or even having to go elsewhere first to get treatment for his problem behaviour. In a group setting, a time-out may consist of an individual member not attending the group session and instead working with one of the therapists to analyse which mode was triggered and why. They can also discuss how the client might explain this to the group and what kind of support he needs to do it. In cases where it becomes apparent, for example, that the whole group is contributing to secrecy or reticence, it's possible to give the whole group a time-out. The group is then put on hold, and individual discussions take place with the aim of unravelling and challenging the group's pattern.

CASE STUDY

Group schema therapy: Reveal under external pressure

Amber has had a time-out because her reactions in the group were led by an angry protector, and she has worked with the therapist to prepare for her return to the group. The therapist begins:

>> Therapist: "Amber would like to say something."

Amber continues:

>> Amber: "In the individual session I focused on the reasons why I've been so angry and withdrawn over the last few weeks. This is to do with my angry protector. It's something I learned as a child when I was growing up in and amongst violence. My parents argued a lot and my father used to hit my mother. My mother had an angry protector too, and she used to attack my father by making nasty accusations. I started to copy that. Now, whenever I feel insecure, I shut myself off and become really mean. It helps me to avoid feeling lonely. At the moment I'm in a violent relationship. History is repeating itself and I feel insecure again, so I'm not able to show my vulnerability in the group. I need your help with this."

Whilst disclosing all this, Amber is sat next to the therapist and holds her notes in front of her to help her remember the main points she wants to get across.

…and go for it, especially when things are tense.

No matter how familiar a coping pattern feels for the client, ultimately it is a destructive behaviour that he wants to get rid of and the reason why he started therapy. In the long term, avoidance will cause anxiety. Or he may suffer from loneliness, caused by an angry protector or approval seeker. Bearing all this in mind will help the therapist overcome his own barriers and face the confrontation. The higher the tension, the more there is to be gained. For example, a client might say: "I didn't like that time-out at all. I felt like I was being told off and abandoned. With hindsight, though, it was the most helpful part of the whole therapy process. If it wasn't for that time-out, I don't think anything would have changed." The therapist benefits too; he frees himself from tension and caution, he'll most likely find the client more pleasant to work with after the intervention, and it gives him the chance to feel more open-minded and unprejudiced again.

3.6.3 When is it time for the next phase?

Towards the end of phase 2, the following guidelines should be used to determine whether or not the client has made enough progress within the six-month timescale to move into the phase 3:

- The client is ready to change his behaviour. Outside the therapy he is struggling, as he keeps repeating certain behaviour patterns. He is motivated to practice with different behaviours and he feels the need to get on with shaping his life outside of therapy.

- He is able, to some extent, to acknowledge and regulate his own emotions. He can show and share with others what his child mode is going through.

- He can cope with some separation, he is not afraid to go against the flow, and he is willing to get involved in a debate. He stands up for himself if something is bothering him.

- In the majority of sessions, he is in his vulnerable child or healthy adult mode. He can tolerate it when the therapist challenges his coping behaviour, and he can put it to one side when the therapist asks him to. He no longer hides behind the dysfunctional modes.

Chapter 4:
Phase 3 – Do it yourself

Chapter summary
4.1 Basic needs
4.2 The therapy environment
4.3 Goals in this phase by schema mode
4.4 The therapeutic relationship
4.5 Exercises
4.6 Areas of focus and tips

Chapter summary

In the third phase of therapy, the client moves towards doing things himself. He experiments with changes in his behaviour, in search of a life that will improve his well-being and make him happier. He discovers that this may have consequences both for himself and for others, and that he must take responsibility for this. The client explores his own identity, which will go hand in hand with anger and sadness and result in him having to try to make choices. This requires the therapist to take a reassuring, encouraging stance that promotes enthusiasm. This phase also has a greater focus on life outside therapy. The therapy entails a constant balancing act between the client doing things himself and the therapist taking control. The goals, exercises, tips and tricks all correspond to this.

4.1 Basic needs

4.1.1 Adolescence

Over the previous phases, the client has gained an insight into his pattern and the first steps have been taken towards strengthening healthy schemas. The client feels sufficiently supported by the therapist; throughout his struggles and moments of crisis the therapist has stood by him, providing support and understanding, but has also given him guidelines and created the necessary conditions for him to make progress. As the client has had opportunities to express himself whilst maintaining a sense of security and connection, he has developed a new identity and a growing need for independence and autonomy. In this part of the therapy, these needs will further evolve.

The healthy base that has been built so far is adequate for the client to begin to explore alone. The parallel with a child who transitions from primary to secondary school comes to mind. It's a scary thought for every parent but, at the same time, there is also belief and trust in the child's abilities to face these new challenges. Parents want their children to develop into independent individuals, and to make this happen they must give them room to grow and respect their uniqueness. At the same time, parents must be mindful that their children are still children and not fully independent yet; therefore, a good parent will continue to provide a safe and secure base that the child can always rely upon and come back to. Maintaining structure and setting limits will enable the child – and here, the client – to experience that he is in a safe place where he has the opportunity to develop himself. In doing so, he will gain sufficient self-confidence to lead his own life (table 4.1).

In a similar way, the therapist must try to achieve a balance in this phase. It is vital that autonomy and self-appreciation can be developed within a therapy environment in which there is trust and scope to grow, but also guidance along with limits when necessary. So on the one hand the therapist must give the client room to get to know himself and develop self-confidence; on the other he must set limits and make adjustments. This means that, alongside autonomy and self-appreciation, realistic limits are once again an important basic need. The therapist must differentiate the guidance he provides and the limits he sets and adapt them to the client. After all, a parent has different expectations from a twelve-year-old compared to a sixteen-year-old, or a girl compared to a boy.

This combination of needs also leads to conflicts. There is no doubt that the client will clash with the therapist or other group members about issues related to his autonomy, just like an adolescent who argues with his parents over what time to be home at night, or what music he likes. The client can feel his self-confidence grow; he wants to explore, experiment, be independent and stand on his own two feet, but at the same time he's not yet ready to do this all by himself and he feels insecure ("Am I capable enough?"). He wants to assert and further explore his own identity, and he feels stifled when the therapist restricts his actions, so he becomes rebellious and recalcitrant.

If the client allows himself to practice new behaviour within the set limits and structure, he will be able to develop sufficient self-appreciation and autonomy to get through this 'adolescent phase'. He can then begin to internalize these realistic limits. It's all part of the learning process; discovering that he can make his own choices, within realistic limits, forms a corrective experience that will aid his development and serve as a resource that he can draw upon throughout the therapy process.

Table 4.1: Overview of the components of phase 3	
Theme:	Do it yourself
Basic need:	Autonomy, self-appreciation
Limited reparenting:	Adolescence
Overall goal:	Doing means learning
Important exercises:	Using anger
	Repairing the damage
Empathic confrontation:	Low
Group development phase:	Reciprocal phase
Mode model:	Customised and personal
Role of the therapist:	Encourage

>> **Client:** "I often feel unsure and I think to myself 'I'll never be able to do that'. I believe that my insecurity is proof of my inability. I know what I don't want any more but I don't know how to do things differently. Until now, I didn't realize how much I was hurt by what happened to me. I can't use my protector as much as I used to. Sometimes I wish I could! My therapist often brings me face to face with myself. Very annoying, I'd rather she left me alone! At the same time, she shows me that I'm stuck in self-doubt: I haven't got the courage. I do want to. But I can't. She doesn't stop, she perseveres and keeps asking what my ultimate goal is. She also helps me to come up with new, small steps to take and she encourages me to give it a go. I feel that I can be myself with her."

4.2 The therapy environment

4.2.1 Intrapersonal and interpersonal

In the first two phases, the client was struggling with himself and his destructive personality characteristics. He discovered how his past keeps repeating itself in his schemas and dysfunctional modes. This was mainly an intrapersonal process whereby the client learned to express his feelings and needs in order to create opportunities for schema corrective experiences. By encouraging him to work hard and persevere, the therapist helped the client to have these corrective experiences within the safe therapy environment. As a result, the client's schemas are now healthier. The old pattern is less rigid and the client is more in control of his modes and schemas. The healthy adult mode has become stronger, and the client is better able to tolerate anxiety.

The next step consists of connecting the inside world with the outside world. Again, a parallel may be drawn with a teenager who is exploring life outside the family environment more and more actively. The child/client no longer has an egocentric view of the world. He becomes part of larger contexts to which he contributes with his own identity. Themes associated with this are self-image, intimacy, sexuality, relationships, career choice, place in society, norms and values – but also insecurity, a feeling of belonging, peer pressure and rebellion. In this phase, the client practices staying in touch with his identity and inside world and, at the same time, making contact with the outside world. He uses the therapy to analyse the experiences he has in his day-to-day life, and to try out new behaviour.

> ### Discussing themes in therapy
>
> At this point in the therapy, the outside world starts to require more attention. Therefore, themes such as work, daytime activities, finances, general health, relationships, social network, lifestyle, housing, sexuality and parenting should be discussed. The client may not initiate a conversation about these things; if so, it is important that the therapist does it. It may be helpful to use a checklist to make sure that key topics are included. Starting to discuss themes now enables the therapist to spend plenty of time on it, giving each topic the attention it deserves and helping the client to overcome any barriers in these areas of life. A therapy process can only be complete when sufficient attention has been paid to the client's life outside therapy.

4.2.2 From 'old and familiar' to 'new and strange'

The client uses his matured individuality to take new steps. He is more aware of how his pattern dictates his life, and what advantages and disadvantages result from this. He also understands better what he actually needs. This increased awareness goes hand in hand with increased responsibility; expectations rise as a person becomes more knowledgeable and more capable, but at the same time the client still struggles with his patterns, feelings and inabilities. He still finds it difficult to integrate these aspects and to defend his own needs.

The increased expectations put him under pressure, and it's not easy for him to live a conscious life and fight against continual destructive urges. Not surprisingly, this evokes lots of emotions and schemas are triggered. Feelings of insecurity and fear emerge ("Will I ever be able to do it? Will I ever be happy?"), but also feelings of self-reproach and high demands ("You know how it works! Just do it then!") or irritation and loss of discipline ("I don't want to work this hard all the time. It's not fair! I'm not doing anything at all then!").

For every emotion triggered, the client's coping is on standby to numb it again. At the same time, the client senses that this coping is no longer functional; its replacement isn't quite ready yet, but it has changed from something comfortable to something that feels uncomfortable and unwanted. This requires the therapist to adopt a stance with which he shows empathy for the client's struggle but also keeps applying pressure on the client to practice new behaviour. Moreover, it's important that he keeps an eye out for recurring schemas that still need to be modified.

CASE STUDY

Individual therapy: Grieving for the deficiency

>> Linda: "I'm really upset about the fact that I didn't manage to talk to my partner. I know full well that I don't want him to treat me in the way he does."

>> Therapist: "It sounds like you're angry with yourself?"

>> Linda: "Yes, definitely! Honestly, under these circumstances it's never going to work out. I'd be far better off moving out and living on my own. That would solve everything."

>> Therapist: (makes eye contact with a sympathetic look in his eyes): "Hey, I completely understand your reaction. It's not a nice feeling when you have the intention to do something and then, for one reason or another, you don't manage it."

(Linda makes eye contact and nods.)

>> Therapist: "But what do you think? Which of your personality traits can you hear when you listen to yourself?"

>> Linda: "Well, I guess it's that punisher who's telling me off. And the avoider who wants to go and live by herself."

>> Therapist: "Yes, very good, that's what I think too. I'm impressed that you're aware of the different personality traits that play a role and that can make this part of our conversation. Just tell me about little Linda. I could hear her in your first sentence, when you said that you don't want your partner to treat you like he does?"

>> Linda: "Yes, that's right. I'm really fed up with the way he treats me. But I'm also annoyed with myself for not saying anything and changing my ways just for him. And it makes me really sad that I keep getting hung up on this. Why is life so tough?"

(Linda cries and seeks eye contact with the therapist.)

4.2.3 Trial and error

Although there are now many different emotions on lots of levels, the client is better able to handle this. He can tolerate more feelings without quickly becoming anxious, and is more able to experience and process different feelings at the same time. There will still be times when he gets overwhelmed by unprocessed feelings and pain, but usually he can keep things under control. He has a greater range of options; falling back on his pattern is no longer the only way forward. He knows for example what would be good for him when dealing with these emotions, even though he may not yet manage to do it all the time. In this phase, it is important that the client sets out to further increase this range of options and widen his behavioural repertoire. He needs to progress from 'consciously incompetent' towards 'consciously competent'. It's also important that unprocessed feelings are addressed and new feelings are validated, in order to continue to strengthen the healthy schemas.

All this is a process of trial and error. It is a quest in which the client flips back and forth between desire and fear. A yearning for the old and familiar alternates with a fear of relapse, and a wish for a new, happier future prospects co-exists with anxiety about what that unknown future might bring. However, the inner belief that he truly wants things to be different, along with the fact that he has already developed some healthier schemas, gives both client and therapist more confidence. Knowing that wrong turns are fine, and the therapist will keep faith no matter what, is a corrective emotional experience. This leads to the formation of a reciprocal spiral, starting with internal changes that pave the way for behavioural changes. Subsequently, by practicing with new behaviour, the client is able to let go of his pattern. In responses, he gets new reactions to his behaviour that he hasn't experienced before. For example, his fear of abandonment if he tries to be himself in the company of others isn't confirmed. This is then another schema corrective experience that can reinforce internal changes.

>> **Therapist:** "It's great to see how much my client has developed in the therapy so far. His hard work has paid off. At the same time, he's definitely still struggling as he's now encountering the most difficult obstacles. I enjoy motivating him to tackle these issues. I say things like: 'Good on you for trying. It's the trial and error phase and it's part of the process, you're learning new things. Of course, that's not easy. After all, you haven't done this before, have you?' I also often say: 'Give it a go – it's no problem if it doesn't work. The only battles we're sure to lose are those we don't join. It's fine to try things out.' I also want to know: 'What's your goal? What do you want?' and I encourage him to go for it! He no longer needs to settle for less than he is hoping for."

4.2.4 The environment of group schema therapy

The group offers an excellent framework for practicing new behaviour, as there are 'peers' present with whom clients can experiment and compare themselves. Being part of a group allows them to experience that everyone is different and people make their own choices. The clients now feel free and strong enough to be critical of each other. After all, they have developed sufficient individuality, they know that the atmosphere in the group will remain safe and secure, and they also now know that openness can actually be helpful for others. They are more keen to express their feelings and opinions. They want to practice transforming their emotions into behaviour in order to boost their self-confidence. The therapists encourage this but, in this phase, there is less need for them to interfere. The clients are more aware of and sensitive to what is acceptable and what isn't, and they are better at showing suitable behaviour – just as children know 'that's how we do things in our family'.

At the same time, irritations are more overt. Participants are more able to sense what is healthy and what isn't. They recognize their own triggers, emotions and basic needs. Their coping is less effective and they find it more difficult to numb their feelings. They respond to dysfunctional behaviour with defiance and resistance. Developing an own identity means that they start to differ more and more from each other. This may lead to an intimacy crisis, which has the benefit of creating scope for the differentiation between someone's opinion and someone's personality. The group practices with bonding and letting go, but also with integrating the two. This forms the foundation of the group developmental phase of reciprocity, which goes hand in hand with relative calm and acceptance of each other and each other's peculiarities (Hoijtink, 2001).

Now that there is sufficient intimacy and cohesion, it's possible to use the group to enhance the identity of each participant and to expand behavioural alternatives (Farrell & Shaw, 2012). Instead of avoiding a conflict, the clients are willing to face up to it and take risks. They compare themselves to each other, and work hard to overcome feelings of embarrassment. They experience that their fears are not necessarily confirmed when they share something with the group, and they sometimes even enjoy being different. At times their ways of sharing and responding to each other isn't yet perfect; there is still room for progress with regard to healthier schemas and more appropriate behaviour. The therapists support and encourage the clients in achieving this. After all, each of the clients is trying out new feelings and new behaviour against the background of an old pattern. This requires the therapists to monitor the frameworks, set limits if necessary and encourage clients to persevere and be themselves. Schemas and unprocessed feelings are addressed and, if appropriate, the therapists will help clients to actively seek a confrontation in order to deal with pain from the past. By encouraging the group members to break away from patterns, both during the sessions and as part of their homework, they provide opportunities for new, schema corrective experiences and ensure another step forward in the clients' process of change.

> **CASE STUDY**
>
> **Group schema therapy: Revealing a secret as a result of internal pressure**
>
> Kim has worked hard on her detached protector. She has discovered that he appears when she's feeling down, and makes her believe that her sadness is a selfish overreaction. As a result, she starts to feel even worse. She used to deal with this by switching her feelings off. In the therapy she has learnt to take her emotions seriously, and to express herself. She has noticed how relieved she feels when a fellow group member listens and tries to understand her.
>
> However, the other group members don't know that Kim also suffers from a binge eating habit to suppress these feelings. In recent weeks she has felt torn by this dilemma. She wants to say what's bothering her, as it is nice to share things and it helps her to feel less lonely. But she's also afraid of rejection. The more she hesitates, the more she binge eats. This is fuel for her punisher: "You see! You'll never succeed." At the same time, she feels the need to rebel: "I no longer want to be controlled by my protector and I no longer want to be knocked down by my punisher!"
>
> Kim realizes that she only has one option: choosing healthy behaviour. She decides to take the plunge and asks her therapist by email to help her to tell the rest of the group.

4.3 Goals in this phase by schema mode

This phase of the therapy is a turning point; the end is now in sight, so it's make-or-break for the client. Some clients arrive at this realization themselves, as in the case study above; others need the therapist to help by suggesting it as a next step. Therapist and client can then decide together how the client may be able to use the therapist's healthy adult for his battle. In group schema therapy, individual conversations can be used to discuss how the client can go about sharing this with the group, and how he can use the other group members' healthy adults – for example, to challenge his own punisher. As a result of the changes that have taken place and his psychological and emotional development, the client is now able to take more responsibility for his own choices and for his own therapy process. Exhibiting different behaviour is a way of creating opportunities for schema corrective experiences, and this manifests itself in the goals for this phase.

4.3.1 Overall goal: "Doing means learning"

Towards the end of this phase, the client realizes that he himself plays a key role in his life: "What do I find important? How can I achieve it?" His emotional and practical independence, his identity and his sense of reality have all grown. He can see his feelings and dysfunctional behaviours as symptoms of a need that's now in jeopardy, and he knows it's up to him to break his pattern and choose whether to embark on a process of gaining schema corrective experiences. He can weigh up the advantages and disadvantages of different options, and he is able to consider various behavioural repertoires. He has experienced that he can step out of his pattern in more than one way – that ignoring destructive modes is an option too, and that practice is useful when learning something new. He has also experimented with the application of his new skills outside of therapy.

In a group situation, the clients are able to support, challenge and encourage each other. They are capable of establishing reciprocal relationships and they respect each other's differences. They are also able to give and receive feedback, and to incorporate this into their self-image.

4.3.2 Child mode: "Come on, I see you"

By the end of this phase, the client has processed most of the feelings associated with a primary schema. The vulnerable child mode can still be overwhelming at times, but the client knows that this symbolises a need. He recognizes the need and knows that he must take it seriously, but he also knows that he himself is in charge of fulfilling it. He doesn't yet succeed every time, but he is able to reflect on his actions afterwards. Furthermore, he takes a different stance with regard to his angry child mode. He can connect with this mode and he knows that the anger is a symptom of: "I sense a limit" or "this is important to me". He has become more assertive, and has practiced using his anger when setting limits and defending his needs. He has practiced connecting with his undisciplined child mode, and understands which stance and message this mode needs in order to change. If other child modes also play a role, then he has practiced adopting a suitable stance towards these too.

4.3.3 Coping mode: "Oh, there you are again… what does that tell me?"

By this phase the client's coping mode has become egodystonic (i.e. not consistent with his needs and goals). The client understands how it links to his symptoms, and the advantages and disadvantages of using it. This enables him to make a choice: he can deliberately set his coping mode aside or he can keep using it. The client understands that the recurrence of the coping mode means that a schema has been triggered that goes hand in hand with intense emotions; coping is a signal that means a basic need is at risk of being compromised. As a result, he can respond to his own pattern in a mild and empathetic way; he understands and appreciates the reasons behind his actions.

4.3.4 Parent mode: "I can conquer you and I can ignore you!"

The parent mode too is now egodystonic. The client knows that the child mode is at its most vulnerable when the parent mode is triggered. He can sense his own anger about this, and use it to oppose the parent mode and protect the child mode. At the same time, he is also capable of pushing past the parent mode; he can ignore it and focus directly on his basic need instead. The parent mode is more differentiated and more personal. The client is able to detect when this mode is triggered, where it originates from, which part of the message is demanding and which part is punishing. He can recognize both elements, and he is capable of overcoming them.

4.3.5 Healthy adult mode and happy child mode: "I'm here and I'm not going away anymore."

The client's healthy adult mode is significantly stronger than it was, and it is capable of simultaneously overseeing several things. Therefore, the client often succeeds in fulfilling his needs. This mode has a strong bond with the inner world through the different child modes. There is a constant connection; the healthy adult mode acknowledges and validates the inner feelings and uses them as signals for a basic need. At the same time, this mode is also connected with the outside world. It takes other people's feelings into account, thinks about the impact of behaviour and considers the consequences with regard to important aspects of life. Last but not least, this mode is aware of the fact that it requires discipline and perseverance to defy dysfunctional personality traits.

CASE STUDY

Individual therapy: The healthy mode is always there

>> Linda: "I'm really fed up with my husband. I've talked to him but he doesn't understand me. We're just not on the same wavelength."

>> Therapist: "Well done for trying, and I'm sorry it hasn't led to what you were hoping for. Shall we have a look at how it went?"

>> Linda: "We were sat at the table and I asked if we could talk. Then I told him that I'd like him to talk more about his feelings too. He said that I always get angry or upset when he's being honest. I said that that's because he says things in such a blunt way. I always think about how I say things and how it will come across – surely he can do that too? But then he said that he's always walking on eggshells, scared to say the wrong things. We started arguing because he blamed me again."

>> Therapist: "How awful Linda, that sounds really frustrating. It seems to me that you got stuck in your pattern. Is that right?"

>> Linda: "Yes. But asking him to adapt, is that really too much to expect? I don't want it to have to be me all the time. I have to battle every day. I just want someone to take note of my wishes for a change.'." →

>> **Therapist:** "Yes, I understand that and well done for saying what you want. It's a very healthy need! It's a need that wasn't fulfilled when you were a little girl. Your parents didn't take enough account of your needs, and therefore this has now become an issue for you. You can feel a lack of consideration for your needs in the interactions with your husband, and that's horrible because it's as if what happened in the past is playing out all over again. At the same time, you're no longer just that little girl. You're much more than that. There's now also a grown-up Linda, who knows what she needs and who is learning how to stand up for herself. And that grown-up Linda is always there, even if she seems far away: she is there and she's not going away anymore. Shall we make her stronger through an exercise? An imagery rescripting or a chair technique perhaps? What do you think? What would help you the most at the moment?"

4.3.6 Mode model in this phase

The mode model continues to be the foundation of the therapy. It's still possible for issues that until now have been untouched or hidden to rise to the surface in this phase. Or a schema that seemed resolved might reappear, requiring attention again. If that's the case, the mode model will help to understand this. Moreover, there is now a differentiated and customized model, specifically set up for the individual client, that can be used as direction indicator. What does the client want to achieve? Which schemas are still present? What are the symptoms like now? This approach also includes 'reading between the lines'; the therapist, or the other group members, now know the client well enough to be able to sense and understand unintentional or implicit signs. Doing this contributes to a further deepening of the therapy and helps ensure that any remaining issues are dealt with.

Parent mode: Any elements that are new are added to the model. It's not uncommon for clients to take until this phase to be able to define what their parent mode actually sounds like, which may result in a 'penny dropping' moment: "Oh! That's how my punisher says that!"

Child mode: The different child modes that play a role in the client's life have been identified. The corresponding basic needs and their historic origins are clear. New elements that haven't been discussed before, such as a history of abuse or feelings of shame, can potentially be addressed and then added to the model to increase the client's understanding of himself. The angry and/or undisciplined child has now been given a clear place in the model. Furthermore, the client is better able to describe his emotions in a subtler way (e.g., "I feel unsure" instead of "I'm scared").

Coping mode: It remains important to keep an eye out for any changes in the client's behaviour. For example, it's possible that he may start to drink more alcohol now that he is more in touch with his feelings. Also, a change that at first seems healthy can sometimes veer towards coping – such as a client who at first avoids doing his paperwork and decides to address this, but then becomes overcontrolling. A relapse into old coping is also possible. If a client reports an increase in symptoms, then this may be an indication that something isn't quite right and a coping mode is at work.

Healthy adult mode and happy child mode: These modes now deserve a more prominent spot in the model. Important elements of the healthy adult mode in terms of discipline and ability to learn can be supplemented with expressions such as "perseverance pays off" or "I don't find confrontation easy, but I can do it and afterwards I feel relieved." The happy child mode reflects the client's increased individuality and self-appreciation: "I enjoy drinking coffee in the sunshine" or "I'm someone who loves to read."

4.4 The therapeutic relationship

4.4.1 Limited reparenting

The increasing importance of self-appreciation and autonomy also applies to the therapeutic relationship. The therapist takes less upon himself and lets the client experience more things for himself; however, he does keep an eye on him so that he can intervene if necessary. He also approaches the client with optimism: "You can do it. I have faith in you." The relationship between therapist and client evolves correspondingly and becomes more equal. The therapist still plays an exemplary role, but no longer as a controlling authority; he is now more of a role model for the client to follow in developing his own identity. The therapist is aware that the client sees him in this way and his contributions are mainly for educational purposes, to give the client opportunities to try things for himself: "Look, this is how I do it. That's one way. Other people may do it this way. Your parents did it that way. Every way has advantages and disadvantages. What do you want now? What suits you the most? Which direction do you want to go in?" The therapist does intervene firmly if a clear limit is necessary, for example, when it concerns destructive behaviour with which the client puts himself, the therapist or the continuation of the therapy at risk: "I really want you to stop stealing from the supermarket now. You're putting yourself in danger and I don't want you to. You're way better than that. We've discussed this too many times now. Enough is enough."

Translating parenthood to the therapeutic relationship

This phase of the therapeutic relationship has parallels with parenting an adolescent child. A teenager needs his parent in a different way to a young child, and the relationship between the two evolves correspondingly. Adolescents are more independent and less reliant; they are able to and allowed to do more. At times the child's dependency can re-emerge; the teenager may struggle with insecurities and turn to his parents as a safe haven. A good parent understands this and is always there for him. At the same time, parents must encourage their children to face their insecurities, explore and take risks. There may also be times when a child systematically chooses to cross the limits of what's acceptable and puts himself at risk, for example with drug use that goes beyond experimenting. In those cases, a good parent will intervene and set appropriate limits. Showing understanding, setting limits and encouraging positive behaviour are three important aspects of parenthood in the adolescent phase of a child's life, and they are also important aspects of the therapeutic relationship in this 'adolescent' phase of the therapy.

4.4.2 Limited reparenting in a group setting

In group schema therapy, the therapists are like the parents of a group of adolescent children. This requires quite a lot from them; they must be resilient and consistent, both as individuals and as a duo. The response to questions such as "What sort of behaviour requires a limit?", "When do you intervene as therapist?" and "How much do you reveal about yourself?" can often be very personal. For one therapist certain behaviours are totally unacceptable; for another quite understandable. Similarly one therapist may be comfortable talking about his own struggles, while another is anxious. The clients are able to sense these differences and react to them, either explicitly or implicitly, for example by playing the therapists off against each other. Just as in an ordinary family, where parents must provide the guidance and structure needed for adolescents to safely develop themselves, it is therefore vital that the therapists ensure consistency with regard to key issues. Being transparent about differences of opinion is good, as long as it remains clear that they present a united front.

The clients go through a similar process; they too notice mutual differences. This phase offers an excellent atmosphere for the clients to learn to deal with these differences in a respectful manner. The group members help each other with this; they express their thoughts on certain behaviour and are straightforward with the group when they're feeling inhibited, just like children in a family. Again, the therapists take more of a backseat and encourage the participants to take more responsibility.

4.4.3 Empathic confrontation and limit setting

The end of the therapy is in sight, so the goal is now to make noticeable improvements. Awareness of modes and schemas must be turned into changes of behaviour. The way the empathic confrontations are now formulated fits with this. The client is familiar with his pattern, so usually it's no longer necessary to dwell on the origin of the coping and its advantages and disadvantages. Spending less time on this is a way of imposing limits on this destructive personality trait, and also creates more scope for a constructive approach: "You know that your coping isn't doing you any good. You're now on your way to change, to meet your needs." This approach requires discipline and perseverance: "It is important not to get distracted. Use your healthy adult mode to stay in control."

This means that the empathic confrontations now consist of a greater focus on confrontation and less on empathy. The 'minimal' and 'low' empathic confrontations described in the previous chapter (table 3.2) are well suited to this. 'Standard' empathic confrontations are now mainly implemented by the client himself, with support from the therapist. He's familiar with his coping, he knows what it comprises, he knows what its advantages and disadvantages are and when and why it surfaces: "Oh, there you are again, my adapter. I'm aware that I start to adapt to others when I think I'll be rejected if I try to be myself. That's what I learned to do in childhood. But my own needs aren't met when I adapt to others. I'm allowed to be myself, it's okay." Falling back into coping is part of life; everybody's reactions, at times, are driven by coping. However, for clients it's the parent mode that determines the automatic response to this: self-reproach, self-criticism, and feelings of guilt. Instilling a more sympathetic stance with regard to coping enables the client to oppose the parent mode, and this then creates more scope to carry on learning and making progress.

Dealing with a relapse

Being able to show yourself compassion is an important part of the healthy adult mode when it concerns practicing new behaviour and dealing with a relapse. Learning something new doesn't happen overnight; it's a process of trial and error. It is vital that the client learns to stay calm, rather than getting overwhelmed by feelings of panic or desperation. Instilling a healthy adult perspective is therefore essential. This requires a conscious approach; without any instructions, the parent mode will respond to a mistake or a relapse. The therapist may say to the client: "It might not work out, but you're going to try. You can't expect to be successful immediately when you try something new, and it's important that you can look at it that way too. In your childhood you learned to automatically see the glass as half empty, and you now need to learn to see it as half full. You might compare it to shaking someone's hand. You've learnt to use your right hand and now I want you to use your left. It won't necessarily go well the first time, and it will feel strange because it's new and different. But with practice you will master it."

As outlined before, it may be necessary in this phase for the therapist to impose limits on destructive behaviour via 'high' level empathic confrontation. This shouldn't be the first time (Arntz & van Genderen, 2020) as it's make-or-break with regard to limit-setting too. For example, a client continues to shoplift despite having had extensive discussions with her therapist about her destructive modes and the role they play in this. The therapist has also devoted several individual sessions to teaching her self-control skills. None of this has had an impact, and when the client admits to having stolen yet again the therapist says: "It's really important that this stops now, otherwise there is no point in carrying on with the therapy. We're going to have a time-out from your Schema Therapy, like we discussed before, so we can arrange for some treatment to help you make better choices. I'll pass you on to a colleague of mine and we'll pick up where we left off and get back on track again when you stop the shoplifting." The limit goes hand in hand with a consequence that is actually carried out. However, there is scope to restore the relationship as the therapy will be resumed once the client takes the limit seriously.

The empathic confrontation in a group setting

In a group setting, the focus in this phase is the same; on the one hand, clients must learn to be more sympathetic and understanding with regard to their own coping, and on the other they must learn to limit their destructive personality traits by paying them less attention. The group members are capable of helping each other with this. As a result of their increased individuality, they get annoyed more easily with each other's coping and parent modes. They have less patience, and they are less tolerant towards clients who avoid, show off or just obey and comply. They can no longer accept each other's destructive behaviour and they can't hide their feelings of irritation anymore. By practicing in the therapy, they learn that anger has an important purpose: it shows that someone has reached their limit and there's something they can no longer cope with. Moreover, it's easier to feel angry with someone other than yourself. Explaining the difference, and creating opportunities to practice expressing anger in a confrontation with (the coping of) someone else, teaches clients to recognize and validate the anger within themselves and to see it as a sign. If necessary, the therapists will take on a guiding role, in order to make sure that expressing irritation towards each other turns into a corrective experience and takes place within a context in which the clients feel safe and secure.

4.4.4 The therapist's perspective

The components of limited reparenting as outlined above require the therapist to be firm and confident. Firstly with regard to self-disclosure; many of the issues that clients struggle with also trouble the therapist, or have troubled him in the past. What is the therapist's attitude towards autonomy, intimacy, sexuality, pushing limits and experimenting? What are his norms and values, for example with regard to a relationship with a married man, drug use at parties, or skipping breakfast in the morning? What did he get up to when he was a teenager himself? The therapist is required to set an example, but at the same time he will be confronted with himself.

Secondly, the therapist must show understanding, set limits and encourage. Finding the right balance between stimulating independence and offering help is not easy. The ability to show empathy and understanding and a readiness to take over are usually well-developed skills among therapists. Setting limits and stimulating independence and behavioural change tend to be more difficult, especially when the client feels insecure and looks to the therapist for answers. The therapist's own schemas reappear, for example self-sacrifice ("It'll harm the client if I ask him to do that"), high demands ("I need to offer him more skills training first") or failure ("Oh no, that's not going to work"). It can sometimes be necessary in this phase for the therapist to sit and wait for things to happen – to provide the client with opportunities to practice and make mistakes, and to continue to have confidence in the client's development, even if it goes against his own feelings.

Thirdly, in this phase every possible emotion will surface: anger, defiance, impatience, failure, sadness, insecurity, fear and shame, as well as love, pride and appreciation. The client rejects the therapist as an example and attachment figure, rebels against the frameworks and the structure and is impatient with regard to his own progress. He makes mistakes and poor choices. He is faced with his primary schemas again, and he can no longer avoid this. At the same time, he is also proud of his achievements to date and grateful for all the new experiences. He has bonded with the therapist and finds warmth in their relationship. Moreover, he feels relief and euphoria when he manages to overcome a barrier. All this requires a therapist who can keep both feet firmly on the ground in this storm of emotions. To be able to do this, the therapist needs to stay in touch with his team or co-therapist and discuss his own feelings and experiences with them. This will also enable him to analyse ways in which he can apply his own feelings and experiences in his contact with the client.

4.4.5 Thinking, feeling and doing

In this phase there are plenty of opportunities for experiential exercises based on imagery and chair techniques. Furthermore, the client takes another step towards independence. Encouraged and supported by the therapist, he himself plays the role of healthy adult in a rescripting or chair technique.

Behavioural change

Behavioural change is an important focus. The idea is that behaving differently leads to feeling differently and thinking differently. It's all about teaching the healthy adult mode to adopt a new approach with respect to the other modes. This healthy adult approach is actively shaped in role play exercises. In doing so, it is vital that the goal – meeting the client's need – is achieved. The therapist and client discuss, for example, what a healthy adult mode should look like in terms of posture, facial expressions and tone of voice. Then the therapist models and the client copies. The therapist provides feedback: "Is that correct? Do I believe it? Does it come across as authentic and credible?" Practice continues until it's just right and there's no room for avoidance: "What do you need to be able to succeed?" The options and alternatives are endless; changing behaviour, walking away, ignoring and so on. Every exercise concludes with an agreement or plan: "How will you use this for your own benefit?"

> **>> Therapist:** "I encourage my client to practice now. Previously, I was happy if she managed to say something to her employer and wasn't just adapting. It's now time for her to make sure that her needs are met in that type of relationship as well. She knows her own pattern and its pitfalls, she knows what she needs and she can build on experiences in which her needs were met. I really want her to become strong enough to make choices that are right for her. That's why we'll use the sessions to keep practicing for as long as it takes for me to believe her: "I can see now that you really want to make that clear to your boss, and that you'll manage to do it." Then we also agree on what new behaviour she's going to try and, if necessary, we practice that too. We both enjoy it when she manages to take a step forward. It's great to see the sense of pride on her face."

The client also learns to adopt a different approach to the way he deals with anger, so that he can be a good parent to an angry child. There are two elements to this process, just as there were in the process of changing his attitude towards the vulnerable child that he practiced in phase 2. One element focuses on the inner world, whereby he learns to acknowledge the anger and see it as an important sign: "I'm angry and I've had enough of the fact that you always ignore me!" This leads to the second element: connecting this emotion to a desirable effect. After all, something has to change. The change may be focused on the external world, for example a partner who refuses to do chores. Or it may be focused on the inner world, such as a demanding parent mode that constantly criticises.

So, on the one hand, the client learns to adopt a validating approach towards his anger and, on the other, he learns to translate this feeling into new, more assertive behaviour. Here too, practice continues until the new limit is clear and something is really changing. When analysing new behaviour to see if it has an impact, it may be useful for the client to hear from the therapist or the other group members how they think it comes across. In a group setting, the therapists may ask the participants to give each other feedback and share with each other how they feel about the client's new behaviour; in individual sessions, the therapist can do this himself.

Psychoeducation

With regard to cognitive techniques, psychoeducation continues to be important. Appropriate information that matches the client's perceptions, and his cognitive and emotional level, increases independence and self-confidence and makes the client feel he is being taken seriously. Specific topics in this phase are: What does a good relationship look like? How do sexuality and intimacy relate to each other? What is a healthy lifestyle? When does experimenting become dangerous? What is the importance of meaningful daytime activities? The client has a clear input into the topics. It may be worthwhile bringing in an external specialist, for example a colleague who works in addiction care or a marriage counsellor. This again increases the client's feeling of being taken seriously, it may remove some of the burden for the therapist and, at the same time, it sets an example in terms of asking for help and the importance of collaboration.

Information about having a healthy amount of discipline and determination, and how to cope with frustrations, is an extra point of focus in this phase. In many cases the client doesn't know what this means. He has usually experienced pressure from a demanding personality trait, or has become used to not achieving anything as he's driven by an undisciplined child mode. He may also feel lost when a demanding parent is no longer there to 'guide' him. The therapist reflects on the differences between healthy, realistic demands and relentless standards. He may also use exercises to enable the client to experience these differences. The focus at the end of a session, on coming to an agreement or making a plan to be carried out at home, automatically becomes an exercise in perseverance. Finally, by learning to ignore destructive personality traits, discipline is practiced at the same time.

CASE STUDY

Individual therapy: Information about high demands and a lack of discipline

Linda blames herself for not having completed her tax returns again. She's had the forms for a few weeks now and they're ready to be filled in, lying next to a pile of other paperwork that needs sorting out. She also hasn't managed to change the bedding for over two weeks.

>> Therapist: "Well Linda, it sounds like you're having trouble with your demanding personality trait. It's putting more and more pressure on you. Completing your tax returns is just one thing, but then there's a whole list of chores added to that. It's checking all the loose ends with a fine tooth comb and confronting you with everything that's not good enough."

>> Linda: "Yes, that's right." →

>> **Therapist:** "Because of that demanding personality trait, the pressure just keeps increasing. Think of it as a tyre that's being pumped up; the pressure increases with every blast of air. As long as it keeps pumping, the only ways for the pressure to go down is if the tyre bursts with a big bang or air leaks out through a broken valve. Do you recognize that?"

>> **Linda:** "Yes! I have days where I run around like a headless chicken to get everything done. Then I'm exhausted. The last few days I haven't managed to do anything, I've just laid on the sofa."

>> **Therapist:** "Your collapse is like the burst tyre and you not being able to do anything for a week is like the broken valve. When that happens, all discipline goes out the window and you get into trouble. You do need to complete your tax returns, otherwise you'll get fined, you know that?"

>> **Linda:** "Yes, that's why I'm so annoyed with myself."

>> **Therapist:** "And on top of that you get your parent mode. Your lack of discipline is actually regulating the pressure from that mode, like the leaky valve."

>> **Linda:** "Hmmn, that sounds about right. I was so fed up with all the 'must do this and must do that'. I just wanted a bit of peace and quiet."

>> **Therapist:** "Sure, I get that. You've had so much to deal with lately, it's not surprising that your undisciplined child mode decides to rebel against that demanding personality trait."

The therapist looks at Linda with an encouraging smile on his face. He lets her talk about everything that has been too much for her over the last few weeks. Then they have a discussion to decide what she actually needs to enable her to meet her obligations in a healthy way. They agree to identify a list of priorities, and for Linda to get some help with her administration.

4.5 Exercises

The Phase 3 exercises can be organized into the following categories:

1. **Learning to adopt a healthy adult stance:** exercises of this kind are most suitable at the start of this phase; however, repeating them at a later stage can certainly be necessary and useful.

2. **Using the angry child mode in a constructive way:** in these exercises the client learns to use his angry child mode in order to set limits towards others and towards his parent mode. The exercises build on the ability to reflect on the most difficult emotions. Tension needs to be high whilst doing these exercises, and it is therefore recommended that they be carried out approximately halfway

through the phase. In group schema therapy, there needs to be sufficient stability and security again (after an intake moment).

3. **Addressing topics that have led to damage:** these exercises explore the connection between the inner world, including the client's schemas, and the outside world in which he has to live with these. They serve as preparation for the transition into the next phase, and therefore they are most appropriate towards the end of phase 3.

4.5.1 Exercises around learning to adopt a healthy adult stance

Exercise 4.1: Discussing homework	
Goal:	Incorporating homework into group schema therapy.
Category:	1: Learning to adopt a healthy adult stance
Preparation:	Take a ball.
Instructions:	This exercise should be done standing up.
Step 1:	The therapists ask the clients to share what they've managed to do differently.
Step 2:	Client 1 gets the ball and tells everyone what he's done differently since the last session. This may be a small change in behaviour.
Step 3:	Client 1 throws the ball to client 2.
Step 4:	Client 2 catches the ball and repeats what client 1 said. He may add his own words and pay client 1 a compliment.
Step 5:	Client 2 keeps hold of the ball and now moves on to tell everyone about his own change in behaviour since the last session. He then throws the ball to client 3.
Step 6:	Client 3 catches the ball and steps 4-5 are repeated until everyone has had a turn.
Notes:	■ This is an exercise that can be done at the start of a session as a warm-up, and as a way of quickly discussing homework. Having the opportunity to add their own words stimulates the clients' autonomy.

Exercise 4.2: Making the child mode a promise	
Goal:	To acknowledge the child mode and make it a promise.
Category:	1: Learning to adopt a healthy adult stance
Preparation:	None
Instructions:	
Step 1:	Ask the client to do a brief imagery exercise in order to connect with himself when he's in a certain mood (angry, sad, ashamed, insecure). Ask him what his need is when he's in this mood. The client tries his best to keep his position as healthy adult, whilst observing the emotion and need of his child mode. He describes what he can see in the image: Little [client's name] feels sad because people have dropped out of his birthday party and he wants to be comforted.
Step 2:	Ask the client to use his healthy adult mode to stay connected with the child mode, to acknowledge it and to make it a promise: "I can see that you're feeling lonely, Little [client's name]. I really don't want you to feel like that anymore. Something has to change and I'm going to make sure it does."
Step 3:	Ask the client to open his eyes, then discuss together what kind of new behaviour would match this promise. The client will practice this, in the session but also at home. The therapist and client could, for example, write a WhatsApp message inviting the client's friends to his party, within which the client expresses how important it is to him to celebrate his birthday with loved ones.
Notes:	■ In a group setting, the group members can share their thoughts and join in with the exercise. ■ The exercise can also be done with positive feelings like contentment or happiness. Here, too, the healthy adult mode makes a promise, for example: "I enjoy seeing you so happy, and I'm going to make sure that you feel like this much more often."

Exercise 4.3: A new attitude to the undisciplined child mode	
Goal:	To learn how to deal with the undisciplined child and to react to it.
Category:	1: Learning to adopt a healthy adult stance
Preparation:	None
Instructions:	
Step 1:	The group members stand opposite each other in two lines. One line acts as the undisciplined child, while the other uses their healthy adult mode to respond. Therapist 1 supports the undisciplined child line, and therapist 2 supports the healthy adult line. →
Step 2:	Ask the first client in the child line to do the following: "Show us the undisciplined child inside you and let it speak. What is it you don't feel like? What do you not want to do? What do you feel like?"
Step 3:	Ask the client opposite in the healthy adult line to do the following: "Try to respond to the child opposite you from a healthy adult perspective. How would you position yourself? What would your tone of voice be? What would you say?"
Step 4:	Next, ask the client who acted as the undisciplined child: "What is nice or not nice about this healthy stance?"
Step 5:	Client 2 in the line of the undisciplined child has his turn, and the exercise proceeds until all clients have taken a turn in both roles.
Notes:	■ The exercise can be done in individual therapy. In the first round, the client acts as his own undisciplined child and the therapist models a healthy response. Then they swap roles for the second round: the therapist acts as the client's undisciplined child and the client expresses a healthy response. The therapist supports the client in doing this. ■ This exercise often leads to the parent mode making an appearance. In most cases, clients have primarily experienced punishment and high demands in response to a lack of discipline. It's important for the therapist to describe clearly the difference between a parent mode and the healthy adult mode. He also needs to support the client in adopting a healthy adult stance: motivate and encourage, don't punish or demand, use verbal and non-verbal techniques (look, posture, tone of voice, facial expressions and gestures).

Exercise 4.4: Discovering a new attitude to the coping mode	
Goal:	Discovering and practicing a new attitude towards coping
Category:	1: Learning to adopt a healthy adult stance
Preparation:	Take a soft ball
Instructions:	This exercise should be done standing up.
Step 1:	The clients and therapists stand up. Client 1 takes the ball and tells everyone about a situation in the past week in which his coping mode re-emerged. He describes the event in terms of concrete behaviour: "I did it again… I did what my girlfriend asked me to do. I just said 'yes' and abandoned my own plans."
Step 2:	Therapist 1 supports client 1 in describing his coping in a gentle way (tone of voice, facial expressions, posture).
Step 3:	Client 1 throws the ball to client 2, who summarises what client 1 said in a kind and sympathetic way: "So he turned up again, your adapter. That's a shame."
Step 4:	Therapist 2 supports client 2 in adopting a gentle stance (tone of voice, eye contact, facial expressions).
Step 5:	Therapist 1 asks client 1 how client 2's response makes him feel: "How does a gentle and sympathetic reaction, instead of a punishing one, make you feel when you've had a relapse? Does it help? Or not?"
Step 6:	Client 2 keeps the ball and tells everyone about a situation in the past week in which his coping mode re-emerged. He then throws the ball to client 3 who responds kindly, and the exercise continues until all clients have had their turn.
Step 7:	Follow-up: The therapists explain why it is important to be able to have sympathy and show understanding with regard to coping and having a relapse.
Notes:	■ In individual therapy the client throws the ball to the therapist, who responds in a kind and gentle way. Next they swap roles, enabling the client to practice responding in a gentle way to his own coping, as expressed by the therapist.

Exercise 4.5: Adopting a new attitude to the coping mode	
Goal:	Learning to adopt a different attitude to the coping mode
Category:	1: Learning to adopt a healthy adult stance
Preparation:	The exercise builds on exercise 3.4: Empathic confrontation of the coping mode. Get two chairs ready: one for the coping mode and one for the healthy adult.
Instructions:	
Step 1:	The client briefly talks about a situation in which his coping mode re-emerged or in which he had a relapse. He also describes how that makes him feel. It may be useful to instruct the client to take a moment to completely lose himself in this coping mode, as if the mode is what he wants again (to increase the tension). →
Step 2:	The client sits on the healthy adult chair and uses the healthy adult mode to respond to the coping. He incorporates the four steps from the previous phase into his reaction (set a gentle limit, validate, disempower, provide hope), in order to make the message come across as gentle and sympathetic but also restrictive. The therapist is on standby to support the client and model the different steps; however, it's vital for the client to experience that he himself plays a key role.
Step 3:	To make this exercise more difficult, the coping mode can fight back. Either the therapist or the client himself sits on the coping mode chair and answers. Then the client has another go at responding with an empathic confrontation.
Step 4:	When the client has practiced this a few times, he can try shorter reactions, such as: "Ah, there you are again. I'm not going to listen to you now, I know what's right for me." Or, even shorter: "Ah, there you are again, not now thanks."
Notes:	■ In group therapy, participants can take turns to play the role of the coping mode or to support the active client. Group members can also be used as judges, by asking questions such as: "So you think the limit is gentle enough? Can you sense a connection with the child mode when she says that?"

Exercise 4.6: Preparing for change

Goal:	Learning to adopt a different attitude to change
Category:	1: Learning to adopt a healthy adult stance
Preparation:	Take a ball
Instructions:	Steps 1 and 2 can also be done separately as part of a warm-up exercise.
Step 1:	Play an association game based on the question: "How was change dealt with in your childhood? Think about a new class for example, or a new teacher or a new hobby." The therapist and client throw the ball to each other and take turns to say what comes to mind in relation to this theme.
Step 2:	Play an association game focused on needs: "What does a child need when something changes? How does a good parent deal with this?" Again, the therapist and client throw the ball to each other and take turns to say what comes to mind.
Step 3:	The therapist and client sit down. The therapist asks the client to use a brief imagery exercise to return to a moment of change in his childhood. The therapist asks questions to make the image as vivid as possible and increase the tension.
Step 4:	The client briefly portrays the scene on the basis of questions such as: "What happened? What did you see in the image? What message did you get from it? How did that feel?"
Step 5:	The client and therapist discuss what kind of message would work encouragingly to be better able to deal with the change.
Step 6:	The client portrays the image again and he himself (or the therapist) acts as the healthy adult mode and adds the encouraging message from the previous step.
Step 7:	Follow-up: The therapist asks how it makes the child mode feel to receive this encouraging message. The client also agrees to take another step forward: "What are you going to do next that will enable you to eventually change your life for the better?"
Notes:	■ This is an excellent group exercise. In the warm-up (steps 1 and 2) the clients throw the ball to each other. In step 3-6 they take part in portraying the image and contribute to the discussions about the encouraging message and the client's next step forward. They can also take on the role of the healthy adult who steps into the image. ■ This exercise can also be done in earlier phases of the therapy, for example when there's an intake moment in an open group, or when the therapist is going on holiday. In this case, the →

| | question in the follow-up may be: "What step are you going to take with regard to the changes within the group/therapy?" In earlier phases, the client does need extra support from the therapist to help him shape the healthy adult mode. The therapist can model this and then ask the client to just copy him. |
| | ■ The encouraging message and/or the next step forward can also be written down or recorded on the client's phone, to make it more tangible. |

4.5.2 Exercises in the context of the angry child

Exercise 4.7: Learning to be sincere when setting limits	
Goal:	In the previous phase, the client built a repertoire of skills for setting limits. Now that he has more alternatives to choose from, he can start trying to develop his own, authentic ways of communicating assertiveness.
Category:	2: Using the angry child mode in a constructive way
Preparation:	Take a soft ball.
Instructions:	Steps 1 and 2 are warm-up exercises that can also be done separately.
Step 1:	The therapist and client stand up and play an association game based on the question: "How can you defend your limits in the sincerest way possible?" They take it in turns to express their thoughts then throw the ball to each other. The therapist makes sure that they focus on a variety of aspects, such as: "What can you say?" "What kind of facial expression could you have?" "What could your posture and body language be like?" "When would you be fierce?" "When wouldn't you be?" "What do you do with your emotions?"
Step 2:	When several aspects have been mentioned, the therapist writes them on the whiteboard. If necessary, he adds any elements that are missing.
Step 3:	The client chooses what he wants to practice in a role play. This is based on an actual situation that the client is struggling with (e.g. with a partner, colleague).
Step 4:	To finish the session, the therapist and client agree on a plan to be carried out by the client outside of therapy.
Notes:	■ This exercise can also be done in a group setting.

Exercise 4.8: From anger to assertiveness

Goal:	Learning to regulate the angry child internally, and use that when setting limits externally. Components of the healthy adult mode are also strengthened.
Category:	2: Using the angry child mode in a constructive way
Preparation:	Have a hoop ready. Put three chairs in a row – one for the angry child, and two for the healthy adult.
Instructions:	See figure 4.1 for a visual representation of the exercise.
Step 1:	Ask client 1 to use a brief imagery exercise to connect with a recent situation that made him angry. Ask him to briefly explain what happened. Focus on the details: "What is it exactly that makes you so angry? What is the specific trigger for the anger?" For example: "When she rolled her eyes", or: "When she called me useless". Highlight this trigger and ask the client to repeat it.
Step 2:	Client 1 stands inside the hoop and portrays the trigger.
Step 3:	One of the group members takes over from client 1 and stands inside the hoop. He portrays the trigger and, if necessary, exaggerates it as the tension needs to be high for client 1. Therapist 2 supports him.
Step 4:	Client 1 sits on the angry child chair and uses this mode to respond to the trigger. Therapist 1 asks questions such as: "What are you really fed up with? What do you not want anymore?" He also connects the trigger with the client's personal life: "In what way do you recognize this in your life? How often have you felt like this?" He supports client 1 in feeling and expressing his anger; the tension needs to increase. It's also important to find out what his actual need is. What should the limit be about?
Step 5:	One of the group members takes over from client 1 on the angry child chair.
Step 6:	Client 1 sits on the middle chair. This chair represents the healthy adult who keeps in touch with the inner world. Using this part of the healthy adult mode, client 1 acknowledges the child's feelings and considers how he would like to influence them. This creates some distance between the client and his emotion. The whole group discusses: "What do you want? How can you achieve it? What do you think the other person's reaction will be? What can you do then?" For example, the client's need may be to restrict his mother's nagging. Sometimes this behaviour can be stopped, but at other times the only option is to walk away.
Step 7:	Client 1 says out loud what his conclusion is. →

Step 8:	Client 1 sits on the third chair, symbolising the healthy adult who takes action and practices behavioural change. Client 1 now shows how he can behave in a different way in response to the trigger from step 1, so that the child mode's need can be met. The other group members support and encourage him. This response may be more elaborate and in-depth, and may include a dialogue between the 'trigger' and the healthy adult. The 'trigger' role is used to analyse the impact of the healthy adult's reaction. For example, therapist 1 asks the client portraying the 'trigger': "Would you stop now, in response to this limit? What do you notice in yourself? Are you starting to listen? Are you calming down?"
Step 9:	The therapist also asks the client on the first (angry child) chair: "How does this make you feel?" The aim is for the child mode's emotion to fade away.
Notes:	■ In individual therapy this exercise works in exactly the same way, although the therapist does have to 'multitask' – he portrays the different modes, helps the client to devise and practice a healthy response and generally stimulates and encourages him throughout the process.
	■ The anger needs to be expressed while standing inside the hoop, as this contains it but also provides freedom of movement and does the emotion more justice. It also makes it easier for group members to step in and out of it. As already indicated, the tension needs to be high. Participants can step out of the trigger if they become overwhelmed by it, and another group member (or the therapist) can take over if necessary.
	■ It is important that the child mode gets the chance at the end of the exercise to relax, and to feel a sense of relief when its need is fulfilled. The client has never experienced this before; as a child he was always stuck with the emotion and there was no regulation. The feedback from this mode is therefore an important indicator of the exercise's success.

Components of the healthy adult mode

The healthy adult mode consists of many different components. In this phase, clients learn to connect their inner world with the outside world. This involves two key components of the healthy adult mode. One regulates the internal emotion: "I feel the emotion, take it seriously and see it as a sign." This component also takes the other person into consideration: "if I say it like that, nothing will change." Based on this, the second component starts to take action, investigate, and practice to make sure that his need will be fulfilled: "I'm going to do this now."

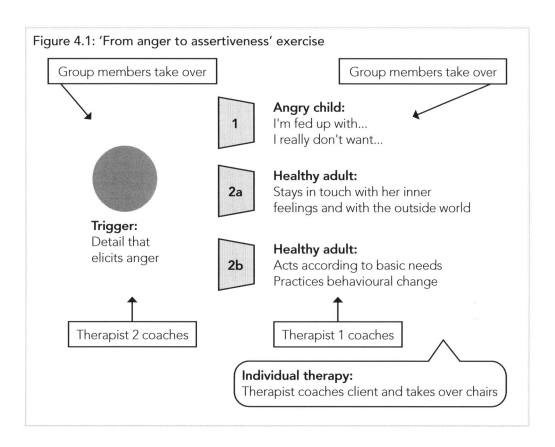

Figure 4.1: 'From anger to assertiveness' exercise

Exercise 4.9: Overcoming the parent mode with regulated anger	
Goal:	To regulate the angry child internally, and use it to overcome the parent mode.
Category:	2: Using the angry child mode in a constructive way
Preparation:	Get one chair ready for the vulnerable child mode and two hoops for the parent modes (one for the demanding parent and one for the punishing parent).
Instructions:	See figure 4.2 for a visual representation of the exercise.
Step 1:	The therapist asks client 1 to use a brief imagery exercise to connect with a recent situation in which he felt vulnerable. The aim is for him to experience the emotion that goes hand in hand with his primary, most intense schema, as this will trigger the parent mode in the most powerful way. The therapist focuses on sensory information and details; the tension needs to increase in order for the client to immerse himself in the emotion. →

Step 2:	Client 1 portrays his vulnerability verbally and non-verbally, including its accompanying beliefs and consequences. For example: "I feel useless. I will always be by myself. I'm a bad person."
Step 3:	One of the group members steps in and takes on the role of the vulnerable child. He is given the instruction to act as much as possible like a child.
Step 4:	Client 1 stands in the first hoop and uses the demanding parent mode to express a reaction, including features and connotations that are specific to the demanding parent. Therapist 1 supports him in this: "Go for it. What does he say? What are his comments? What is his body language like? How does he look?" Then another group member steps into the first hoop and takes over.
Step 5:	Client 1 stands in the second hoop and uses the punishing parent mode to express a reaction, including features and connotations that are specific to the punishing parent. Therapist 1 supports him in doing this: "Go for it. What does he say? What are his comments? What is his body language like? How does he look?" Then another group member steps into the second hoop and takes over.
Step 6:	Client 1 stands between the two hoops and the vulnerable child mode chair. The therapist then says the following: "You're now going to look at what's actually happening inside yourself. There's a small child (points at the group member acting as a child in the vulnerable child chair) and these two (points at the group members in the parent mode hoops) are attacking it from different directions."
Step 7:	The group members who are sitting on the chair and standing in the two hoops act out the client's pattern. They are allowed to add any extra bits they may know about the client. The aim is for the client to watch this, feel the tension and become angry with the parent modes. For example: "That's completely unacceptable, you can't treat a little child like that!"
Step 8:	The client now learns how to use this anger towards the parent modes in a constructive way. Therapist 1 encourages him: "And now you're going to say that to these parent modes. Use your emotions. Go for it: 'That's not the way to treat a child!'" If necessary, the therapist models this so the client can copy him. In this step, it may be useful for the client to be quite elaborate in what he says to the parent modes, without it becoming a dialogue. The more substance, the higher the tension: "You can't treat him like that! He's a lovely child, who tries his best to not make his mother more ill. Rolling your eyes is just derogatory!" →

Step 9:	The aim is for client 1 to have a genuine impact on the parent modes. The group members playing the different roles form a reference framework. The parent modes are asked questions such as: "Does it come across? Would you back off? Would you go away?" The vulnerable child mode is asked questions such as: "Do you feel protected? Do you feel relieved? Are you able to relax?" The exercise doesn't conclude until client 1 has successfully managed to create a change in the dynamics; the other group members decide when this has happened.
Step 10:	The group members and the therapists all give client 1 a big cheer.
Notes:	■ This is also a vital exercise in individual therapy, done in exactly the same way but with the therapist multitasking.
	■ This exercise does require some explanation beforehand. For example: "We're going to do it this way. This exercise will feel like you're walking a tightrope. We'll do it once, in order to change all your deepest areas of pain. We'll focus on your most vulnerable feeling. We're doing that because we know that the parent mode targets this feeling in the meanest possible way. And today, we're going to overcome that."
	■ The use of hoops is important in this exercise, as it provides the opportunity to step in and out of a mode. The clients who take on the roles of the parent modes are able to regulate the tension by stepping in and out of the hoops. It also makes it easier to take over from each other. If necessary, the therapists can also step in and out of a hoop to take over. Of course, the same effect can be achieved by other means (e.g. sticky tape on the floor, chalk, paper).
	■ In this exercise, the difference in connotation between the demanding and punishing parent modes becomes clear. This is necessary to enable the client to differentiate between the modes and it's helpful in 'catching' the triggers for the vulnerable child and the angry child as effectively as possible.
	■ This exercise evokes all kinds of emotions, with a lot going on, and the therapists persevere and be vigorous to enable it to succeed. After all, the client must win. Even when there's a barrier, they keep going. It's often necessary to help client 1. Anything is possible: for example, one or more group members can stand next to him, take his hand and join the rebellion against the parent modes. Ultimately, though, the aim is always for client 1 himself to overcome his parent modes: "I'm an adult too, I can take care of the little one myself, I'm no longer allowing you to tell me what to do!" →

- The props that were previously used to symbolise these modes can be used again here, especially in an individual setting. For example, a photo of the client from his childhood as the vulnerable child, a skeleton as the punishing parent, animals or dolls. The co-therapists each support one part of the exercise. Therapist 1 focuses on client 1, while therapist 2 focuses on the other group members.
- For this exercise to be used successfully in a group setting, it's vital that there is a secure and cohesive atmosphere within the group.

Figure 4.2: 'Overcoming the parent mode with regulated anger' exercise

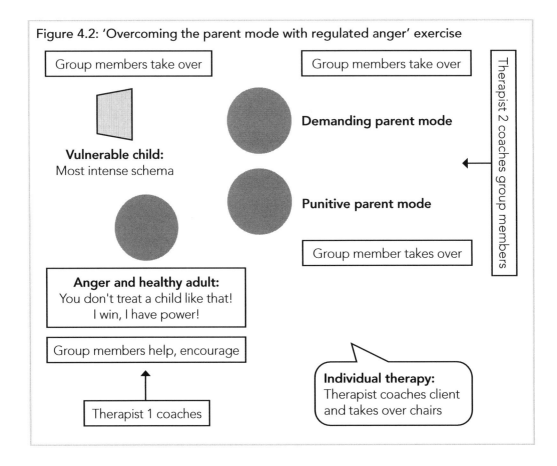

4.5.3 Exercises relating to repairing damage

Exercise 4.10: Reparing the damage related to various themes	
Goal:	To gain insight into unprocessed feelings and develop the ability to repair this.
Category:	3: Addressing topics that have led to damage
Preparation:	Have a few extra chairs ready: one for the parent mode, one for the coping mode and one for the child mode. Take a sheet of paper.
Instructions:	
Step 1:	Together with the client, choose a theme he wants to work on. Anything is possible, as long as it's a topic that has led to damage in the past. A few examples might be: sexuality, self-image, relationships, work, the future and lifestyle. The therapist writes the chosen theme on a sheet of paper.
Step 2:	A sensitivity stocktake: The therapist puts the sheet of paper on the floor, in front of the client, and asks him what thought comes to mind when he reflects on this theme: "go on and tell me: I'm afraid that…". In doing so, the therapist and the client gain an insight into the sensitivities that still surround the topic.
Step 3:	Next, the therapist asks: "What does your parent mode have to say about this? What are you then tempted to do?" The client briefly portrays these destructive traits (verbally and non-verbally: posture, key message, tone of voice) whilst sitting on the corresponding chairs.
Step 4:	Interaction with the vulnerable child. This is the most important part of the exercise. The therapist asks the client to sit on the vulnerable child chair and reconnect with the vulnerable part within himself. The client portrays this and expresses his feelings and needs, as if he is a child.
Step 5:	The client returns to his own chair, the healthy adult chair. First, he validates the emotion and considers what may be required: "What did you notice? What can you do to defend this?" Together with the therapist, the client ponders over these questions and voices his ideas.
Step 6:	Change of behaviour: The client now tries to put his ideas from the previous step into action. He can practice in the session, but then definitely at home as well.
Notes:	▪ This exercise can also be done in a group setting. The clients can take on different roles and take over from each other when necessary. They can also reflect on ideas and practice together. →

> - The interaction between the healthy adult mode and the vulnerable child mode is the key part of the exercise. This means that the therapist and client shouldn't spend too much time and attention on the dysfunctional traits. In this phase, the client is expected to be familiar with the parent mode's core message and his coping's initial reaction to this.
> - Finally, it's essential to finish the exercise with a tangible change of behaviour. For example, a client will tell her partner that making love four times a week is too much for her.

4.6 Areas of focus and tips

4.6.1 Areas of focus

Keep in mind the following areas of focus during the third phase, with its emphasis on 'Do it yourself'.

- The development of individuality and autonomy plays a major role. On the one hand, the client benefits from the fact that some of his schemas are already healthier; on the other, he still struggles with primary schemas, insecurity and a lack of skills. Through trial and error and lots of practice, he starts to notice that things are really beginning to change for him. This requires plenty of encouragement from the therapist.

- The client practices his new skills in the outside world and brings themes from that world with him into the therapy. His world is expanding, and he plays a role in it. He reveals more and more about himself. He can no longer keep it all in, because he's now aware of the regulating effect that expressing yourself and thereby fulfilling your needs can have. This requires the therapist to provide lots of encouragement and motivation, and to show sympathy and understanding.

- The therapeutic relationship is becoming more equal. The client has more individuality and responsibility, which takes some pressure off the therapist. At the same time, the therapy isn't over. Increase the pace and the tension, to guide the client towards genuine behaviour change.

- Make use of the positive bond and be a healthy role model, like the parent of a teenager. This includes disclosing own struggles and stumbling blocks, as well as reassuring the client and providing him with opportunities to experience things for himself. At the same time, it's important to stay alert and intervene if necessary, with an empathic confrontation or by setting limits.

■ For many clients it won't come naturally to have a kindly, gentle attitude towards themselves. Incorporate exercises that are aimed at developing this attitude, linking emotions, thoughts and behaviour, learning to assess how things may appear to someone else, and building a healthy amount of discipline and perseverance.

■ Reinforce the constructive and open atmosphere within the group. The clients now have the confidence to express themselves and they know that it helps. They encourage each other and learn that this also has a positive effect on themselves. They give each other feedback and, in doing so, help each other to progress. They read between the lines and hence help the therapists to ensure that important issues are not missed.

■ In this phase, it can be difficult to handle the client's individuality and autonomy while at the same time trying to deal with a sense of responsibility and concern for him. It's not easy to find a balance between observing and intervening. Moreover, increasing the tension to make sure the client can't avoid facing his deepest pain is a highly intense experience. Peer support and group learning are therefore once again vital elements of the therapy process.

4.6.2 Tips

Avoidance is not an option…

In this phase, it's all about making a genuine change: avoiding this is no longer an option. This is necessary for two reasons. First of all, every schema that is present needs to be tackled on every level. The therapy no longer leaves any room for avoidance behaviour or attempts to cover things up. This means that the tension needs be at an optimal level. Working at the maximum bearable degree of tension leads to a high potential for change. Developing the ability to tolerate tension and practice new behaviour results in great relief and a boost for the client's self-confidence. Often this means that the tension needs to be increased in the session, in order for the client to be able to completely immerse himself in the emotion. This may require the therapist to deliberately make the client connect with sensory information, for example, or to expose him for a longer period of time to messages from the parent mode. In the previous phase the client could board the rollercoaster and get off again; in this phase he's firmly strapped in and must stay on till the end of the ride.

…but you can do it…

Secondly, this pressure is necessary to ensure that the client will genuinely practice new behaviour. After all, trying something new is difficult and scary. At the same time, motivation is now high: "This is the moment!" All this triggers insecurity and high demands, which up the pressure even more. As a result, the undisciplined child mode may be triggered to escape from all the obligations. Practicing can mean that the therapist, or another group member, models the behaviour first, after which the client chooses what part of the behaviour he wants to try out in his own way. The point is that he does have a choice. This combination of pressure ("you will practice") and autonomy ("but you can choose") makes it easier for the client to move forward. An encouraging, positive attitude from the therapist ("try it, you can do it") lowers the demands and increases the intrinsic motivation. At the same time, the healthy adult mode is strengthened by focusing on the things that go well, no matter how small. By doing all this, every painful issue is addressed and, at the same time, destructive traits are ignored, kindness is practiced and a healthy amount of determination is acquired.

…and I'm here to encourage and support you…

Deliberately and purposefully practicing constructive behaviour and a constructive attitude is part of this change. It starts with structure: every session ends with an agreement or plan for what will be done in the time between sessions. The next session then begins by looking at what the client has managed to change. Every small step counts, and talking about it ensures that the client is aware of his achievements. This provides hope and a sense of direction and control. It also means that the client learns to focus his attention on the positives. Moreover, he notices that by doing something differently his life becomes different, and he learns that this is another way to manage his anxieties.

The client's plans are practiced in the session so as to increase his chances of success when trying to fulfil his needs outside of therapy. By doing this, the client gets feedback on his approach and hears the response from other group members to his plan. It also enables him to better predict how the other person will react and consider what his own reaction to this might be. After all, the reality is that having a need fulfilled is often not easy. The client might lack the necessary skills, there may still be traces of coping in the way he defends his need, or the other person may lack the ability to meet the need. This is all part of the learning process of the therapy. Lots of practice results in change.

…because this is really important to you.

After a disappointment, clients often say "just leave it" or "I can live without it." However, once again the therapist won't let the client escape: "No, this is really important to you!" He explains: "When you know the reason why something seems difficult, it causes you less stress. You have a better understanding, and you take your feelings and needs seriously." The therapist isn't like a parent mode ("You're useless! You've done it wrong again!"); instead, he has a caring and interested perspective that is aimed at helping the client to make progress: "By understanding your needs, you can be kinder to yourself and to the other person." Once again, coping is a sign that's something's wrong; and understanding exactly what is wrong that is causing the coping may be helpful. Alongside analysing such situations in the session together with the therapist, it may be useful to keep a schema and/or schema mode diary to gain a better insight into the interaction.

In many cases this analysis will indicate that it's still difficult for the client to show his vulnerability in a constructive way and to share why something is so important to him. After all, the risk of rejection continues to exist – that's part of life. Therefore, the client tends to use his coping to express his feelings: somewhat subdued, with a lot of bravura instead, or from an underdog position. To practice this effectively, it's necessary for the client to stay connected with his feelings, desires and needs. He will then experience that he can manage his anxieties when he shows his vulnerability, and that it increases his chances of having his needs fulfilled. If it should turn out that the other person isn't able to meet his need after all, then that provides more practice material yet again.

CASE STUDY

Group schema therapy: Have a dry run

Nico has sent an email to a good friend to invite her over for his birthday. She has replied that, unfortunately, she won't be able to make it. Nico is disappointed.

>> Nico: "I'll just leave it. I won't bother celebrating my birthday."

>> Jenny: "Oh come on. You've been looking forward to this for ages – you definitely want to celebrate your birthday with her. And now you fall back on your coping and just give up?"

>> Therapist: "Let's find out why this hasn't worked out, and why you've now fallen back on your coping. You'll feel better when you understand what's going on and the reasons why the other person reacted how she did. There might even be things you want to do differently then."

Nico reads the email he sent to his friend out loud. A group member gives him feedback:

>> Mia: "Your email sounds quite formal. She might not realize how important this is to you. Maybe you could mention how much you were looking forward to celebrating the day with her, and why you particularly wanted to do it now, after all these years."

Together with the other group members, Nico writes a new email in which he speaks from the heart. The other participants decide: "Yes, I would definitely come after reading that!" As soon as he gets home, Nico sends the email. In the next session he tells everyone about the response he has received from his friend. She wasn't aware of how important it was to him to celebrate his birthday with her. Unfortunately, she is still busy that day, but they've arranged to meet up the night before. Nico has also managed to find another friend with whom to spend his actual birthday.

4.6.3 When is it time for the next phase

Alongside the fixed period of time set aside for this phase, the following guidelines may be helpful in deciding whether a client is ready for the next and final phase of therapy:

■ The client wants to start integrating his newly learned skills into his life outside the therapy and has already taken initial steps towards doing this.

■ He is more concerned with what he wants for himself, and less inclined to adapt to others. He isn't afraid to express his frustrations, with or without support, and he's able to use these in a constructive way to defend his needs.

■ He can step out of his coping mode independently, or with minimal support, and he can overcome his parent mode. He can also choose to ignore these modes. He has increased his behavioural repertoire and range of options, and he is better able to regulate his emotions.

■ He is better able to cope with separation; his self-appreciation and autonomy have grown. He is ready to start doing things his own way, with the therapy there to support and encourage him.

Chapter 5:
Phase 4 – Live your life

Chapter Summary

In the end phase of therapy, the client learns to make independent choices with regard to the direction he wants his life to go in, and to be happy despite his vulnerabilities. The goal is to generalise and integrate the changes that have been made into everyday life. The client is now aware of his dysfunctional modes, and he is learning to use his healthy adult mode to make better decisions. At the same time, nearing the end of therapy and looking to the future generates new feelings of insecurity, and old schemas can flare up again. This requires the therapist to express and instil confidence in the client's ability to overcome his difficulties. Moreover the therapist fulfils a coaching role, which includes a certain amount of openness about his own struggles in order to teach the client what it means to lead a 'normal' life. The chapter also outlines the goals linked to each mode in the end phase, as well as examples of exercises and guidelines for the therapist.

5.1 Basic needs

5.1.1 Flying the nest

By the final stage of therapy, most basic needs have been sufficiently met and healthier schemas have been developed. The client is experiencing the rewards of this development, and he's starting to get ready to leave the therapy behind him. The time has come for him to make his own choices and live the life he wants to live, with the people he chooses around him. Autonomy and spontaneity, in the sense of being able to feel happy and content, are the key basic needs in this phase (see table 5.1).

> **>> Client:** "I've noticed that I've learned a lot. I'm stronger and braver and I don't feel so insecure and inferior to others anymore. I'm also better able to talk about my feelings, with my next-door neighbour for example. That's nice. However, I'm also very aware of the fact that the therapy is coming to an end and I find that scary. What if I can't do it on my own? What if I start to feel like I did before the therapy again? And what if I don't manage to cope with it?"

The foundations are now in place and robust enough for the client to be able to make his own choices; however, he still often lacks self-confidence. Anxiety rears its head when he is confronted with the reality of life not always running like clockwork, all human beings having their own individual struggles and the fact that there will always be vulnerabilities. The realisation that the therapy will end soon increases this anxiety: "Will I be able to cope, on my own?"

Just as a child leaving home is on the one hand happy to be independent, but on the other insecure without a dependable source of help and advice, the client must make his own choices by trial and error and either be pleased with his decisions or learn from them. The child faces up to his limits through new-found independence ("What is feasible for me? What have I achieved? What do I still need to learn?") and develops more connections by choosing new friends or entering into a steady partner relationship. From the moment he flies the nest, he has the opportunity to further develop his ability to fulfil his own basic needs, while the safety net of home remains in place.

The client's development in this phase of the therapy generally mirrors the child's development. The progress he has already made means that he is more skilful, he is able to take more responsibility and his actions are more autonomous. The task before his now is to integrate everything that he has achieved so far into his own life, personality, abilities, opportunities and preferences in connection with others outside of the therapy. If he manages to do that, he will be better able to fulfil his own basic needs and he will learn to appreciate life – with all its highs and lows – and to be happy.

Table 5.1: Overview of the components of phase 4 (end phase)	
Theme:	Live your life
Basic need:	Autonomy, spontaneity
Limited reparenting:	Young adult
Overall goal:	Goodbye and good luck
Important exercises:	What's your plan?
	Saying farewell
Empathic confrontation:	Minimal
Group development phase:	Separation phase
Mode model:	Everyday language
Role of the therapist:	Coaching

Translating therapy into everyday life

The early stages of therapy were characterised by the use of schema therapy language as a means to create guidance and connection. In the end phase, it's important to partly let go of this language so as to aid integration into everyday life. After all, an employer would find it odd if an employee started talking about his 'punisher'! At the same time, most people are familiar with the underlying concepts and have their own bad days, when things aren't going their way. In this phase the client learns to normalize his struggles, share them with others and face the reality that a perfect life doesn't exist. Coming to realise this assists with translating the core lessons of schema therapy into everyday life and helps answer the question: How does someone who isn't in therapy deal with vulnerability?

5.2 The therapy environment

In the previous phase the client gained a lot. Alongside the inevitable insecurity that comes with taking new steps, he also developed feelings of pride and gratefulness for new experiences. He brings these feelings with him into the end phase, in which he develops confidence in his ability to deal with life. He takes further steps toward independence, and is increasingly able to rely on his own skills and capabilities without needing support from the therapist or other group members. The end is in sight; the time has come for him to let go and to learn what life without his difficulties means.

5.2.1 Separation and individuation

In many cases, separation doesn't cause any problems. As there are healthy schemas present along with a secure attachment relationship, the therapist and client are able to reduce the therapy at the agreed pace. Saying farewell to it requires considerable attention. The relationship with the therapist (or with group members in group schema therapy) is quite possibly the very first healthy attachment relationship for the client, and he also has little or no experience in ending a relationship in a healthy way. Moreover, his contact with the therapist has generated many new memories.

Phasing out the therapy step by step, and paying attention to all the different positive and negative feelings that are involved in this process, enables the client to have a schema corrective experience. A farewell isn't just the end of something; it's also the start of something new. The client has internalized the image of the therapist, and this may help him gauge the direction in which he is heading and make good decisions: "What would my therapist say about this?" He can refer back to what he has learned from the therapist, just as a child who has flown the nest refers back to what he has learnt from his parents when shaping his life as a young adult.

During the process of separation and individuation that takes place in this phase, many of the client's experiences take place outside of the therapy. In rebuilding his own life, he encounters situations that provide him with opportunities to further strengthen his healthy adult mode. It is the therapist's task to support the client in developing his self-confidence, and his belief in the client's self-reliance empowers him to use his own healthy adult mode to respond to feelings that have been triggered.

5.2.2 Feelings are evoked

The impending end of therapy often evokes difficult feelings in the client. One emotion that often surfaces is a feeling of sadness associated with bereavement. The client looks back at his life from the perspective of the relative calmness of his current situation. He comes to realize what he has missed, and the impact of his difficulties on his life thus far. He is also confronted with any lasting effects; or it may become clear that there is some irreversible damage. Furthermore, with the end of therapy now a reality, old schemas may flare up. The client's vulnerability to abandonment may cause him to fear loneliness: "You see, everybody leaves me eventually, even you." Or emotional neglect may cause him to rebel against independence: "I've always had to do everything myself, and I don't want to anymore."

Fear of the future is another emotion that may play up in this phase. This often goes hand in hand with ruthless standards: "My life should be perfect now, flawless, and I should be able to deal with everything without any problems. I'm sure I'm going to fail and then I'm back to where I started!" The client expects that all his problems have been solved and is shocked when he's faced by struggles and insecurities. This puts wind in the sails of the parent mode again. Previously hidden unresolved traumas can also come to light in the end phase. On the one hand, the client feels a sense of time pressure knowing that the therapy is nearing its end. On the other hand, he has already overcome a lot and his self-confidence and resilience have grown. The combination of these facts makes him brave enough to jump into the deep end ("It's now or never") and seek attention for traumatic memories that, until now, were too embarrassing or too deeply buried to share.

The powerful feelings evoked in the end phase can make both the therapist and client feel hesitant. They may wonder if they missed something, or didn't pay enough attention to a certain topic. However, it must be remembered that these feelings are flaring up in the light of a new situation – the prospective end of therapy. This brings new topics, or new dimensions of the main schemas, to the surface. Just as in previous phases, an extra individual session focused on an experiential exercise, such as an imagery rescripting, may be appropriate to help the client process these feelings. This will usually take less time than before, as the client is stronger, steadier and has gained resourcefulness.

CASE STUDY
Individual therapy: Coping with grief

Linda has worked hard to get her life back on track. Her finances are in order, she and her partner are more on the same wavelength, and she's working part-time. She has agreed with the therapist that this is the final stage of the therapy. She attends sessions every other week instead of every week, and the final goodbye is planned for five months' time. At the same time, she's been feeling very sad and despondent lately. She cries a lot and feels like she has lost control over her emotions.

>> **Linda:** "You see, I'm never going to succeed. It hasn't worked, I'm crying all the time."

>> **Therapist:** "Yes, I've noticed. You're really feeling very sad. Just let those tears come out. You can handle it. You know very well that keeping it in doesn't resolve anything. Now tell me, what's affecting you so much at the moment?"

>> **Linda:** "Well, I keep thinking about the past. When I'm at home with my husband and the kids I feel happy. But, at the same time, I see how things used to be at home when I was a child and also the way I behaved when my own children were little. Then I feel so sad. My mother couldn't give me that sense of safety and security, and I was so depressed after the birth of my youngest."

$\rightarrow$

>> **Therapist:** "Oh Linda, it sounds like you're grieving now for what you've missed in your life. And also for how that loss has impacted on your life. That's quite something."

>> **Linda:** "Yes, that's right. But shouldn't I have come to terms with all that by now? We've done so many of those exercises."

>> **Therapist:** "Yes we have. But processing a trauma goes in steps. It's not a straight line. So far in the therapy, you've worked hard on overcoming your traumas and you've felt the anger about what you've missed, the injustice of it. Now the time has come to feel the sadness, about the fact that this was your fate, that your needs couldn't be met by your mother. And that this means that you have to live with those experiences. It is important that these feelings come to the surface now, so you can come to terms with them."

Linda talks to the therapist about her grief. She's now better able to connect with it in the session. At the end, she says:

>> **Linda:** "Thank you. It's a relief to be able to talk about it. I'm going to do the same with my friend when I see her tonight."

5.2.3 Have confidence in self-reliance

To the client, the feelings evoked in the end phase can come as a surprise. Having done all the exercises, his expectations were for the negative feelings to have been processed and resolved, and for his life going forward to be pain-free. The therapist isn't always prepared for strength of these feelings either; they may shock him and make him doubt his own capabilities or those of the client. This shared sense of shock can make them both lose confidence in the client's healthy adult mode. They fall back into their patterns: for example, the client becomes dependent again and the therapist takes on the role of healthy adult. The more regressive the client's behaviour, the more difficult it becomes for the therapist to keep faith that the healthy adult mode is still there too.

Yet that's what it's all about in this phase: promote autonomy and boost the client's confidence. With this in place, all old and new feelings that are triggered can be dealt with by the client's healthy adult mode, supported and encouraged by the therapist like a loving parent. The therapist acknowledges the client's feelings and struggles, but preserves his autonomy by not taking control of the solution. Instead he teaches the client, through experiential exercises, to look at the problem from the perspective of the healthy adult mode and to use these insights to come to an answer. In doing so, the client learns that he is strong enough to handle a relapse or difficult feelings, that he himself is a good parent to his vulnerable child, and that he can cope with whatever the future brings.

>> **Therapist:** "I recently had a client who showed a recurrence of severe avoidance behaviour. I recognized it from the early stages of the therapy, but she'd had it under control for quite a while. However, when we began working towards ending the therapy, she started to call in sick. Or she just didn't turn up to the session without any notice. It took a while before it became obvious to me what was going on: nearing the end of therapy evokes something. I discussed this with her, and she recognized it: 'As a child I was always left to my own devices. Now I'm going to lose you and I'll have to do things all by myself again.' With the help of a chair technique we were able to look from a distance at the distressed child and the avoidant coping. It made us both realize that this was an old pattern that had resurfaced in full force. However, my client also found that she was able to perceive and recognize this from the new perspective of her healthy adult, and that she knew how to deal with it. That gave her a lot of confidence and encouragement, which in turn enabled her to use her healthy adult mode to look after that frightened little girl."

5.2.4 Accepting reality

The end phase confronts both therapist and client with a reality: primary schemas form an ongoing vulnerability, for every human being, and it's unrealistic to think that schema-related feelings will never be triggered again. However, schemas are flexible, not rigid, and when one is functioning in a healthy way it is quicker and easier to switch from a dysfunctional mode to a functional mode.

The fact that the protective environment of the therapy is increasingly replaced by the outside world is also part of reality. For sensitive people, which applies to the majority of clients, this means coping with an environment in which their old schemas will be nudged. The client notices his vulnerability in his contact with the outside world. These confrontations evoke feelings of uncertainty: "Is what I feel normal? When will I be done with the therapy? Will I ever be able to cope by myself?" The client's healthy adult mode is now able to acknowledge these unhelpful feelings, undermine them and replace them with hope, but the client still needs the therapist's support to acknowledge that his vulnerability will always be part of him, and that he can learn to detect and use it.

In a healthy upbringing, a child learns that it takes perseverance and determination to deal with ongoing vulnerabilities in life. For the client, who has not had the benefit of a healthy upbringing, the therapist is an important role model in this. Through specific self-disclosure with regard to his own struggles, the therapist can show the client that being vulnerable is part of life and the triggering of schemas is perfectly normal. In doing so, he defies the client's parent mode, lessens feelings of frustration and helps the client become more tolerant towards imperfection: nobody is perfect, the therapist isn't and neither is the client.

Moreover, he provides a sense of realistic hope for the future: the client sees that taking charge and staying on track is becoming easier and more natural, and he comes to understand that a person can be happy despite the setbacks and struggles he faces in life.

CASE STUDY

Group schema therapy: Reality test and self-disclosure

Today Amber and Nico are entering the end phase of group schema therapy. They're looking forward to it; finally, it's going to happen! They're going to learn how to keep their lives calm and quiet, and how their healthy adult can always be in charge. Therapist 1 opens the session:

>> **Therapist 1:** "Welcome Amber and Nico! Just a quick question. Now that you're in phase 4, you're probably thinking that life will never cause you any more setbacks! Is that right?"

(Amber and Nico nod and some of the group members give them a knowing smile or wink.)

>> **Therapist 2:** "Well, it sounds like we've got some demanding standards here!"

>> **Therapist 1:** "Let's just do a quick reality check. What do you think my life looks like? Do you think I sometimes hide behind my protector?"

>> **Amber:** "Yes, for sure."

>> **Therapist 2:** "And for how long might I hide, do you think? An hour? A day? A week?"

>> **Nico:** "An hour maybe, no longer than that."

>> **Therapist 1:** "Well, let me enlighten you. My life has its ups and downs too, I do indeed hide behind my protector every now and then and sometimes this can last of a few days." (looks around at the other group members) "Can you remember, a little while ago, when Anna asked me if I was tired? I was actually feeling quite worried about a few things that are going on at home."

>> **Nico:** (looking puzzled) "Oh, okay, but then you can't really work with us like that, can you?" missed in your life. And also for how that loss has impacted on your life. That's quite something."

>> **Therapist 1:** "My protector isn't that destructive anymore. In the past I'd sometimes stay in bed and let the situation deteriorate, which meant that things would go wrong. Now I'm able to function, even when I'm worried or fretting over something. However, I'm more introverted and withdrawn in those situations. My little self is struggling then; she's sad and scared. My healthy adult doesn't always notice that straightaway." (asks Therapist 2): "Do you recognize that? Do you experience the same sort of thing sometimes?" →

>> **Therapist 2:** "Most definitely I recognize that. I have days too when I can function but everything seems to be more difficult."

>> **Therapist 1:** "And yet I'm more capable than ever of recognizing the signs and moving that protector out of the way. For me personally it helps to talk about it, with a colleague or a friend. I also take other people's signs more seriously. If a close friend asks me if I'm alright, I'm instantly alert and ask myself that question. That's how I learn – through trial and error."

>> **Therapist 2:** (to Amber and Nico) "What's it like to hear this?"

>> **Amber:** "Well, I'm not sure yet. On the one hand it's nice to know that I'll continue to learn new things, but on the other hand I was hoping that it'd be done now."

>> **Therapist 2:** "Oh I completely understand. Who recognizes that?"

(all the other group members nod)

>> **Therapist 1:** "We'll come back to this quite a lot and do plenty of practicing. Let's start with that now, in our warm-up exercise."

5.2.5 The environment of group schema therapy

Letting go of the therapy, and coming to terms with the corresponding feelings, plays a major role in group schema therapy, just as it does in individual therapy. Saying farewell to the group as a whole and to individual group members is a form of grieving, and it may evoke a separation crisis. Learning to cope with loss is thereby a key topic in group schema therapy, and it is important that there is scope within the group to process different experiences of loss (Hoijtink, 2001).

Focusing on a positive goodbye is also important. Group schema therapy is for many clients their first successful experience with a group of people, and the strong bonds they develop with each other can lead to friendships for life. In a (semi) open group there is a constant flow of incoming and outgoing group members, and this means that clients have previously gone through small separation crises when members they were close to departed from the group. This time though, saying farewell has a bigger impact; the client himself moves on without the therapy, the fellow group members or the therapists. This creates opportunities for processing a variety of emotions in relation to saying farewell and grieving, and for schema corrective experiences.

The healthy adult mode is further developed in this end phase, as clients use this mode to approach each other (Farrell & Shaw, 2012). They encourage each other's healthy adult mode and, in doing so, strengthen their own healthy adult too. Clients also practice connecting their inner world with the outside world, and they are active on multiple levels at the same time; they are group members as well as autonomous individuals. For example, they can recognize when a peer is in distress, but they also sense ways in which they themselves are different. They try providing the other person with suitable tips and advice and they practice supporting each other, without losing themselves.

A phase-oriented group (see the Introduction of this book: Example of phase-oriented group schema therapy) or a closed group has the advantage that all the clients know each other very well by the time they reach the end phase. They have shared their joys and sorrows with each other, they have managed to solve interpersonal conflicts and they are well aware of each other's dysfunctional modes. They can 'read between the lines' in their interactions, which means that they are able to help each other work through any remaining issues that have been hidden away in the therapy so far.

CASE STUDY

Group schema therapy: Giving each other advice from their own perspective

The group session starts with a round in which everybody has two minutes to speak about the following. Which basic need or mode are you struggling with? What have you tried so far using your healthy adult? In which mode did you get stuck? Which basic need is the focal point?

>> **Anna:** "I'm struggling to make room for myself. I feel like I'm being swallowed up by my job and the housework and I suffer a lot from self-sacrifice. It makes me feel agitated and restless. I tried to ignore my adapter; unfortunately I failed, and I was afraid to do things wrong. I think that self-expression is my focal point and that I need to say more often what I think."

>> **Therapist 2:** "Okay, that's very clear."

Next, the other members take turns to answer the questions. Then, the group does the exercise 'imagination of the future' (see further on). When this is finished, the therapists get back to Anna.

>> **Therapist 1:** "Anna, you told us about your struggles to make room for yourself. Let's get the other group members involved." (to the group): "You might not totally recognize Anna's struggles, but there surely is something that strikes a chord in her story. What would be your advice?"

>> **Amber:** "To start with, I want to say that I'm sorry to hear you feel like that Anna. But it's good that you can see things so clearly. What would help me, if I was in your situation, is make a list of all the tasks I'm supposed to do and then cross out half of them."

>> **Nico:** "Well, I recognize what you're saying. I can't make time for myself very easily either. When I notice this in myself, I do a brief concentration exercise, in which I look at an image of little Nico. I, as grown-up Nico, go and sit next to him and ask him 'What would you really like to do today? Whatever it is, I promise that's what I'll do. You're good the way you are." →

>> **Therapist 1:** "It helps me to allow myself two nights a week to do absolutely nothing. Especially when I'm really busy, I explicitly make that agreement with myself. I don't always find it easy, but I know it makes me feel better."

>> **Therapist 2:** "Okay Anna, there's a few tips for you. Which one would you like to try for yourself?"

>> **Anna:** "I quite like the sound of Nico's suggestion. I think it helps me to purposefully connect with little Anna. I know she's a good benchmark for working out what I actually need."

>> **Therapist 2:** "That sounds like a plan! Little Anna is indeed a good compass. I'm confident that the connection with her will enable you to choose what's right for you in order to fulfil your own needs. Good luck!"

5.3 Goals in this phase by schema mode

5.3.1 Overall goal: "Goodbye and good luck..."

In the end phase, the final goals of the therapy are achieved. The client has developed a sufficient number of healthy schemas, and he is able to establish and maintain healthy relationships. He is engaged in meaningful daytime activities, and he has a healthy lifestyle. The symptoms he was suffering from at the start of the therapy have been reduced or resolved. If there is an additional disorder involved, such as an anxiety disorder, then this has been resolved or primed for treatment in a supplementary therapy. The client is able to use colloquial language to talk about his vulnerabilities; for example: "I know you don't mean it like that but I just tend to feel excluded. It's a sore spot from my past." Finally, the client manages to say farewell in a positive way to the therapist, the therapy and, in the case of group schema therapy, the group.

5.3.2 Child mode: "I take you seriously and I take care of you"

The client is more aware of and better able to accept his own vulnerabilities. The emotions related to his child modes are less intense and less overwhelming. He can recognize these feelings as a sign of an unmet need, he takes these signs seriously and he responds in an appropriate manner. Underlying traumas have, for the most part, been addressed.

5.3.3 Coping mode: "I can deal with difficult feelings in an appropriate way"

The coping mode has become significantly less destructive, and the behaviour that goes hand in hand with it is now part of the client's array of ways to deal with difficult feelings. The healthy adult mode is in charge of deciding which way is best for a given situation. At times the coping mode is still capable of luring the client back and causes a relapse. However, the client is able to be gentler with himself when this happens and switch back to the healthy adult mode, with support from the therapist if necessary. He takes signals from other people seriously when they point towards the presence of destructive behaviour.

5.3.4 Parent mode: "I'm in charge of you!"

The client knows when a parent mode has been triggered, as he recognizes the accompanying feelings and reactions. In those moments he can better recognize and acknowledge what his need and vulnerability are, and take care of them by ignoring the parent modes. At times when the parent modes are too strong and ignoring them isn't an option, the client can fight and overcome them.

5.3.5 Healthy adult mode and happy child mode: "I feel, I think and I do"

The healthy adult mode is now in charge. He is able to deal with difficult feelings. He is aware of his needs and their telltale signs, and he knows the best way forward. He can be gentle with himself in case of a relapse; however, he can also adopt a more restrictive stance (i.e. be more disciplined, or say sorry when something has gone wrong). He is able to distance himself from situations he finds overwhelming. He knows when he veers towards a destructive mode, and he may sometimes even choose to do this, but he also knows how to veer away from it again. He is able to ask for and accept help and support from others. He is capable of integrating his thoughts, feelings and actions as well as his inner and outer world. He feels happier and more content, and he is able to enjoy life.

5.3.6 Mode model in this phase

So far, the mode model has served as a guiding framework for the therapy. It enabled both therapist and client to better understand what was happening. It also helped to monitor the main goals of the therapy. In the end phase, the mode model is changed into a kind of roadmap for everyday life, one that supports the client in staying on track as the key elements are summarised. It is important that the presentation and language are adapted to the individual client as much as possible, in order for the transfer of these insights into daily life to run as smoothly as possible. See figure 5.1 for an example of a translation of the model.

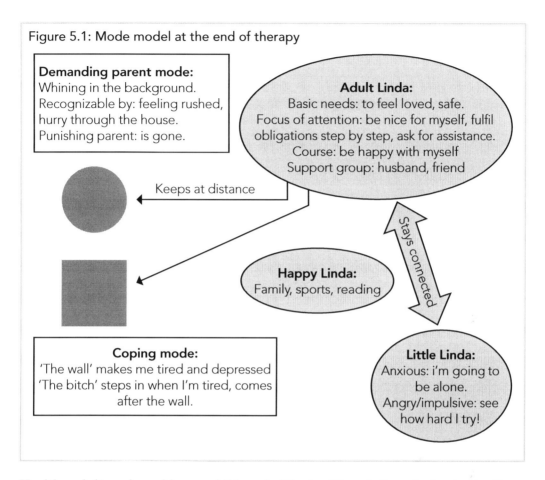

Figure 5.1: Mode model at the end of therapy

Demanding parent mode:
Whining in the background.
Recognizable by: feeling rushed, hurry through the house.
Punishing parent: is gone.

Adult Linda:
Basic needs: to feel loved, safe.
Focus of attention: be nice for myself, fulfil obligations step by step, ask for assistance.
Course: be happy with myself
Support group: husband, friend

Keeps at distance

Stays connected

Happy Linda:
Family, sports, reading

Coping mode:
'The wall' makes me tired and depressed
'The bitch' steps in when I'm tired, comes after the wall.

Little Linda:
Anxious: i'm going to be alone.
Angry/impulsive: see how hard I try!

Healthy adult mode and happy child mode: The healthy adult mode dominates the model. This mode has grown considerably and is in control of the other modes and schemas, making sure that there's sufficient room for the happy child.

Parent mode: The space in the mode model that's taken up by the parent modes is significantly reduced, which means that they are immediately identified when they arise. The healthy adult mode knows what to do to keep it that way.

Child mode: The child modes with their corresponding feelings are sufficiently regulated by the healthy adult mode. The healthy adult mode stays connected with these feelings, recognizes the signs and knows what they mean.

Coping mode: The coping modes are also reduced in size and less intense; they are subordinate to the healthy adult mode. The healthy adult mode has a clear grasp of the advantages and disadvantages of the coping modes, and decides when it is appropriate to use them.

> **The mode model as a roadmap for everyday life**
>
> Working with the client to define and depict his current mode model is an excellent exercise. Key questions to consider are: What's the size of the healthy adult mode now? What is it heading for? How does it relate to the child mode? Which feelings and needs should be monitored? Who can the healthy adult mode rely on? What kind of behaviour or symptom is an important sign? Which parent mode is sneaking around below the surface? How can you recognize this?
>
> The size of the sketched-out modes, as well as the colour of the background, can be used to depict how large and powerful a certain mode is. This model can then be compared with the models from previous phases (see for example figure 3.1 for Linda's previous model). The comparison will serve as a visual history of the client's personal development.

5.4 The therapeutic relationship

5.4.1 Limited reparenting

With the client's healthy adult mode now substantially developed there is a shift towards a more equal relationship, with the therapist acting more as the client's coach. The client is able to share his feelings and experiences with the therapist, and the therapist is obviously available for support if either party deems it necessary. The therapist doesn't recap much on what he has taught the client in previous phases. He mainly focuses on the skills that enable the client to recognize dysfunctional modes and strengthen his healthy adult mode. He provides the client with opportunities to come to mature and carefully balanced solutions by himself. This requires the therapist to be patient when he can see that the client is struggling. He needs to refrain from giving him advice too quickly, and instead question and support the client's healthy adult mode: "How could you tackle this issue? What would the consequences be of that scenario? Are there any other possibilities?" The therapist can also mention something about his own relevant struggles, if it's helpful to the client.

> **>> Therapist:** "In this phase, I regularly focus with my client on his baggage. I ask him to look back and reflect on the past: "What was it like when you first started?", but I also concentrate on the things he's experiencing and feeling right now: "This vulnerability will be coming with you when you leave. How can you make sure that you'll stay on the right track?" It's nice to see how clients respond when I share something with them about my own insecurities in life. After all, the truth is that we all have our own baggage. I also feel proud when the client is able to take care of his vulnerable child by himself in an imagery exercise; most of the time there's no need for me to step in and help. I can just give him a big thumbs up at the end.

The therapist is still partly responsible and it's important that he points out any concerns he may have. A parent whose child announces that he wants to travel the world, and is therefore quitting his studies with immediate effect, will say: "I don't think you're fully aware of the consequences of that decision." Similarly, the therapist should question a dubious choice: "You've only just recovered from that break-up. Do you think it's a good idea to go on a new date so soon? What does your healthy adult mode think about that?" The therapist is still warm and empathetic; however, at the same time, he is creating more distance and becoming more detached. The client is learning to stand on his own two feet and needs space to make his own decisions and deal with the consequences.

The client might no longer tell the therapist about everything that's happening to him. He is able to decide on what he wants to share, for whatever reason, and what he wants to keep to himself. The therapist can respond in an encouraging way to signs indicating that the client is beginning to live his life outside of the therapy: "You're reshaping your life, that's great. There's no need for you to tell me everything. You're allowed to, and I enjoy listening to you, but it's up to your healthy adult mode to decide what you want to share with me and what you want to keep to yourself. I'm here for you regardless. You can share your success stories with me, but you can also share your mishaps."

5.4.2 Limited reparenting in a group setting

The group operates to a large extent on a healthy adult level, and the clients apply the principles of limited reparenting to themselves and each other. They feel connected with each other but they're also individuals, just like adolescent children who are moving out of the parental home. They merge the group norms with their personal norms and values. In a closed or phase-oriented group, the therapists utilise their group interventions to strengthen and stimulate the healthy adult. They mainly play a coaching role and act like supportive parents at a distance. They also create opportunities to process emotions and are proactive, if necessary, in monitoring the schema therapeutic environment and the structure of the session. They prevent clients from avoiding important topics and they facilitate a positive farewell for clients who are leaving. Moreover, they keep an eye on the clients' specific needs, for example when the feelings described above flare up or when a client has only just entered this phase. Using a fixed structure for each session may be helpful in this (see box below).

Continuing to provide sessions with depth in the end phase of group schema therapy

In this phase the therapy is gradually being reduced, and the group members meet perhaps only once a fortnight. A potential pitfall to avoid is the tendency for group sessions to become catch-ups in which there's a great deal of chatting, experiential exercises are forgotten and little progress is made. In order to make sure that sessions continue to be of a high standard, it's helpful to use a fixed structure, whereby each session is divided into the following parts:

- Start: a brief concentration exercise to enable clients to connect with themselves.
- Warm-up: every client has two minutes to talk about:
  - What basic need or mode are you struggling with?
  - How have you used your healthy adult to do something about it?
  - In what mode did you get stuck?
  - Which basic need plays a key role?
- Exercise (preferably experiential) in which the group members work on a certain topic. This could be a joint theme that applies to several clients, or it could be more individual with one person forming the centre of attention. The therapists make a decision on this together with the group members.
- A period of time is set aside for whenever someone is saying farewell to the group.
- Finish with a brief exercise full of energy; e.g. the clients give each other a high five.

Being able to talk about an issue or a question in a clear and concise way is important for the pace and depth of the group sessions. However, it's also a useful skill to have in everyday life situations, for example when asking a colleague for help.

5.4.3 Empathic confrontation and limit setting

Using empathic confrontations to strengthen the healthy adult

There's less need for empathic confrontations in the end phase. The destructiveness of the coping is significantly reduced, and the client is better able to switch, either by himself or with a little help, to a more constructive stance. The minimal empathic confrontation (see table 3.2), whereby the therapist or one of the group members uses a minor intervention to make the client aware of the fact that his coping has been triggered, is the most appropriate.

Nevertheless, it is still possible for a client to get stuck in his dysfunctional behaviour. As described above, this may mean that an old schema is flaring up because the client is nearing the end of the therapy. For example, the therapist encourages a client with an emotional neglect schema to do things by himself: "Go on, you don't need help to do this." However, the client interprets this as a recurrence of the neglect he has previously experienced: "I have to cope on my own again." Or the therapist tries to stimulate the client by saying: "The ball is in your court now, it's your turn to take action", but the client interprets this as a high demand: "I have to do it all myself!" At such moments, an empathic confrontation requires more space and attention.

In this phase, the therapist is less focused on a connection with the vulnerable child and more on a collaboration with the healthy adult. In order to establish a positive collaboration, he may actively point out what he's noticing and experiencing and, at the same time, call upon the client's healthy adult mode as much as possible. For example the therapist might begin by explaining his stance: "This stance, whereby I try and encourage you to do things by yourself, is appropriate for this phase of the therapy. Can you see why I'm doing this, and how it might help you?" It's also important for the therapist to acknowledge the client's reaction: "This stance clearly evokes a lot of emotions. Do you know which mode or which schema is being triggered and why that happens?"

If the client really struggles to use his healthy adult mode to respond, then it may be helpful for the therapist can describe his own feelings: "This process of letting go is nerve wracking for me too. It feels like I'm taking my child to school for the first time. But at the same time, I know that we won't achieve anything if I don't let you go. You need to stand on your own two feet. When I see you struggling it worries me, but it also frustrates me because I know you can do it." Then the therapist creates another opportunity for the client's healthy adult mode to step in: "What are you thinking and how does it make you feel when your healthy adult mode hears me say all those things? What do you recognize?" Finally, an exercise can help to stimulate the development of a healthier schema.

CASE STUDY

Individual therapy: Collaborating with the healthy adult

Linda is struggling to socialize with her friend in a relaxed way. Again and again her friend gets annoyed about the way Linda interacts with her. Linda doesn't understand why things are so complicated. The therapist asks her to recount one of their conversations.

>> **Linda:** "I asked if she could get me some coffee. She was going to the shop anyway but I didn't have time as I had to go to work. She said: 'I don't really want to, as it means I'd have to drive past your house and I can't because I'm too busy.' I replied: 'Oh. Well leave it then. I'll just have tea.' Then she responded: 'Yes, that's what I do sometimes.' And then there was this awkward silence."

>> **Therapist:** "That's a good example. Let's zoom in on it. Which of your personality traits do you recognize in your reaction?"

>> **Linda:** "I felt sad and angry, so that's little Linda. I thought to myself: If it was the other way around and she was asking me to do something for her, then I'd do it even if it wasn't convenient. I'm clearly not important to her. I can hear my punisher in that thought."

>> **Therapist:** "Yes, me too. And what other trait can you hear?"

>> **Linda:** "Well… I think maybe an angry protector. I sounded snappy when I said 'Leave it then'."

>> **Therapist:** "And what do you know about the derivation of these modes?"

(Linda thinks about this for a while, then speaks cautiously; the therapist waits and listens patiently)

>> **Linda:** 'I'm still scared to be rejected. I actually assume that she'll dump me one day… I've been through that so many times, why would it be different now? I've learned to protect myself from disappointment by being moody with people and keeping them at a distance."

>> **Therapist:** "So do you understand now why your relationship with her is so complicated?"

>> **Linda:** "Yes, I think so. It's actually quite hypocritical… I act as if it's fine for my friend to say no, but when she actually does say no I feel rejected again and I make that very clear."

>> **Therapist:** "Do you also know what your basic need was and if it was being fulfilled?"

>> **Linda:** "I'm happy with her friendship, and I enjoy being in her company when I feel comfortable with her. That wasn't the case in that situation. I felt lonely."

>> **Therapist:** "Wow Linda, well done. I do understand why it has such an impact on you, I know your background. I suggest we now have a think about how you can use your healthy adult to express yourself in such a a way that little Linda's basic needs are better met and the other person has a better understanding of your feelings."

Setting limits with regard to dependency issues

In some cases, a client fails to move towards healthier behaviour despite empathic confrontations carried out by the therapist. Likewise, emotions that keep flaring may not be processed, despite the input of imagery rescripting or other interventions. Situations like these may be an indicator of dependency issues that are only now coming to light. The client persists in regressive behaviour and, time and again, manages to coax the therapist into taking over responsibility. This capitalizes on and amplifies the therapist's uncertainty: "Am I doing it right? Have I missed something?" It is important for the therapist to ask his peer coaching group to support him with his insecurities as usually, at this stage, the client's behaviour is related to his pattern; it's not personal.

The therapist also needs help to enable him to persevere in his supportive stance, whereby he sticks to his role and to the limits of the therapy. The therapist can explain this stance and acknowledge the client's response: "I have faith in your solution. I've seen plenty of times how much you can achieve by yourself. You've grown as a person and I want you to grow even further. I know you feel insecure, and I understand that it's hard for you to tolerate those feelings. Your dependent self wants me to take over." He also specifies a limit and calls upon the healthy adult mode to collaborate: "I'd like to help you but I don't want to take over from you because I don't think you would learn anything that way. Why do you think that is? Which basic need do I reinforce by not taking over?" Next, a chair technique can be used to encourage the healthy adult: "Let's put the problem and the modes that are involved in it on chairs. Then we can use our healthy adults to analyse things together."

Discussions about extending the therapy can be another point at which the client's dependency resurfaces. Here, too, the therapist should continue to seek collaboration with the healthy adult: "I know that you feel 'unfinished' and believe you need more therapy. What makes your vulnerable child so vulnerable? Let's look at it together using a chair technique." The therapist and client discuss which modes and schemas have been triggered and place these on a chair. Then the therapist asks: "What does that vulnerable child need?" If necessary, he can offer suggestions: "I believe he needs more autonomy because he wants to make his own decision. What do you think?" Next, the therapist tries again to establish a collaboration: "How could we achieve that? How can we make sure that we strengthen your autonomy?" If the client, in his position as healthy adult, persists in his wish to extend the therapy, then it's important for the therapist to agree but, at the same time, persevere in his efforts to strengthen the client's autonomy. He may suggest for example: "I'll discuss it with my colleagues, but let's make it more specific. How many extra sessions, and what should we focus on?"

>> **Therapist:** "Last year I had a client with dependency issues that came to light when we were about to finish the therapy. She'd already had a lot of therapy and I know for a fact that her Schema Therapy, which lasted for almost three years, has done her a great deal of good. Still, she made it clear in verbal and non-verbal ways that she wasn't ready for the therapy to end. During conversations she would hyperventilate, and she kept trying to ring me between sessions. It made me feel very insecure, and as if I was making her suffer. I regularly discussed the situation with my peer coaching group. One colleague showed me a clip of a baby bird. The mother bird pushed it out of the nest. It looked like the baby was going to fall to its death but, at the very last moment, just above the ground, it spread its little wings and flew off. That became the image I then kept in mind with my client. I managed to come to an agreement with her over finishing the therapy. She's been going without therapy for a few months now and, from what I've heard, she's doing pretty well."

Setting limits by ending the therapy

Often, ending the therapy proves to be quite difficult. Developing healthy schemas continues in this phase, but also in everyday life. It is not easy to determine when these schemas are healthy enough, whether there is still a significant shortage or when a client's behaviour is sufficiently functional. In addition, a continuous stream of loose ends can come to the surface requiring attention, especially in clients with a severe personality disorder. At the same time, the capacity for recuperation has a limit, especially in clients who have suffered serious damage, and it isn't always clear when that limit has been reached. The therapist's own insecurities play a role too: "Have I missed something? Have I done it well enough?" Also, a so-called 'deserve-factor' may have to be taken into consideration: "He has been through so much. I really think he deserves to make a bit more progress."

The ultimate limit, which is the fact that the therapy and the therapeutic relationship will end at some point, can be felt constantly in this final phase. It's important for the therapist not to avoid this and to mark the separate stages of the road towards the end, just as he does in other forms of limit setting (Genderen & Arntz, 2012). Think of a child who, together with his parents, prepares in stages to move out of the family home. Agreeing on a set time frame, six months for example, establishing how often a session is needed, and discussing which topics still need to be dealt with, will all facilitate a successful ending to the therapy. For clients with a borderline personality disorder, it's important not to be too rigid in adhering to this limit, and to agree on an extension with a specific goal for example. Meeting up occasionally for a set period of time, just to keep in touch, can be an option too.

5.4.4 The therapist's perspective

This end phase requires a clear shift of stance from the therapist; he no longer takes over control. He acts like the parent of a child at university; that child might come home for the weekend, but on Monday morning it's back to lectures, even if it's going to be a tough week. Every now and then, for example if something traumatic happens, the child might stay at home for a week to be looked after; but life will quickly return to normal after that. Just like a parent, the therapist will sometimes go the extra mile if necessary. For example, when a trauma still needs to be processed or when a client is stuck in his pattern. The therapist will tell the client explicitly that situations like these are an exception to the norm, and he will explain why that is the case.

For many therapists this carries risk; they may be too quick to go the extra mile or respond too swiftly to their client's question or problem. They find it difficult to let go and allow the client to 'muddle on'. They are inclined to take over. In doing so, they encourage dependency and fail to think in terms of the client's autonomy and self-reliance. It is essential for the therapist to adopt the appropriate stance and show faith in the client's ability to deal with difficult situations and painful emotions by himself. All that is left for the therapist to do now, in the end phase, is to help and strengthen the healthy adult, discuss subtleties and refinements with the client, and support him in his own approach. He does have the option to discuss his urges with the client: "I want to give you tips and advice, but I don't think this will help to strengthen your healthy adult. Shall we have a look back at what's happened between us; the reason why this pattern continues to be there?'"

This stance requires the therapist to be highly disciplined: he must sit back and wait, and not intervene unless necessary. Like a football coach standing on the touchline, he observes and monitors the client's progress; he doesn't run on to the pitch to play himself. This also means that the therapist may have to tolerate uncomfortable facts: not everything can always be resolved, a client may opt for less functional behaviour, and there may sometimes be such significant deficiencies that the client will be permanently restricted in his daily functioning. In those cases, it is important to maintain a positive approach: "What is going well? In which aspects has the client made progress?"

>> **Client:** "I've noticed that the therapist had a lot of confidence in me. Sometimes that can be frustrating, for example when I had a lot of doubts about my relationship. I felt like I couldn't be myself in that relationship, but I didn't have the guts to finish it. I repeatedly asked my therapist for advice; however, she said that I was able to make my own decisions. She also said that there was probably a reason why I couldn't make up my mind. We then used a few of our sessions to discuss my struggles. In doing so, I felt that the therapist supported me, regardless of the decision I would make. After a couple of months, I came to a final decision and, for the first time ever, I managed to end a relationship in a positive way. I now live on my own and that suits me. I'm still in touch with my ex. We're good friends, he just wasn't the right life partner for me."

5.4.5 Thinking, feeling and doing

The end phase is all about integrating the new learning into the individual and their everyday life; after all, saying what you think privately to a friend is very different from expressing your opinion confidently to a stranger. It's now for real – it's about the client himself and his own personal life.

Empowering the client

If a lack of skills in a specific area comes to light, then these are developed in order to empower the client and increase his capacities. In the previous phase, the client learned to deal properly with things that were important to him. Now there is scope to refine that approach, fine-tune it and integrate it into his personality. Role play exercises provide guidelines that help the client shape his healthy adult: "Here's your partner. What do you want? Shall we also look at his basic needs at this moment in time, and at how you can take those into account as well? What would you say then? I would do it like this; how would you do it?" Psychoeducation, in the form of self-disclosure by the therapist, watching films or enquiring about the ways in which others deal with certain issues, is an important resource to help increase these skills. Moreover, if necessary these interventions can contribute to a reality check; when a client learns that his friend has also experienced loss and struggled to cope with it, then that validates his own feelings and disempowers his parent mode.

Regular schema-focused interventions, such as a chair technique or imagery rescripting in the past or the future, are carried out as much as possible with the client in the role of his healthy adult. Such exercises remain important in order to process feelings and make schemas healthier. In this phase the exercises provide relief more quickly than before. The client is also better able to translate them into real-life situations ("How can I do this with my employer?"). The therapist or another group member can help the client by mirroring him and acting as his 'double'. This enables the client to distance himself from his feelings and the situation, and to look at the interaction from an outsider's perspective. As a result, the healthy adult mode is better able to oversee the various elements of a situation, to connect them with each other and to come to a balanced decision. This mode is also becoming more robust by practicing difficult everyday life situations within the therapy. The client's self-confidence grows when he learns from experience how well he already knows himself, and how much he can achieve by himself. This learning pathway can be put in place by allowing the client to continue to experiment in a safe way until he manages to reach a solution with which he is satisfied.

Integration

The clients learn to identify what is important when deciding whether or not to tackle a particular issue. They practice estimating the intensity and urgency of their feelings and needs. They gain experience, for example through being allowed to decide for themselves what they do and don't want to share in therapy: "If it bothers me so much, then there's evidently an urgent need for action", or: "I'm obviously not determined enough to go through with it at the moment; there must be a reason for that." In every aspect there is a greater focus on the client's everyday life, and the correct use of Schema Therapy concepts is thus less important. The emphasis is on integration, and enabling the client to use his healthy adult mode to get an insight into what's happening by seeing the bigger picture ("That's my vulnerability, this is what I need and that's what I can do to achieve it"). In order to facilitate this integration into everyday life and pave the way for separation from the therapy, it's essential to reduce the frequency of sessions. This may evoke a range of emotions for the client; this can itself then become a topic of conversation where necessary or desirable.

5.5 Exercises

In this phase there is no planned build-up of appropriate exercises. Instead, in every session, the therapist and client choose an exercise together. However, the therapist must ensure that all relevant topics are addressed, and no issues are deliberately avoided.

The end phase exercises can be organized into the following categories:

1. **Relapse and reality:** life is defined by recurring confrontations with vulnerability. These exercises help the client learn to cope with relapse and to accept himself with all his strengths and weaknesses.

2. **Staying in control:** these exercises teach the client how to use his healthy adult mode as director.

3. **Saying goodbye:** focusing on all the changes and the progress the client has made, or highlighting and celebrating his achievements, allows for a positive farewell.

5.5.1 Exercises focusing on relapse and reality

Exercise 5.1: Confidence exercise	
Goal:	To develop confidence in the ability to cope with complicated fears
Category:	1: Relapse and reality
Preparation:	None.
Instructions:	
Step 1:	The therapist asks the client if he has further developed his confidence in the therapy or felt confident with regard to his ability to deal with difficult issues.
Step 2:	The therapist describes on what basis he, as the therapist, has developed confidence in the client.
Step 3:	The therapist explains that he is going to represent both his own and the client's confidence.
Step 4:	The therapist asks the client to express his worst fears for the future. He supports the client in generating his fear: "Just keep talking, release your biggest doubts and worries, just let it all out into the open." He continues to do this until the client's anxiety has reached the maximum level.
Step 5:	The therapist switches to an encouraging, reassuring role. For example: "When you look at me, can you feel my confidence in you, that I believe you're able to cope with these kinds of emotions? You can do it. You can feel it. You can handle it. You'll survive. I've seen you take difficult steps before; you can manage this too. I have faith in you."
Step 6:	The client takes it all in and the therapist asks him explicitly to accept his message of confidence: "Please accept what I'm saying to you."
Step 7:	The therapist asks the client, whilst he is still caught up in his fear: "Can you handle it now?"
Step 8:	The therapist checks: "Just keep talking. Have you reached your fear yet? Just let it all out." Steps 5 to 7 are repeated, more than once if necessary. The aim is for the client to truly feel what he is scared of in the future and for the therapist to witness that. It often takes a while for the client to reach his deepest fears; usually this goes hand in hand with a few tears. ➡

Step 9:	A sense of relief and alleviation is created when the client manages to connect with the deepest layer of his fear then gain a feeling of confidence in his ability to cope with that fear. It is important for the therapist to remain confident that the anxiety will ease off by itself, as long as the client is able to stay connected with his fears and, at the same time, accept the messages of confidence.
Step 10:	Follow-up and explanation. How was it for the client to go through this? What has he learnt from it? The therapist explains that if the client is capable of dealing with these feelings now, then he will be capable to deal with them at any time.
Notes:	■ In a group setting, the clients work in pairs. Client 1 expresses his fears, and client 2 instils confidence. Client 2 doesn't help client 1, he just reassures him by being there and convincing him with words such as: "You can do it." One of the therapists will sit with the pair and coach them, instilling faith in client 2 ("Have you noticed that he can deal with difficult situations?") and maximizing anxiety in client 1 ("Keep talking... what would be the very worst thing that could happen then? Can you feel your heart beating?")
	■ In a group setting, this exercise can be used when client 1 is about to say farewell, provided the composition of the group has been stable for a while.
	■ Maximum anxiety levels are essential for this exercise; the objective is to make the core of the schema emerge. This increases the impact of the new experience, which leads to a greater sense of relief and a higher probability of the client changing his behaviour.
	■ Provided that it has been agreed in advance, physical contact (holding the client's hand, for example) can be a way of providing further reassurance.

Exercise 5.2: The struggle	
Goal:	To practice a healthy response to a permanent, difficult situation
Category:	1: Relapse and reality
Preparation:	Provide an extra chair representing the struggle.
Instructions:	This exercise can be used when a client talks about a situation in which he gets stuck.
Step 1:	The therapist asks the client to sit on the struggle chair. Whilst on this chair, he is allowed to completely let himself go and indulge in his struggle: "How does it make him feel? Where does he get stuck? What are his doubts?" The therapist supports the client in making the struggle as specific as possible. An example might be: "I struggle with the fact that I'd like more time for myself, alongside my family and my job. I'd like to go to the cinema more often, but arranging a babysitter makes me feel guilty. So I end up not going, which is what I actually don't want anymore, but I don't want to leave the kids on their own either."
Step 2:	The client returns to his own chair which, in this phase, is always the healthy adult chair.
Step 3:	The therapist supports the client in taking on a conscientious, healthy adult stance. He says for example: "You're taking on a different stance. You're opening up, you're responsive, accepting and understanding towards that struggle and you're trying to watch and listen with affection but also with a degree of hindsight. I only want you to respond from that position and perspective."
Step 4:	The therapist sits on the struggle chair and mirrors the client's struggle. In doing so, he adds his own interpretation of the client's feelings, including feelings that haven't been expressed out loud by the client. He may also add things based on his knowledge of the client, that haven't been mentioned by the client himself.
Step 5:	The client observes the therapist mirroring him from the position and perspective he's been instructed to take on.
Step 6:	When the therapist has finished mirroring, he invites the client to use his healthy adult stance to respond to the struggle, by asking him questions such as: "How does it feel to observe that struggle? What would you like to say about it from your perspective?" The therapist encourages the client to put his reaction into words; what would the healthy adult say to the struggle? For example: "Oh dear, I can see that you're stuck between your own needs and your feeling of guilt. You're so used to having to adapt to others. But you know what, you're still a good parent, even when you take some time for yourself." ➔

Step 7:	The therapist stays on the struggle chair and analyses how it feels to listen to the reaction from the client's healthy adult, by thinking out loud about questions such as: "How does it make me feel, the words he's saying to me, as well as the way they come across? Have I, in my role as the struggle, been reassured? Is this an appropriate reaction? Does it emphasise the need? Does it cover everything?" The therapist explains his thoughts and feelings.
Step 8:	The client has an opportunity to respond again, from the perspective of his healthy adult.
Step 9:	The exercise is complete when the anxiety that goes hand in hand with the struggle has been sufficiently reduced.
Notes:	■ This is an excellent group exercise. One of the group members can mirror the struggle. The therapists focus on their role as coaches, one for the client who is the centre of attention and one for the other group members. The group can act as a jury ("Do we believe the reaction from the healthy adult? Is it authentic enough?") and also provide input ("How does this struggle come across when you look at it from the perspective of the healthy adult? Are you familiar with a struggle like this, or do you recognize certain elements? What would you do in that situation? Or what do you find helpful on such occasions?"). Each group member is allowed to give only one piece of advice. The client then chooses one tip that he's going to try for himself. ■ Alternatively, in step 7, the client sits on the struggle chair (role switch) in order to experience for himself how his own healthy adult reaction to the struggle comes across. ■ In this exercise, the emphasis is on gaining a bird's eye view and the ability to observe from a healthy adult perspective. Implementing lots of role switches, whereby the therapist repeats but also adds to the struggle chair, helps the client to make step-by-step progress. ■ This task works really well when the client brings up a typical, existential problem in which the therapist can pinpoint input from a range of different modes. The use of Schema Therapy language is less important. It is particularly essential that the client doesn't keep any issues to himself.

Exercise 5.3: Realism and acceptance	
Goal:	To develop a realistic and accepting self-image: "Who am I?"
Category:	1: Relapse and reality
Preparation:	This exercise is suitable for the last few sessions of the therapy. Take three chairs; one for 'realism', one for 'vulnerability' and one for the healthy adult.
Instructions:	See figure 5.2 for a visual representation of this exercise.
Step 1:	The client takes a seat on chair 1, 'realism'. The therapist asks him to talk briefly about the following: "What is your character? What are you like? How would you describe yourself?" The aim is for the client to define his personality and temper. The therapist (or group) can add to this if crucial information is omitted.
Step 2:	The client sits on chair 2, 'vulnerability'. The therapist asks him to talk briefly about the following: "What is your sore spot? What will always be your difficulty or vulnerability? What will you always remain self-conscious about?" Here too, there is room for amendment or expansion by the therapist or the group.
Step 3:	The client sits on chair 3, the healthy adult – an accepting, empathetic stance.
Step 4:	The therapist sits on chair 1, realism, and copies what the client said when he was sitting on that chair.
Step 5:	The client acknowledges the realism by saying things like: "That's right, you're an energetic and passionate person who always rushes headlong into everything. I completely accept you the way you are."
Step 6:	The therapist sits on chair 2, vulnerability, and copies what the client said when he was sitting on that chair.
Step 7:	The client acknowledges the vulnerability by saying things like: "That's right, it will most likely continue to be one of your vulnerabilities for quite a while, but that's not a problem. Everybody has their own issues and you're no exception. I completely accept you the way you are."
Step 8:	The therapist can provide feedback about the way the realism and vulnerability were perceived and interpreted through the reaction from the healthy adult. →

Notes:	■ An extra role switch, whereby the therapist sits on the healthy adult chair and the client sits on chair 1 then chair 2, is an option if it's crucial for the client to experience for himself the impact of the healthy adult.
	■ This exercise can be made more difficult by letting chair 1 and chair 2 'talk back'. The client then has to persevere in providing his acknowledging and accepting healthy adult response.
	■ In a group setting, the clients themselves take on the role switches.

Figure 5.2: 'Realism and acceptance' exercise

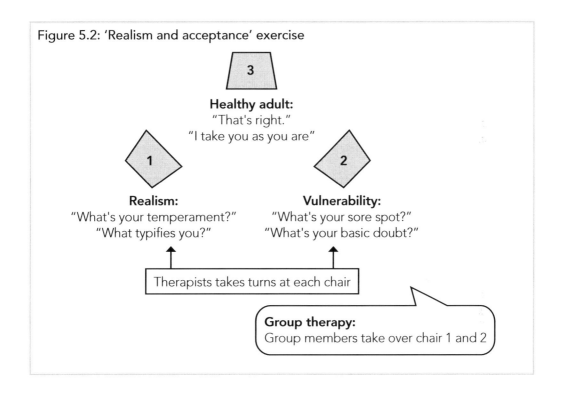

Exercise 5.4: Make a flashcard based on a chair technique	
Goal:	To create a guideline for dealing with destructive modes
Category:	1: Relapse and reality
Preparation:	Take three extra chairs: one for the trigger, one for the pitfall or destructive urge and one for the healthy adult.
Instructions:	
Step 1:	The client sits on the first chair, the trigger. He talks about a recent situation in which painful emotions were triggered, by answering questions such as: "What was the reason? What happened? How did you feel?"
Step 2:	The client sits on the second chair and talks about his reaction: "What was the pitfall you fell into? What was spurring you on? What was your destructive urge?"
Step 3:	The client sits on the third chair and comes up with a range of ideas that might help to deal with the situation in a more constructive way. The therapist can give advice from his own experience ("What helps me in a situation like that is…"); if so, the client decides for himself if he wants to make use of the advice or not.
Step 4:	The client writes on the flashcard: When [trigger] happens, I tend to [destructive urge] but it would be better to [more constructive response].
Notes:	■ In a group setting, the group members give advice from their own experience. The client decides which of the recommendations he wants to take with him in his healthy adult rucksack. Several clients can have a turn in one session. ■ This exercise can also be used earlier in the therapy, with the second (destructive urge) chair being more about the biographical context of the coping ("Where did you learn that? Tell me something about your past"). ■ The exercise can be concluded with a plan relating to behavioural change.

5.5.2 Exercises focusing on staying in control

Exercise 5.5: What's your plan?	
Goal:	To stay in control and, at the same time, stay in touch with triggered modes.
Category:	2: Staying in control
Preparation:	Take three chairs: one for the vulnerable child mode, one for the parent or coping mode and, in front of these two, a chair for the healthy adult mode.
Instructions:	See figure 5.3 for a visual representation of this exercise. The exercise is described in a group format, but can be used in individual therapy (see notes).
Step 1:	The therapist asks client 1 about a recent situation in which he felt that a parent or coping mode was making demands on him. He asks for example: "How do you feel? What is your urge? Which mode is making demands on you?"
Step 2:	Then he asks client 1 to briefly describe the situation and sit on the vulnerable child chair, chair 1. Therapist 1 asks client 1 questions such as: "Try to connect with your vulnerable child. Which of your vulnerabilities was affected? Did you get that feeling you recognize from your childhood? Or did you have that typical feeling of uncertainty, that your vulnerable child still often struggles with?"
Step 3:	Client 1 then sits on the parent or coping mode chair, chair 2. Therapist 1 asks: "Which mode is making demands on you? Which mode wants to remove you from that feeling?"
Step 4:	Other group members take over chairs 1 and 2. They briefly recap on what client 1 said when he was sat on those chairs. Therapist 2 supports them.
Step 5:	Client 1 sits on chair 3, the healthy adult mode chair. Therapist 1 asks him: "Do you have a connection with the two other modes?"
Step 6:	Therapist 1 explains: "This is what's going on internally, but now your healthy adult mode is in charge – it's taking control. So I'm asking your healthy adult: What's your plan with this difficult situation? How do you want to approach it?"
Step 7:	Client 1 talks about his plan of action in whatever way he feels comfortable. The plan may be a rough, concise outline, or already quite concrete and specific. →

Step 8:	The therapist and the other group members question the client about his plan, with the aim to make it as specific as possible. Questions may be for example: "What steps are you going to take? Who do you need to talk to about this? What will you say? Who will you call? What are you going to put in your email?"
Step 9:	Client 1 is given time to think about the questions and to formulate answers.
Step 10:	The other group members take turns to sit on chairs 1 and 2 and continue to question client 1 about his plan and the practical implementation of it. Therapist 2 supports them, but he himself can also sit on chair 1 or chair 2. The aim is to increase the pressure for client 1 to formulate, refine and troubleshoot his plan.
Step 11:	Steps 8-10 are repeated a few times. Client 1 is consistently given time to come up with an answer. The other clients keep walking back and forth between their own chair and chairs 1 and 2. As a result, this exercise is somewhat chaotic and disorganised – but that's the idea behind it. The therapists make sure that client 1 doesn't become too overwhelmed by the rapid-fire questions and pressure.
Step 12:	In this way, client 1 repeatedly practices using his healthy adult mode to stay in control whilst destructive modes are causing trouble. Therapist 1 supports him.
Step 13:	The exercise ends when the therapists or clients decide that it's a good time to stop. Sometimes, they will consider it enough when client 1 is able to retain some form of control; in other cases it may be important for client 1 to have a specific plan, or for him to secure a 'clear victory' over the problem modes.
Notes:	■ This exercise can also be used in individual therapy, with the therapist questioning the client in order to increase pressure but also supporting him in taking and keeping control. ■ In this exercise the client learns to counter obstacles and use his healthy adult to make decisions. Often, the healthy adult will want to pull out as soon as he loses a 'battle' with the vulnerable child mode and the mode that is making demands. The exercise teaches the client to persevere and increases his confidence in his own abilities to stay in control as the healthy adult. ■ It's important in this exercise that the client comes up with his own plan or solution, whatever it may be. The therapist needs to make sure that it's not him, or any of the other group members, who devise the solutions.

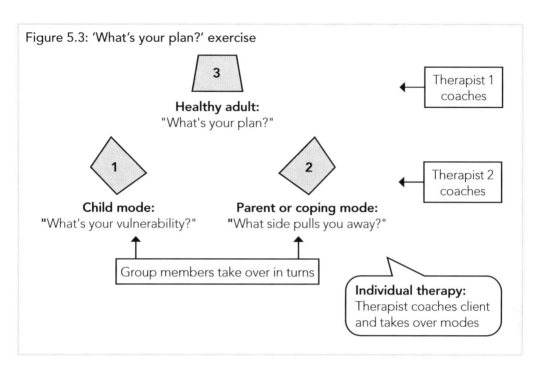

Figure 5.3: 'What's your plan?' exercise

Healthy adult:
"What's your plan?"

Therapist 1 coaches

Child mode:
"What's your vulnerability?"

Parent or coping mode:
"What side pulls you away?"

Therapist 2 coaches

Group members take over in turns

Individual therapy:
Therapist coaches client and takes over modes

Exercise 5.6: Imagining the future	
Goal:	To practice taking control as healthy adult in a difficult situation, and to recognize dysfunctional modes.
Category:	2: Staying in control
Preparation:	None.
Instructions:	
Step 1:	The therapist asks: "Is there anyone who's avoiding something at the moment? Something you should get on with, but keep delaying? For example, a discussion you really need to have with someone, but lack the courage to start?"
Step 2:	The clients who are affected briefly explain what they're struggling with. Together they decide who is going to be the centre of attention, or how they're going to handle things if several clients have an issue.
Step 3:	Client 1 is the focal point and the others join in. Everyone shuts their eyes.
Step 4:	The therapist asks client 1: "You're going to use your imagination to tackle this issue. Start playing your internal 'film' for us. Choose a starting point. →

	Take us there and describe the situation with regard to who, what and where. Who are you with? Where are you? What is your plan of action?"
Step 5:	Client 1 describes the image, with his eyes still closed.
Step 6:	The therapist says: "Let the film keep playing, talk us through the steps you're taking. Tell us what you're doing and what you can see. If you notice that your intended actions aren't going according to plan, describe the mode that's getting in the way. Is it your punisher? Or your protector?" (client answers the question). The therapist gives the client a compliment and tells him he's doing really well.
Step 7:	The therapist says: "Now switch to your healthy adult and let him take over."
Step 7a:	If the client manages to use his healthy adult to stay in control, then the therapist says:" Excellent, carry on. Let the film continue."
Step 7b:	If the client fails, then the therapist asks again: "Which mode has been triggered?" and then: "Now switch back to your healthy adult. Has it worked? Great, carry on and let the film continue."
Step 7c:	If the client really isn't getting anywhere, then the therapist asks the other group members: "Who can support client 1's healthy adult?" The clients can take it in turns to respond and provide advice, based on the question: "What do you find helpful in a situation like that?" After this, the client goes back to the image and uses the advice he's been given to try again and carry out his plan. The therapist may ask: "Is it working? Can you do it now?"
Step 8:	While the film is running, the therapist regularly asks: "What's happening?" If the therapist notices that the client is no longer using his healthy adult mode, he says: "Which mode has been triggered?" then "Now switch back to your healthy adult."
Step 8a:	If the client presents a scenario that sounds too perfect, then the therapist should counterbalance this with something he knows about the client. For example: "I know you find it difficult to express your opinion freely when you're with your mother. That's when your punisher tends to make an appearance. Are you managing to do it now without your punisher?"
Step 9:	The clients all open their eyes when client 1 has successfully carried out his actions and used his healthy adult mode to stay in control. They take it in turns to say what has inspired them, and what they will take with them for future reference.
Notes:	■ This is a group version of the 'Imagination in the future' exercise that's used in individual therapy.

Everything is brought down

Sometimes, clients systematically use a certain verbal repertoire or make excessive use of peculiar phrases. They are unaware of the effect this has on others – who back off because they've heard it all before, because their previous attempts to counter the negativity haven't worked, or because it seems impossible to disempower the underlying message. So, the effect of the client's 'mantra' is that everything is brought down, as it were. The therapist is out of ideas and feels powerless and unable to stamp out this persistent, destructive pattern – a pattern which manifests itself not only in the therapy but also in everyday life. It is vital for the client to become aware of this, so that he can then find a way of turning the helplessness into control.

Exercise 5.7: Everything is brought down

Goal:	To enable discussion of a persistent pattern in a low-threshold manner, and to make progress towards overcoming persistent coping and parent modes.
Category:	2: Staying in control
Preparation:	None. The therapist uses this exercise if he notices that the client has relapsed into regularly behaving or expressing himself in a distinctive, destructive way.
Instructions:	
Step 1:	Client 1 portrays the mode that is constantly making demands on him. For example, the desperate child, a persistent avoider or a discouraging punisher.
Step 2:	Client 2 takes over from client 1 and portrays this mode. He is allowed to exaggerate and add a little drama.
Step 3:	Client 1 joins the rest of the group. The group serves as a forum of healthy adults. Therapist 1 says to the group members: "Just watch client 2, who's portraying client 1's destructive mode, and open yourself up to this mode and the impact it may have."
Step 4a:	When client 2 has finished, client 1 asks: "What are your thoughts and feelings with regard to this mode?"
Step 4b:	Client 1 also connects with the impact the mode has on him ("How does it come across? How does it make me feel?").
Step 5:	Next, the members of the forum debate with each other, for example: "What message does this mode actually carry? Which emotion isn't acknowledged because of its presence? What does client 1 really need? How could he use his healthy adult to be more assertive?" →

	The aim is to draw up a plan that will help client 1 stand up for his needs. This debate doesn't need to take long – 5-10 minutes is sufficient. Client 1 joins in with the discussion, but client 2 stays in the role of the demanding mode.
Step 6:	Client 2 portrays client 1's persistent mode one more time.
Step 7:	Client 1 responds to this. Encouraged by the discussion with the forum, he uses his healthy adult to take the lead and focuses on the persistent demanding mode. In doing so, he uses the following phrases: "Because I feel [e.g. insecure], I tend to [e.g. reject compliments]. What I actually want to say is [e.g. that I appreciate you trying to help me]."
Step 8:	Follow-up: As a healthy adult, how can you be mindful of your own needs as well as someone else's? How do you react if the other person veers towards his coping? It's possible to link this to a role play.
Notes:	■ If necessary, someone can make a note of the client's problematic phrase in step 7, or perhaps turn it into a plan of action that he can use as practice material for the following weeks.
	■ This exercise is similar to an empathic confrontation and can be used when the therapist finds himself reacting in a certain way, for example with a weary groan or a sigh, or when he finds himself thinking: "Here we go again!" It can also be used when other group members express such reactions.
	■ In individual therapy the therapist has to switch roles a few times. First, he takes the role of the persistent mode. Next, he consults with the client's healthy adult in order to draw up a plan. Finally, he supports the client in taking the lead and standing up to the persistent mode.

5.5.3 Exercises focusing on saying goodbye

Exercise 5.8: Past, present and future	
Goal:	For the client to become aware of the progress he has made.
Category:	3: Saying goodbye
Preparation:	Take three chairs; one for the past, one for the present and one for the future.
Instructions:	
Step 1:	The client sits on the past chair and talks about how things were when he started the therapy: what life was like, what he looked like and what symptoms he had. ➔

Step 2:	The client sits on the present chair and talks about what life is like for him at the moment: what has he left behind, what has he already achieved, what he still finds difficult and what he still needs to work on.
Step 3:	The client sits on the future chair and talks about how he sees himself going forward into the future.
Step 4a:	The therapist adds to this by saying how he has seen the client develop, in the therapy as well as outside it. He also points out what he has learnt from the client and describes any lasting impressions the client has made on him. He writes a few of these messages on a card.
Step 4b:	In a group setting, the other participants add to this by saying what they've noticed in terms of development. They also outline what they've learnt from the client. They write their own messages on a card for the client to take with him.
Notes:	■ This exercise can also be used earlier on in the therapy to evaluate how the therapy is going. ■ An extra step can be added between the present and the future, representing what the client wants to be and what he needs to get there.

Exercise 5.9: Warm shower	
Goal:	To shower the client with positive feedback.
Category:	3: Saying goodbye
Preparation:	Take an extra chair.
Instructions:	
Step 1:	The departing client sits on the extra chair.
Step 2:	The group members and the therapists take turns to say what they respect the client for, what they believe he's good at, which achievements they admire him for, what they like about him, what makes him special and so on.
Step 3:	The client uses his healthy adult mode together with the happy child mode to accept these compliments.
Notes:	■ The messages given to the client can also be written on a nice card, to give to the client as a farewell gift when the therapy is finished. ■ This type of exercise can also be used earlier in the therapy, for example to increase the client's self-appreciation in his battle against a parent mode.　　　　→

5.6 Areas of focus and tips

5.6.1 Areas of focus

The end phase encourages the client to go and live his life. The following areas of focus can provide extra guidance for therapists:

- Black and white becomes grey and there is scope for modification and refinement. Point out to the client that he has a range of role models to choose from. There is more than one way forward: he has options, and he is allowed to choose his own path. If he appears to head for a dead-end, then it's appropriate to point him in a different direction and try to re-establish the collaboration with the healthy adult. Ultimately, though, the client makes the decisions.

- The therapist is proactive in setting an example by telling the client about his own struggles. In doing this, it's important to promote realism and to not make a situation sound better than it actually is or was. It's also important to make sure that these self-disclosures don't carry too personal an overtone. Peer review meetings can be helpful to do this effectively.

- Separation and individuation are key development goals. The client is leaving the therapy behind and shaping his own life. Taking on the background role of caring parent ensures sufficient support as well as space. It requires time and attention to end the positive attachment relationship on a happy note. If the therapist and client manage to do this together, then that creates another schema corrective experience.

- The healthy adult mode continues to grow and is becoming more robust. The client is learning to oversee situations, to integrate his inner world into the outside world and to stay in control, even when dysfunctional modes make demands on him.

- Nearing the end of therapy may trigger all kinds of emotions. The mode model continues to provide guidelines with regard to understanding these emotions and putting them into context. Developing healthy schemas is an ongoing process that continues even when therapy has ended.

- The client deserves the confidence that will empower him to develop into an autonomous and responsible person who is independent and self-reliant. This requires the therapist to adopt a more detached stance, and to not take over the moment he sees the client struggling. Experiential exercises continue to be useful in strengthening the client's healthy adult.

- In group schema therapy, the clients motivate each other's healthy adult modes by interacting with each other as healthy adults. It is important for the therapist to keep an eye on the Schema Therapy framework by making sure the sessions continue to have depth, so that struggles and emotions can be processed.

- Letting go means a reversal in the therapist's stance, and this may evoke feelings for him too – such as insecurity, sadness or irritation. Adhering to the limit of ending the therapy isn't always easy. It's vital to be accepting and realistic in this, and to ask for help if necessary.

5.6.2 Tips

Do you intervene...

This phase is all about letting go, in order to enable the client to further develop himself. For the therapist, it isn't always easy to sit back and watch and let the client get on with it, especially after such a long, intense and intimate journey. Just as with children, letting go is a dynamic process that involves ups and downs and that goes hand in hand with a range of emotions.

Based on the concept of limited reparenting, the therapist adapts his stance to the client's need. Stimulating individuality and encouraging autonomy are part of this phase of 'moving out'. The client needs space to integrate himself with all his personality traits into his own life, to choose his own path and to make his own decisions. But what if the client chooses a risky path along the edge of an abyss? The therapist should certainly warn him ("Is that a sensible thing to do?"), point out to him that he's responsible for his decisions and actions ("You're the driver, it's your responsibility to take control of your life"), and call upon the healthy adult mode ("What does your healthy adult mode think about this?"). However, if the client's choices create serious doubts and angst in the therapist ("What if it goes wrong, what a waste of everything he's achieved, I have to help"), he may feel the need to intervene ("This is just too dangerous, so you really have to change your decision").

...or do you let go...

The opposite reaction to angst is that the therapist lets the situation run its course. He reasons that the client is now responsible for himself, that he is aware of the advantages and disadvantages of his behaviour, and that it is therefore not for anyone to try to direct him in his decisions.

It is understandable that the therapist wants to intervene and protect the client, just as it's easy to understand the client's desire to fly the nest and achieve autonomy. Yet both reactions ignore the nature of the relationship that the two have built over time. Parents don't abandon their children as soon as they move out, and in the same way it would be inappropriate for the therapist to abandon the client in this phase of the therapy. At the same time, parents generally don't try to directly influence their children's lives, other than where real danger is involved. Even then their power and influence is limited, and the same applies to the therapist. In this phase it's still possible to use empathic confrontations, experiential exercises and step-by-step limits in order to encourage the client's healthy adult mode to take charge. However, if the client still fails to switch to the healthy adult in this phase and doesn't allow the therapist to guide him, then the therapist has not other option than to accept the reality of the situation and end the therapy.

...and how do you know if you're doing well?

In this phase, fortunately, it hardly ever happens that the client persists in unhealthy choices. After all, he has a healthier way of functioning in everyday life and can switch to healthier behaviour, with help if necessary. The therapeutic style is one of pointing out consequences and analysing situations together, but as soon as the therapist sees that the client has managed to use his healthy adult mode to come to a balanced decision on an issue, he steps back and respects that solution. This process of letting go is scary, especially with clients who still lack skills and/or suffer from permanent damage. They are more inclined to veer too close to the abyss and they may still sometimes fall in. Even then it remains important for the therapist to continue to stimulate the client's autonomy, focus on what is going well, tolerate the fact that he can't be completely sure that things will work out for the client, and accept the reality that life – for everyone - will always have its ups and downs.

5.6.3 When is the therapy finished?

Deciding when the therapy has done its work and can safely be ended is not a hard, factual science, and it may be useful to agree on an extension period – especially for clients with a borderline personality disorder. However, if the client has developed and progressed in accordance with the following points, then it is highly likely that the therapy has been beneficial and is ready to end:

- The client makes balanced decisions, taking into consideration various aspects of both his inner world and the outside world

- He is in control of his modes and can switch from a dysfunctional mode to a healthy one, with help if necessary

- He shapes his own life and, in doing so, is aware of his own vulnerabilities and needs

- He has finished the therapy on a positive note and has said farewell to the therapist (and the other group members, in the case of group schema therapy)

Chapter 6:
Pitfalls, frequently asked questions and adaptations

Chapter summary
6.1 Areas of focus and tips
6.2 Advice for therapists
6.3 Pitfalls and FAQs
6.4 Guidelines for other treatment methods

Chapter summary

Every therapist learns through trial and error. Making mistakes is part of the process. But what are the specific pitfalls to look out for when delivering this particular form of therapy? What are the most commonly asked questions? This chapter outlines some useful basic principles, earned the hard way through experience and practice. They may help you as a therapist to stay in control, to collaborate effectively with co-therapists, to manage your anxieties and to enjoy your work. The chapter also looks at adaptations that can be made in order to use the phase-oriented method in different settings, or with different target groups, and presents some supporting exercises.

6.1 Areas of focus and tips

The phase-oriented method in both individual and group schema therapy with people with a borderline personality disorder features several basic principles. These fundamentals can be found across every phase. They relate to basic needs, the therapy environment, the goals of the therapy, the therapeutic relationship and the exercises that help to strengthen learning and development.

6.1.1 Basic needs

- Throughout the entire therapy process, the aim is to connect with the client's emotions so as to fulfil his basic needs. All interventions are means to achieve this overarching objective. By providing a running commentary: "I'm doing this, so that your needs can be met", the therapist is able to head straight for his goal and guide the client through the process.

■ The transformation of schemas and development of the healthy adult start to take effect from the onset of the therapy, or even earlier when the client is contemplating therapy. This is an ongoing process that involves many ups and downs. Every therapeutic intervention, big or small and verbal or non-verbal, is an opportunity to provide the client with a corrective experience.

6.1.2 The therapy environment

■ It's important to make sure that there's an ideal level of tension during the entire therapy process. Too much tension is bad; insufficient tension isn't good either. The level of tension a client can tolerate varies throughout the therapy process. In the final phases in particular, it's important for the client to be exposed to maximum levels of tension in order to achieve a genuine and lasting change of behaviour.

■ If the client is able to step in and out of his emotions during exercises, then this is a sign that he is developing more control over his emotional life. As the therapy progresses, the client is increasingly able to regulate his feelings by himself and there's less need for the therapist to help.

■ In group schema therapy, the therapists focus on safety and connection but also on the expression of feelings and conflicts and the transformation of schemas. The group development phases offer a framework to help gain an understanding of the issues that play a role in the group. They can also guide the therapists' stance and their interventions.

6.1.3 Setting goals

■ Specific agreed limits based on the case conceptualisation and mode model provide the client with clarity and guidance, especially if his own ideas and opinions are taken into consideration when establishing them. A realistic limit means a limit that is clear, comprehensible and reflects the person concerned. This makes the limit feasible and enables the client to learn from it.

■ There is value in determining a specific timeframe within which the client will work on his development. This applies to the therapy in its entirety but also to individual phases and specific agreements. Having a set timeframe helps give a clear direction to the interventions and puts healthy pressure on the therapist and client to produce a realistic plan that will help them achieve the agreed goals within the scheduled time period. Clinical experience shows that, for clients with a borderline personality disorder, scope for deviation from these set timeframes may be needed. If that happens, it's important for the therapist and client to agree on specific reasons for the exception and its conditions: how long will it last and what will we focus on?

6.1.4 The therapeutic relationship

■ Everything is therapy, and perceiving client behaviour and expressions as recurring patterns allows the therapist to see the vulnerable child hiding behind the coping behaviour. Keeping this in mind can help a therapist break his own avoidance and initiate a difficult confrontation. In doing so, it's important to consider the level of tension a client can tolerate. The therapist must also be sure to alternate between showing empathy and putting pressure on the client.

■ Parallel processes and transference and countertransference of emotions are unavoidable. It is important to devote attention to this in peer review sessions and discussions about clients. Analysing a parallel process or a (counter) transference can help the therapist to gain a better understanding of what's going on with a particular client or group. It's also important for the therapist to consider his own schemas and modes in team meetings to help him reflect on his connection with an individual client or the group as a whole.

■ The therapist who is able to challenge his own schema-directed behaviour, permits himself to make mistakes and is satisfied with 'good enough' creates scope for corrective experiences for himself as well as providing the client with a realistic role model of a healthy adult. By tackling important issues and by practising swapping roles, mirroring, acting and impersonating, the therapist supports the client in developing his own healthy adult at his own pace.

■ Every therapist has his own compass and it's important that he has the courage to rely on this. A Schema Therapist is allowed to offer his opinion, in particular if it concerns unhealthy behaviour, and he adjusts the way he does this to the client and the phase of therapy. The therapist-client relationship evolves during the therapy process, just like a parent-child relationship.

6.1.5 Exercises

■ Mode work should be a focus throughout the entire therapeutic process. This means that the therapist and client together identify which modes, and perhaps schemas, have been triggered then decide on a working method that gives the client opportunities to fulfil his basic need.

■ An imagery exercise can generally be applied in any situation – for example when facing a deadlock, when it's unclear how a specific reaction relates to the client's coping pattern or when the client has a particular question. The therapist might say: "It's interesting what's happening now", or "That's a good question. Maybe we can find the answer by analysing the situation in an imagery exercise? Close your eyes and focus on that feeling…". There's a good chance that this will lead to some useful clues or insights.

- Switching roles is useful in every phase of the therapy. At the start it helps to regulate anxiety and enables the client to get to know himself by observing someone else. Nearer the end it helps him look at situations in a holistic way, from a 'bird's eye' or 'helicopter' perspective.

- Various tools can be used to help manage emotions and integrate new skills into everyday life. A hoop, for example, makes it easier to step in and out of emotions. Post-it notes and cards can capture important messages, and if stuck on chairs can help the client recognise different modes. Props or dolls are useful to regulate anxiety. A ball is invaluable to create movement and pace. Laminated sheets with important information captured in an exercise can be used to support the client in portraying certain roles or practicing elements of the healthy adult. These might for example include prompts to remind the client of his various basic needs, the three steps in dealing with the vulnerable child or ways to demonstrate empathy with the coping behaviour.

6.2 Advice for therapists

At times the dysfunctional behaviour of clients with a borderline personality disorder can have an overwhelming effect. Acknowledging this is an important first step in dealing with such feelings.

6.2.1 Don't take it personally…

A negative atmosphere, feelings of hopelessness, resistance, an increase in destructive behaviour and suspicion towards both therapist and therapy are hallmarks of the early stages in particular of helping clients with a personality disorder. Clients complain about the exercises, find them too vague or too difficult, and have to think hard before answering questions. They talk about all sorts of things but avoid the most important topics. All this can make it difficult to be a caring parent. It is important for the therapist to realise that the client's behaviour isn't aimed at him personally. The ways in which clients deal with the therapy are just recurrences of old, dysfunctional patterns. Hidden behind every form of dysfunctional behaviour is a small and vulnerable child.

6.2.2 …React with sincerity and positivity…

If the therapist can keep in mind that everything is therapy, then this can help him respond as helpfully and authentically as possible. For instance, he can give the client a compliment when he expresses himself: "You think it's silly. Well, good on you for having the courage to say so." If he himself gets stuck and is struggling to find a way forward, he can be open about it: "Wow, I'm not too sure about this…". An attack from an angry protector hurts ("Ouch! That's not okay"), and such an attack in a group setting can be a reason to pause the process and, if a sense of security can't be reinstated, finish the session early. It's safer to have a time-out followed by a restorative conversation than to face a deadlock waiting for the situation to escalate – especially as carrying on can actually be damaging. Another important intervention is for the therapist to point out new experiences for the client and to exaggerate their effect on him, especially if they clearly interest him: "I just saw your eyes light up for a moment, let me copy your reaction to show you, it looked like this." He also livens up tough topics and, in doing so, draws upon his own 'dramatic' skills: "I can see that you're suffering, it looks like you're carrying a heavy load" (the therapist stands up and trudges, hunched over, across the room). Alongside this open-minded and unprejudiced attitude, the therapist takes on a confident and proactive approach and remains hopeful of a successful outcome. He serves as a model for a new and different experience, in which needs are being met and every step, no matter how small, counts.

6.2.3 …By freeing yourself from your own burdens…

Peer review sessions are an essential component of the therapy process – for both therapist and client. Therapy demands a lot from the therapist, and he must feel unrestricted enough to compensate for the client's shortcomings. In peer review sessions, there needs to be a safe atmosphere in which the participants can think and act in accordance with schema therapy. A difficult situation with a client is a trigger that evokes emotions and schemas in the therapist, who will most likely respond with schema-directed behaviour. With the aid of a schema therapeutic intervention, for example imagery rescripting or chairwork, the therapist can become aware of this and have an opportunity to meet the needs of his own vulnerable child. This will maximize his ability to provide his clients with schema corrective experiences. Organizing supervision sessions for the team, in which members help each other to reflect on experiences in dealing with a client or each other, is also recommended.

6.2.4 …And by meeting your own needs…

Responding authentically and spontaneously, making appropriate self-disclosures, and showing that it's fine to make mistakes isn't easy for anyone. However, it's even more challenging for those with schemas such as emotional inhibition, pessimism or high demands. For them as therapists, the idea of displaying their dramatic side may evoke feelings of embarrassment and trigger a parent mode: "Don't be so ridiculous… what on earth are you doing?" An experiment that misfires may create a sense of desperation ("That'll never work") or a stern attitude to the client ("Have you actually done what we agreed?"). This can result in the client not having his needs fulfilled and the therapist himself suffering high levels of anxiety. This requires attention in a peer review group, a supervision project or learning therapy, in order to help the therapist find a suitable way of responding with an open mind, self-disclosing and allowing himself to make mistakes. A therapist who doesn't tackle these issues fails his own vulnerable child and, in so doing, fails his client as well.

6.2.5 …Especially in a difficult situation.

The process of schema therapy isn't always obvious or easy. If a therapist gets stuck in a schema, for example fear of rejection, he may struggle to talk openly about his pitfalls in case he is perceived as a failure. Or the parent mode may stop him from sharing his feelings: "Don't be so weak". No matter how hard it may seem, this is precisely the time for the therapist to break the vicious circle. After all, the therapist and client affect each other – so just as schema-directed reactions from the client can seep through to the therapist, the reverse is also true. This is unavoidable; it happens to every therapist, and the goal isn't to try and avoid it. What is important is that the therapist takes himself and his feelings seriously, and ensures that there sufficient safety and connection for him to express himself. With this done, anxiety levels decrease and a reality check takes place: "We all have our schemas, and there's no such thing as a flawless process or a life without problems." This provides a regulating experience, allowing the therapist to be open as well as confrontational with himself, and creates new opportunities to reinforce for the client that it's good to talk about these things.

6.3 Pitfalls and frequently asked questions

Schema therapy is a complex process with clients who suffer from complex issues. The ideas and exercises in this book were developed following many challenging real-world situations. The pitfalls and questions described below are a few examples of the struggles faced by therapists in clinical practice, along with some answers they found. This is not intended to be an exhaustive resource; it is a collection of advice that has originated from personal experience, aimed at normalising struggles and providing the reader with confidence and reassurance first step in dealing with such feelings.

6.3.1 Basic needs

I find it difficult to explain what basic needs are. How can I make this experiential?

It is important to provide the client with information about the different basic needs. He can read books and watch films; however, leaving it at that may mean that the new knowledge doesn't go beyond a cognitive level. For some clients, it works better to make it more concrete and incorporate their emotional life. This can be done by writing the different basic needs on separate pieces of paper and adding a helpful phrase to describe each one. For example "I think you're important" for self-appreciation (see figure 6.1). These pieces of paper are then spread out around the room. The therapist asks the client to use an imagery exercise to connect with a difficult situation from his childhood, and to try and feel what he needed at that moment. When the client opens his eyes, he and the therapist can go and find the corresponding piece of paper and talk about it.

I think 'the safe place' exercise is important – can it be adjusted to the client's level of development?

A visualisation exercise such as 'the safe place' is useful to help regulate anxieties, both in individual and group schema therapy. The therapist asks the client to imagine himself in a place that feels safe to him. Sensory information is used to make this image as realistic and vivid as possible: "What can you smell? Go back to the smell that you're familiar with, the scent of your grandma's house.'" In phase 1, the client needs help to put this exercise into practice. Some clients don't have a safe place. In such cases, the therapist can either explore various possible safe places together with the client, he can use the therapy as a safe place, or he can use the 'bubble exercise' (Farrell & Shaw, 2012).

In phase 2, the client can better connect with his feelings and it's appropriate to encourage him to use his body signals more. For example: "Try to connect with your body. What do you feel? Where is that feeling coming from? Take that feeling with you to your safe place. That's where you're safe. Just take a look around…". In phase 3, the client is more able to do this by himself with encouragement: "We'll start with your safe place. Take a moment to look around. Focus on what you feel and try to analyse it." In phase 4, the following will suffice: "'Just take a minute to find your way of connecting with that feeling of safety inside you.'" When the minute is up, the therapist says: "Now open your eyes."

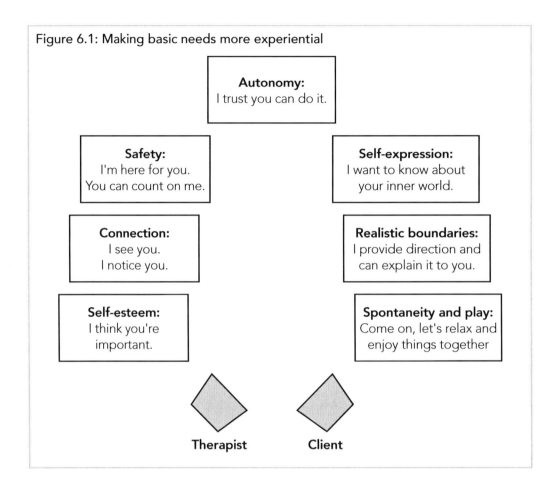

Figure 6.1: Making basic needs more experiential

Autonomy:
I trust you can do it.

Safety:
I'm here for you.
You can count on me.

Self-expression:
I want to know about
your inner world.

Connection:
I see you.
I notice you.

Realistic boundaries:
I provide direction and
can explain it to you.

Self-esteem:
I think you're
important.

Spontaneity and play:
Come on, let's relax and
enjoy things together

Therapist   Client

6.3.2 The therapy environment

I tend to let myself be carried along by the client's story. How can I make sure I stay in control?

The client can be made aware of this behaviour by implementing an empathic confrontation. In doing so, the therapist can tell him what his reaction is ('I get distracted and struggle to work out what's really important and what isn't") and he can explain what the impact is on the client ("this means your needs aren't being met and you'll continue to feel lonely"). He can ask the client if this sounds familiar ("has this happened to you before, people's minds wandering while you talk?") and, if necessary, he can negotiate an agreement ("shall we say that you're allowed to talk freely for the first five minutes of the session, but then we'll move on to an exercise?").

It can also be useful to have a fixed structure for each session. A brief conversation to start, or a warm-up exercise, increases the tension slightly. In group settings especially, or with clients who talk a lot, the structure of a focused (warm-up) exercise can help lay down the rules: "This is not the time or place to talk, this is where we work on our basic needs." In the intervention that follows, it is important to maximise and process the client's anxieties. In the follow-up, the tension is lowered again and there's scope for a discussion about homework. Finishing the session with a game, a physical exercise or a joke can further help with regulation before the client goes home. A break may be considered if the client requires a time-out in the session to avoid tensions running too high.

I struggle to deal with resistance, for example in happy child exercises. What should I do?

It's not unusual for clients to experience resistance towards the so-called 'happy child' exercises. At the start of therapy it's important to accept this reluctance but, at the same time, it's necessary to push on with the exercise, given that it's extremely important for the client to be able to connect with his playful, happy and unprejudiced side. Explaining the importance of play and spontaneity may help to motivate the client, for example: "Being active in a playful and spontaneous way helps you to learn that happy feelings can be created intentionally in a healthy manner." Sometimes, the client finds this kind of exercise 'childish'. If this happens, it's important to take these feelings seriously but also to be firm: "You think this is childish, which makes me think that you feel you aren't being taken seriously. Well done for saying so, and I'm sorry for making you feel that way. It wasn't my intention. I most definitely take this seriously, but I'm going to carry on with the exercise. What do you need now whilst we continue the game?", or, in case of individual therapy: "What do you need now to be able to continue to watch the film that I wanted to show you?" In the later phases of therapy the client is more aware of what suits his happy child, which makes it easier for the therapist to meet his needs.

As the therapy progresses, I find it more and more difficult to 'catch out' coping. The client seems to respond in a healthy way, but at the same time he doesn't. How do I approach this?

As the therapy progresses and schemas become healthier, it can get more difficult to draw on dysfunctional behaviour traits or the deeper emotions of a schema. One way to achieve this is to immerse the client completely in his dysfunctional mode. For example, the client's intention to keep track of his administration contains healthy elements but it also seems overoptimistic: "I'm twelve months behind but I'm giving myself four weeks to catch up." The therapist has doubts: "That sounds very ambitious. Could your coping mode be playing a role in this?" The client persists: "No, I'm sure it isn't. I've thought long and hard about it." The therapist likewise perseveres: "I really do believe I can hear your demanding mode and your controlling coping in this. Shall we have a closer look at it?' The therapist asks the client to sit on the coping mode chair and encourages him to exaggerate and magnify the advantages of this solution: "If I really go for it, as if I'm doing a 10km race, then all my problems will be gone forever. Then I'll have it all under control and everybody will be happy." Next, the therapist asks the client to return to his own chair and analyse the disadvantages. These are also exaggerated: "I did the 10km, but now I'm lying exhausted with torn muscles. So the operation was a success, but the patient died." Using an activity like this to connect with the two extremes of his coping pattern allows the client to become more aware of the dysfunctional elements and take on a healthier stance.

6.3.3 Setting goals

I've noticed that often I just carry on, even though I feel the therapy is no longer generating much value for the client. When is it best to stop?

Stopping the therapy is always a possibility, and working with phases creates natural opportunities to discuss whether or not to continue. After phase 1, it's better to stop if the client doesn't want to let go of his dysfunctional coping. In some cases, the old pattern offers so many perceived advantages that abandoning it doesn't offer sufficient perceived reward. It's also not uncommon for a client to be unable to let go of his coping because of circumstances. For example, a client who has been evicted from his home because of debts; in this case the stress of the situation will be too high, and it's best to pause the therapy temporarily. Last but not least, a different problem or disorder can take priority, for example substance abuse. If it becomes apparent in phase 1 that the client doesn't have control over a problem of this kind, then it's best to go for a different, more targeted treatment first.

After phase 2, the therapist can consider stopping the therapy if empathic confrontations and set limits haven't generated significant change. In some cases, the client may indicate that the insights he has gained are sufficient, and he doesn't require further help to change his behaviour. In phase 3, it's best to stop the therapy if the client fails to change his behaviour as agreed, even after the therapist has routinely encouraged him to do things differently. Clients may also decide for themselves that they are done with the therapy after this phase, in particular those who have been in therapy for an extended period of time and those who have received therapy before. If a client does decide for himself to stop the therapy, it's advisable to ask him to use his different modes to provide feedback on this decision: "What does your vulnerable child say about stopping? What about your angry child? What about your coping? And your parent mode?" Finally, put the question to the healthy adult mode: "Having considered all these different opinions, reflections and reasons, can you try and summarise them – and what's your conclusion?"

If the therapist isn't sure about the client continuing the therapy because of a lack of progress, then it's important to discuss this with the client as early as possible. This gives sufficient time to make plans that may enable the client to turn things around. Extending the time spent on a particular phase can be an option when the client is showing progress but needs longer to achieve his full potential, just like a pupil who needs to repeat a year. In group schema therapy, clients can be offered a few individual sessions alongside the group sessions. All in all, if there are any doubts in the first phase of therapy about its usefulness at that moment in time, then it's preferable to take these seriously and discuss with the client straightaway what the issues are – for his own benefit and, in group schema therapy, for the benefit of the other group members. It may trigger a sense of failure for the client; however, this will only get more intense the longer he carries these doubts. Finally, an early end to therapy makes it possible to set interim goals, paving the way for a potential restart at a later stage. In a group setting, it can be used to counter or prevent negative processes such as exclusion, bullying, procrastination or an increase in feelings of insecurity.

> **>> Client:** "At first, I was shocked when my therapist asked me if I wanted to carry on with the therapy. To be honest, a while ago I did start to wonder: "Is it still effective? Am I still benefitting from it?" I've been in therapy a long time and I've noticed that I sometimes seem to go around in circles. Plus it does cost a lot of energy, time and money to travel to the clinic each time. After I got over the initial shock, I started thinking about it properly and my therapist and I have used a few sessions to talk about it. In the end I reached the conclusion that I've achieved my potential. I'm satisfied and happy with the results I've obtained, and we're going to reduce the therapy."

I often don't get round to working with the happy child. How can I place greater emphasis on developing this mode?

It is important to create sufficient scope for the development of the happy child. For clients with schemas such as high demands and emotional inhibition in particular, it's vital to focus explicitly on the development of spontaneity through the whole therapy process, and also to link this to activities such as homework (Sijbers and van der Wijngaart, 2015). There are various ways to do this. Therapy sessions can be utilised to practice connecting with the happy child by performing different exercises through which the client can experience what suits him and what doesn't – playing games, telling jokes, dancing, performing magic tricks, watching films, reading picture books, drawing, doing craft activities, playing with clay, doing physical exercises or doing visualisation exercises. It's also possible to create room for feelings of joy and happiness in the regular exercises. For example, the therapist can make it standard practice to conclude imagery rescripting exercises with a happy child visualisation. Giggling together or spending part of a session talking about a light-hearted topic, such as a hobby or television programme, also contribute to more spontaneity and play.

Responding to authenticity and spontaneity can be a prelude to the development of the happy child. The therapist can, for instance, watch out for small manifestations of spontaneity: "I just saw your eyes light up for a moment – I think you were enjoying yourself", or: "When you express yourself like that, you seem really in your element." In group schema therapy, the other group members can help a client overcome barriers to participation by demonstrating that they make room in their life for a hobby or allow themselves to show their happy child in the sessions. It can also be useful to focus on the client's identity ("What do you like? What are your preferences? What do you enjoy?"), particularly later in the therapy process so the client is more aware of his happy moments and has a better understanding of what he needs to make him feel that way. Finally, some therapists hesitate to work with the happy child because their own schemas flare up. It's important to look into this and process these schemas, in order for the therapist to be able to find a suitable way of working with this mode.

6.3.4 The therapeutic relationship

I've noticed that I struggle when there are conflicts in the group. What is a good way to deal with conflict?

Dealing with a conflict in the group is difficult. Situations can easily get out of hand, especially in a potentially explosive group containing several clients with an angry protector or a bully-and-attack mode. In such cases the therapist, with his own anxieties, may be inclined either to become over-controlling or to turn a blind eye. The appropriate approach, however, involves a combination of the managing the situation and giving the client sufficient opportunity to express himself in line with the therapy phase. In the first phase, the therapist must intervene firmly ("That's not how we go about this") but also show empathy ("Perhaps that's what you were taught at home, but it's not the way to fulfil your needs") and take the client by the hand ("I'll help you understand what's happening to you on the inside and on the outside"). Then the therapist can ask the client to explain bit by bit what has been triggered and, where necessary, set limits.

In the second phase, the atmosphere is often tense and serious interventions may be needed to prevent clients really falling out with each other. Again, the appropriate approach consists of setting limits ("Hang on, stop") and showing empathy ("There's a reason for the feelings you're having"). At the same time, the therapist also raises the pressure ("Stop. You should know by now that this isn't the way to fulfil your needs"). Now that the client is more aware of his pattern, he can be encouraged to express himself in an appropriate way using the step-by-step approach to interpersonal conflict outlined in Chapter 3. In the third phase, the therapist still intervenes ("Wait a minute") and uses these steps, but the client is expected to do the work: "We'll just go through the steps together. You have the knowledge you need to be able to handle this the right way, and now we're going to put it into practice. You know what's good for you and that's what you're going to do. It isn't easy, so it's fine to follow the steps out loud." In phase 4, the clients will be able to communicate and interact with each other in this way by themselves, and they will barely require therapist intervention at all.

> >> **Therapist:** "I've had to work hard to learn to conduct empathic confrontations in the group. If someone rolls their eyes when another client says something, I tend to ignore it and just carry on with the topic. I feel insecure in those moments: "Is the tension building or is it my imagination? What if I say something that's not right?" and I'm inclined to avoid the confrontation, especially with clients who overreact. However, in the long term the atmosphere only gets worse, and clients are being pushed further back into coping. I can remember group sessions in which my co-therapist and I didn't achieve anything because all of our clients were stuck in their coping style. And we just kept trying to carry on! Afterwards we felt awful. I've learned the hard way that there's no point trying to avoid situations like these; it's better to deal with them as early as possible. My co-therapist and I always review our sessions and prepare together for the empathic confrontations. For example, we decide together which one of us starts the conversation with the client and which one of us involves the other group members in the discussion."

We combine group schema therapy with individual conversations. How can we make sure that these sessions enhance each other in every phase of therapy?

Individual conversations can be particularly useful with a vulnerable target group, such as clients with a severe borderline personality disorder. They can help facilitate the transfer from working in a dyad (pair) to working in a group with several others. The effect is intensified if the individual therapist is also one of the group therapists, or at least works closely with the group therapists. The individual conversations are aimed at facilitating the group process, and it's important to stress that the group therapy is the key component of the treatment. This prevents the client from using individual sessions as a means of escape from having to discuss difficult topics in the group.

In the first phase, individual sessions can strengthen the bond between therapist and client, making it easier for the client to integrate in the group. These conversations also enable the therapist to conduct extensive empathic confrontations to tackle destructive coping, which can be useful if trying to do this within the group is too time-consuming. The individual therapist and the client constantly discuss how the information and agreements resulting from the individual sessions can be fed back to the group. In the second phase, individual sessions allow scope for trauma counselling or systemic therapy which strengthens the therapeutic bond; the therapist can act as an anchor to help the client cope with the intense emotions evoked in the group. Again, it's vital not to have secrets but to create awareness among the group members of the nature of the individual sessions. In the third phase, the individual therapist can encourage the client to use the group to try out new behaviour, in preparation for transferring this behaviour to the outside world. It's important in this phase that the therapist stimulates the client to share his experiences of success with the group. In the end phase, individual conversations usually take place less frequently – although they may be necessary to discuss any final, important issues or to process old schemas that have flared up again.

6.3.5 Exercises

I find it difficult to involve a whole group in an imagery exercise. How can I do that?

Imagery rescripting is a valuable technique that directly addresses the primary schema. It's not easy to turn it into a group exercise. The exercise described below is complementary to existing guidance (Farrell & Shaw, 2012) for involving a group in imagery work.

Exercise 6.1: Imagery rescripting in a group setting	
Goal:	To shower the client with positive feedback.
Step 1:	Therapist 1 asks the group members to close their eyes, then says: "Think over the last week and go back to a situation when you felt sad or scared. What do you feel? Where in your body is that feeling? Put your hand up when you're in that situation.
Step 2:	When almost everybody has their hand up, therapist 1 says: "Stay focused on this feeling and go back to your childhood, in search of a situation that seems to match your feeling. Put your hand up when you have found a suitable image."
Step 3:	When almost everybody has their hand up, therapist 1 says: "Look at that image. Then he begins to increase emotions by asking exploratory questions such as "What do you see?", What do you feel?", "What's happening?" and so on. →

Step 4:	Keep an eye on anxiety levels while asking questions; some clients will quickly reach their limit, which means the therapist can stop.
Step 5:	Therapist 1 asks the group members to open their eyes.
Step 6:	The therapists make eye contact with all the clients and choose a client to focus on for the remainder of the exercise. Often this will be the person who is the most emotional. Alternatively, the therapists can ask the group members to vote or otherwise have a say in who will become the focus of the exercise (client 1).
Step 7:	Therapist 2 says: "We'll continue with client 1. I want to ask the rest of you to keep hold of your own image, like a balloon – we'll get back to it a bit later."
Step 8:	Client 1 briefly talks about the present situation and the image from his childhood. Therapist 1 supports him in this, while therapist 2 keeps an eye on the group.
Step 9:	Therapist 1 says: "Let's all close our eyes and join client 1 in his past. Tell us, where are you? Take us with you into that image of you as a small child."
Step 10:	After client 1 has briefly outlined the image, therapist 1 says: "Now open your eyes again. What comes to mind, watching this from the sidelines? What does that little child need? What do you want to say? What do you want to do?"
Step 11:	The therapists gather ways in which the clients want to intervene in the image. They also offer ideas themselves, and ask client 1 if he has thoughts on this.
Step 12:	Therapist 1 says: "Let's close our eyes again and return to client 1's image. Take your time client 1 to put yourself there. Now imagine that we are all there with you." Therapist 1 lists the names of all the group members who are there with client 1. Therapist 1 asks "Where do you see us?" and "How does it make you feel that we are there?", leaving space each time for client 1 to respond.
Step 13:	Therapist 1, supported by therapist 2, describes all the interventions that the group members have come up with ("Mia says to your mother…", "Nico is coming to sit next to you…" and so on. He repeatedly asks client 1 how all this makes him feel and if there's anything else he needs.
Step 14:	When client 1's needs have been met, therapist 1 says: "Now we're all going to do something fun together. What would you like to do, client 1?" Client 1 answers, and therapist 2 guides everybody into that image. →

Step 15:	Therapist 1 tells the group members that they can now open their eyes, and client 1 is given an opportunity to talk briefly about his experiences.
Step 16:	Therapist 2 says: "We now want to ask everyone – thinking back to the image and all that was said and done for little client 1, was what you suggested something that would be nice for your own little one?" The clients take turns to answer.
Step 17:	Therapist 2 says: "Let's imagine that as well. Close your eyes and return to the image that you kept in your balloon. Take a moment to connect with it again. Now imagine that you, as you are now, together with the rest of the group, enter that image and put into action what you've just said you'll say or do. Look at your little one. How does it make you feel? Now let go of the image and open your eyes." Therapist 2 repeats this for each client.
Step 18:	Follow-up about the different experiences.

6.4 Guidelines for other treatment methods

6.4.1 Using the phase-oriented method in group schema therapy for clients with cluster C personality disorders

With this group of clients, therapists only use three phases and the process is completed in a shorter timeframe (Reubsaet & Sijbers, 2017). The group working method is derived from the individual working method (Bamelis et al., 2014) and has a strong experiential character because of the input of a drama therapist who fulfils the role of co-therapist. This means that, from the very first session, the client is encouraged to connect with his emotions. In contrast to the 'warm bath' that provides a sense of safety and connection for someone with a borderline personality disorder at the start of the therapy, the approach for someone with a cluster C personality disorder consists of more outright confrontations with the avoidant coping style by the therapist. The warm bath quite quickly has cold water added. Of course, this approach remains within the framework and context of a safe and empathic environment, within which the client is able to fulfil his basic needs.

The first phase consists of fourteen group sessions, combined with a limited number of individual sessions in which awareness is the main focus. From the very first session, the client is made aware of the fact that he has a coping mode that pushes emotions away, and that this goes hand in hand with his issues. Emotion regulation is less important. Clinical experience tells us that for this type of client the anxiety level needs to be slightly higher before they can be prompted to experience a connection with their vulnerable child. The second phase also consists of fourteen group sessions plus a limited number of individual sessions. This phase is aimed at changing the client's behaviour within the sessions. The therapist increases the pressure on the coping and encourages the client to challenge his parent mode and fulfil the needs of his vulnerable child in a healthy adult way. The client is supported in doing this by the other group members and the therapist. The third phase consists of seven group sessions, one per month, aimed at creating behavioural change in everyday life. The client has a good understanding of his own behaviour, and has shown in the therapy that his healthy adult mode is well-developed. It's now about applying these skills in the big bad outside world. This is often a difficult time for this client group. Just as in the individual protocol, the sessions focus on what the client is struggling with and what he needs to change his behaviour. Embedding time constraints from the start creates the pressure needed to achieve real change. Avoidance is no longer an option.

6.4.2 Group schema therapy day treatment approach

Day treatment involves an intense form of schema therapy conducted in a group setting over several half-day sessions per week. The treatment team is multidisciplinary and may include expertise from psychiatry, psychology, drama therapy, art therapy, psychomotor therapy, music therapy, sociotherapy, social work and so on. The weekly program contains various elements, drawn from the different working methods – for example, an art therapist will organize a creative therapy session and a sociotherapist will plan for a milieu therapy session. The collaboration within a multidisciplinary team like this requires special attention. Although it is a precondition that every team member is trained in schema therapy, additional coordination and alignment is necessary to make sure that everyone can speak the same language. A potential advantage of an intense programme is that extremely persistent patterns can be overcome more quickly; a potential disadvantage is that too much therapy can wear the client out. Despite a scarcity of data to evaluate the effectiveness of this approach (Reubsaet, 2012; Houben & Arntz, 2011), it is quite commonly applied in the Netherlands.

The phase-oriented approach is well suited to a day treatment format. The program can be divided into phases with decreasing intensity. For example, in the first phase clients have three half-day sessions, in the second they have two half-day sessions and so on. A phasing-out approach of this kind helps prevent clients becoming reliant on therapy and gives them plenty of time to practice and shape their own lives, particularly in the later stages. Since day treatment is demanding and expensive, the benefits must outweigh the costs. Specific targets and agreements can be used to decide if the treatment is having a sufficient effect and the client can move on into the next phase. The integrative nature, whereby thinking, feeling and doing constantly merge into each other, paves the way for successful collaboration between disciplines. Sessions can be carried out by a psychiatrist and an expressive therapist, for example, or by a drama therapist and a sociotherapist. Collaboration of this kind gives the experiential way of working a boost, strengthens the connection between team members and provides a platform for cross-fertilisation between disciplines. Finally, the various components of the programme can focus on different objectives and different topics. For example, in the first session of the week the group can focus on awareness and clients can fill in a schema diary. In the second session chair techniques can be used to encourage more experiential learning. And in the third session a discussion can take place about the translation into everyday life.

Using schema therapy in a day treatment setting requires excellent coordination between the different disciplines and components. The therapists must balance and tailor their working methods to each other to make sure that they embrace and communicate a shared vision about schema therapy and provide clients with a coherent, meaningful programme. In practice this is often not easy, and time and effort in the form of peer review sessions and extra training is required to achieve it.

6.4.3 Using a short-term and theme-oriented approach

The approach described in this book focuses on the primary form of schema therapy: a long and intense treatment for clients with a personality disorder. At the same time, there is also a shortened version of schema therapy (Van Vreeswijk & Broersen, 2017) and there are many clinical psychologists and other professionals who use elements of schema therapy in their work. This latter approach is usually based around the therapist's own perceptions and has not yet been a topic of research.

The working method outlined in this book offers the flexibility to use a more targeted approach and decide together with the client to focus on a specific phase. This means that a client who functions well and has a good understanding of his issues and pattern can focus on elements from phase 3 to help him change his behaviour. A client who only requires a deeper understanding of his pitfalls can opt for the phase 1 experiential case conceptualisation exercise. Elements from phase 4, or exercises to strengthen the healthy adult (e.g. 'empathizing with' exercises in phase 2) can be used in booster sessions, if a client returns because he's had a relapse after he successfully completing the treatment.

Furthermore, specific issues can also be actively targeted within the therapy process. In a semi-open group, new clients can take part in extra sessions aimed at becoming familiar with the language of schema therapy. In these sessions they can practice filling in a mode diary or learn how to recognise their coping. Another available option is for a number of clients who display crisis-prone behaviour to take part in standalone sessions focusing on developing a crisis and safety plan. If the main treatment is group schema therapy, then it's important for the clients to feed back to the group what they've learned in order to preserve sufficient safety and connection.

6.4.4 Using the phase-oriented method in group schema therapy for clients with both a personality disorder and an addictive disorder

In practice, it's not uncommon for a client to present with a personality disorder and, alongside this, an addiction. For cases of repeated relapse in particular an integrated treatment is recommended, so as to avoid a client successfully completes the treatment for his personality disorder but then falling back into drug abuse (or vice versa). The integrative model of schema therapy is well-suited to this type of treatment, particularly when used in an intense way. Currently, this method is the subject of a clinical pilot project. If the initial outcomes are positive, then further investigations will take place.

Twice a week the clients take part in group schema therapy. In the first three months the focus is on creating awareness – clients learn to see their substance abuse as a form of coping, with an underlying basic need. Through brief warm-up rounds a close watch is kept on abstinence and consumption, after which an exercise aimed at processing schemas takes centre stage. In the second phase, which also lasts three months, clients focus on strengthening their healthy adult mode. The objective is for them to be able to make a balanced decision: "I understand what role my drug abuse plays, and I want to leave this behind me", or "the advantages outweigh the disadvantages, I choose to continue using drugs." Clients who choose to change can move on into the next phase.

Appendices

Appendix 1: Overview of elements by phase

	Phase 1: Start phase	Phase 2	Phase 3	Phase 4: End phase
Theme	Safety first	Express yourself	Do it yourself	Live your life
Basic need	Safety, connection	Self-expression	Autonomy, self-appreciation	Autonomy, spontaneity
Limited reparenting	Baby and toddler	School child	Adolescence	Young adult
Overall goal	A platform for change	Recognizing the pattern	Doing means learning	Goodbye and good luck
Important exercises	Experiential case conceptualisation	Mirror exercise	Using anger	What's your plan?
	Basic modes	Strengthen the healthy adult	Repairing the damage	Saying farewell
Empathic confrontation	Standard	High	Low	Minimal
Group development phase	Parallel phase	Intake phase	Reciprocal phase	Separation phase
Mode model	Basic	Scope for differences in modes	Customized and personal	Plain speaking
Role of the therapist	Creating favourable conditions	Encourage authenticity	Encourage	Coaching

Appendix 2: List of exercises

Chapter 2: Phase 1 – Safety first

2.5.1 Exercises concerning safety and connection

Exercise 2.1: Over the line
Exercise 2.2: Portraying the coping mode

2.5.2 Exercises to discover modes and explore connections between past and present

Exercise 2.4: Experiential case conceptualization
Exercise 2.5: Mode flipping
Exercise 2.6: Basic modes
Exercise 2.7: Awareness of child modes

2.5.3 Exercises exploring the impact of modes on each other and on other people.

Exercise 2.8: Coping mode association exercise
Exercise 2.9: Implicit parental messages
Exercise 2.10: Parent mode chair technique

Chapter 3: Phase 2 – Express yourself

3.5.1 Mode dynamics exercises

Exercise 3.1: Mode regulation mirror exercise
Exercise 3.2: Spontaneity in mode regulation

3.5.2 Exercises to strengthen the healthy adult

Exercise 3.4: Empathic confrontation of the coping mode
Exercise 3.5: Empathizing with the vulnerable child mode
Exercise 3.6: Setting firm limits
Exercise 3.7: Blocking the parent mode
Exercise 3.8: Using spontaneity in imagery rescripting

3.5.3 Anger management exercises

Exercise 3.9: Angry child mode warm-up
Exercise 3.10: Empathizing with the angry child mode

Chapter 4: Phase 3 – Do it yourself

4.5.1 Exercises around learning to adopt a healthy adult stance

Exercise 4.1: Discussing homework

References

Arntz, A., & Bögels, S. (2000). *Schemagerichte cognitieve therapie voor persoonlijkheidsstoornissen.* Houten, Nederland: Bohn Stafleu Van Loghum.

Arntz, A., & Jacob, G. (2012). *Schema Therapy in Practice: An Introduction to the Schema Mode Approach.* Chichester, UK: Wiley-Blackwell.

Arntz, A., & Van Genderen (2020). *Schema Therapy for Borderline Personality Disorder* (2nd ed). Chichester, UK: Wiley-Blackwell.

Bamelis, L.M., Evers, S.M.A.A., Spinhoven, P., & Arntz, A. (2014). Results of a multicenter randomized controlled trial of the clinical effectiveness of schema therapy for personality disorders. *American Journal of Psychiatry*, 171(3), 305-322.

Bandura, A. (1986). *Social foundations of Thougt and Action: A social cognitive theory.* Englewood Cliffs, NY: Prentice-Hall.

Claassen, A.M. (2012). Marvelous and great. Groepsschematherapie volgens Farrell en Shaw: een impressie. *Groepen*, 7 (4), 47-49.

Claassen, A.M., & Pol, S. (2015). *Schematherapie en de gezonde volwassene.* (A.M. Claassen, & S. Pol, Red.) Houten, Nederland: Bohn Stafleu van Loghum.

Faßbinder, E., Schweiger, U., & Jacob, G. (2011). *Therapie-Tools: Schematherapie.* Weinheim, Duitsland: Beltz.

Farrell, J. M., & Shaw, I. A. (2012). *Group Schema Therapy for Borderline Personality Disorder. A step-by-step treatment manual with patient workbook.* Chichester, UK: Wiley-Blackwell.

Farrell, J. M., Reiss, N., & Shaw, I. A. (2014). *The Schematherapy Clinicians Guide: A Complete Resource for Building and Delivering Individual, Group and Integrated Schema Mode Treatment Programs.* Chichester, UK: Wiley-Blackwell.

Giesen-Bloo, J., van Dyck, R., Spinhoven, P., van Tilburg, W., Dirksen, C., van Asselt, T., et al. (2006). Outpatient psychotherapy for borderline personality disorder: randomized trial of schema-focused therapy vs. transference-focused psychotherapy. *Archives of general psychiatry*, 63, 649-658.

Hardeman, E. (2017, December). In gesprek met Marleen Rijkeboer: 'Schematherapie is heel effectief". *GZ-psychologie*, 7-8, pp. 8-13.

Hoijtink, T. (2001). *De kracht van groepen: Normen en rollen.* Houten, Nederland: Bohn Stafleu van Loghum.

Houben, M., & Arntz, A. (2011). A quantitative and qualitative investigation of a part-time treatment for borderline personality disorder at Riagg Maastricht. Unpublished master's thesis, University of Maastricht, Maastricht, the Netherlands.

Jacob, G., Van Genderen, H. & Seebauer, L. (2014). *Breaking Negative Thinking patterns: A Schema Therapy Self-Help and Support Book.* Chichester, UK: Wiley-Blackwell.

Kellogg, S. H. (2004). Dialogical encounters: Contemporary perspectives on "chairwork" in psychotherapy. *Psychotherapy: Research, Theory, Practice, Training* , 41, 310-320.

Lafeber, E. (2013). De kracht van het dubbelen bij jongeren met een internaliserende problematiek. . *Groepen*, 8, 25-33.

Levine, B. (1979). *Group psychotherapy, practice and development.* Englewood Cliffs: Prentice Hall.

Lobbestael, J., Van Vreeswijk, M., & Arntz, A. (2007). Shedding lights on schema modes: A clarification of the mode concept and its current research status. *Netherlands Journal of Psychology*, 63, 76-85.

Lockwood, G., & Perris, P. (2012). A New Look at Core Emotional Needs. In M. v. Vreeswijk, J. Broersen, & M. Nadort (Eds.), *The Wiley-Blackwell Handbook of Schema Therapy* (pp. 85-115). Chichester, UK: Wiley-Blackwell.

Meij, H. (2011). De basis van opvoeding en ontwikkeling. www.nji.nl. Accessed April 28,z 2021. https://repository.officiele-overheidspublicaties.nl/externebijlagen/exb-2018-32453/1/bijlage/exb-2018-32453.pdf

Muste, E.H., Weertman, A, Claassen, A.M.T.S. – redactie (2009). *Handboek Klinische Schematherapie*. Houten: Bohn Stafleu van Loghum.

Reubsaet, R.J. (2012, May). The pressure cooker of an intensive Day Therapy Program. In J. Farrell & I. Shaw (Chairs), New developments in groupschematherapy. Symposium conducted at the 5th conference of the International Society of Schema Therapy, New York, USA.

Rijkeboer, M. (2015). De diagnostiek van schema's, copingstijlen en schemamodi. In G. Bosmans, P. Bijttebier, I. Noens, & L. Claes (Eds.), Diagnostiek bij kinderen, jongeren en gezinnen. Deel III: Ontwikkelingsdomeinen in het vizier (pp. 153-173). Leuven, België: Acco.

Rijkeboer, M., & Lobbestael, J. (2014). Unravelling the connection between schemas, copingstyles and modes: Empirical findings. Invited keynote, 6th World Conference of Schema Therapy, June 12-14th,. Istanbul, Turkey.

Sijbers, G., & Van der Wijngaart, R. (2015). Het therapeutisch gebruik van humor in de behandeling van Obsessief Compulsieve persoonlijkheidsstoornis [Workhop]. VGCT 2015: Shiny happy people, Veldhoven, Nederland.

Van der Wijngaart, R. (2015, May). The healthy adult mode; Ways to strengthen the healthy adult of our patients. *Schema Therapy Bulletin*, 1 (1). Accessed April 28, 2021. https://schematherapysociety.org/page-18465

Van Dun, P. (2015). Schematherapie en psychodrama in groepen. *Groepen*, 10, 24-38.

Van Genderen, H., Rijkeboer, M., & Arntz, A. (2012). Theoretical model: Schemas, coping styles, and modes. In M. v. Vreeswijk, J. Broersen, & M. Nadort (Eds.), *The Wiley-Blackwell Handbook of Schema Therapy* (pp. 70-84). Chichester, UK: Wiley-Blackwell.

Van Vreeswijk, M., Broersen, J., & Nadort, M. (Eds.). (2012). *The Wiley-Blackwell Handbook of Schema Therapy. Theory, Research and Practice*. Chichester, UK: Wiley-Blackwell.

Van Vreeswijk, M., & Broersen, J. (2017). *Handleiding Kortdurende Schematherapie*. Houten, Nederland: Bohn Stafleu Van Loghum.

Wetzelaer, P., Farrell, J., Evers, S., Jacob, G., Lee, C., Brand, O., et al. (2014). Design of an international multicenter RCT on group schema therapy for borderline personality disorder. (D. 10.1186/s12888-014-0319-3, Red.) *BMC Psychiatry*, 14: 319, 1-15.

Yalom, I. D, & Leszcz, M. (2020). *The Theory and Practice of Group Psychotherapy* (5th ed). New York, NY: Basic Books.

Young, J. (1990). *Cognitive therapy for personality disorders: A schema-focused approach* (3e ed.). Sarasota, USA: Professional Resource Press.

Young, J. E., Klosko, J. S., & Weishaar, M. E. (2003). *Schema Therapy. A Practitioner's Guide*. New York, NY: Guilford Press.

Yperen, T. v. (2009). Overzicht van opvoedzorgen. www.nji.nl. Accessed Mai3, 2017. http://www.nji.nl/nl/Download-NJi/TabelOpvoedproblemen.pdf